Media, Home, and Family

Media, Home, and Family

Stewart M. Hoover, Lynn Schofield Clark,
and Diane F. Alters

with Joseph G. Champ and Lee Hood

ROUTLEDGE
NEW YORK AND LONDON

Published in 2004 by
Routledge
29 West 35th Street
New York, NY 10001
www.routledge-ny.com

Published in Great Britain by
Routledge
11 New Fetter Lane
London EC4P 4EE
www.routledge.co.uk

10 9 8 7 6 5 4 3 2 1 0

Library of Congress Cataloging-in-Publication Data

Hoover, Stewart M.
    Media, home, and family / Stewart M. Hoover, Lynn Schofield Clark, and Diane F. Alters with Joseph G. Champ and Lee Hood.
        p.   cm.
    Includes bibliographical references and index.
    ISBN 0-415-96916-6 (hardback : alk. paper)—ISBN 0-415-96917-4 (pbk. : alk. paper)
    1. Television and family.   2. Mass media and the family.   I. Clark, Lynn Schofield.   II. Alters, Diane F.   III. Title.
    HQ520 .H66   2003
    302.23—dc22
                                                                    2003016013

CONTENTS

ACKNOWLEDGMENTS

This book could not have been written without the assistance of many people and places. I am grateful to the University of Colorado for the time I have had to devote to this project, and to the University of Edinburgh for hosting me as a visiting professor during a key period in this manuscript's development. At the University of Colorado, I especially want to recognize former dean Del Brinkman and Garda Meyer and Geri Boucher of the Dean's Office for their assistance, as well as staff members Crystal Atkinson, Pat Meyers, and Dave Martinez.

Much of the research in this book was supported by the Lilly Endowment, Inc., of Indianapolis, Indiana. I am grateful to Craig Dykstra for his visionary, intellectual, and pastoral approach to our work, and to Jim Lewis of the Louisville Foundation for his enthusiasm and encouragement.

Perhaps most centrally, it was a great pleasure for me to work with four bright graduate students who became intellectual colleagues over the course of four years of research and discussion. Sometimes it took restraint on my part to avoid imposing my own reading of an interview, because it was clear to me that each member had thought a great deal about each interview, and each member brought a unique set of experiences and knowledge to the project. It became important to me to hear them out and to try to guide their enthusiasm, as I realized early in the project that this group effort could give new shape and texture to the study of media in American life. As a result, I thought it was important to recognize the individual work of each author in the writing process, as well as to acknowledge the group work as a whole. I believe our work is stronger as a result of the varied voices in the text, and I hope that this work serves as a model for the kind of learning that can happen in such large, team-oriented efforts.

—Stewart M. Hoover

As the four research associates brought on to conduct interviews for the research project that formed the basis of this book, we are grateful for the opportunity to be a part of such an engaging research team. Under the direction of Stewart Hoover, each of us was expected to read, analyze, and discuss each interview as quickly as possible after it was conducted and transcribed, and we were to read widely in related fields in order to contribute to the overall thinking about the project. Stewart insisted from the beginning that we contribute intellectually to the project, and he guided and encouraged us, often making subtle suggestions that greatly improved the work as a whole. Our weekly meetings, which went on for four years, were in actuality high-level research seminars, certainly the pinnacle of our graduate education experience, and perhaps the closest anyone can come to an ideal learning environment. We all are grateful to Stewart for his patience, understanding, and encouragement as, together, we wrote this book.

—Lynn Schofield Clark, Diane F. Alters,
Joseph G. Champ, and Lee Hood

I

The Study: Symbolism, Media, and the Lifecourse

1

Introduction

Diane F. Alters
Lynn Schofield Clark

GIVING ACCOUNTS OF THE MEDIA

Nick and Roberta Kandinsky and their sons, Lance and Eric, are gathered around their kitchen table to talk with one of this book's authors.[1] Late in the interview, this good-natured exchange takes place during a discussion about renting videotapes of movies:

Nick [age 52]:	We usually try to get light comedies. When Roberta's out, we get an action movie. You know, I've seen some before. And you know, the kids with their video games, they've seen the violence, and I'm usually there with them. And if it gets too embarrassing, I'll fast-forward it.
Interviewer:	What gets embarrassing?
Lance [age 15]:	You've never fast-forwarded!
Nick:	You know, it's really funny. The violence, I've never fast-forwarded. But sex, I do, and I don't know why I do. It's as harmless as the—[*he is interrupted by the boys, who are making incredulous faces at this. The interviewer laughs.*]
Roberta [age 49]:	[*to the interviewer*] I *know* he doesn't fast-forward.
Lance:	I've never been around you once when you've fast-forwarded!

Nick:	I remember when Eric was there, once I fast-forwarded.
Eric [age 11]:	When was *this?*
Nick [casually]:	Oh it was one of the movies, I forget which.

We heard some version of this conversation in many interviews in our study of families and media in daily life. In this exchange, the father declared that his family did not watch sex scenes in movies because he fast-forwarded through them. Nick Kandinsky thus aligned himself with certain generally accepted notions of media in the United States: that the media are full of violence and sex, and that responsible parents would not let their children watch such things. In identifying himself with these well-known concerns about the media, Nick put himself in the role of father-who-controls-the-media. Earlier in the Kandinsky interview, however, Nick and the other family members had identified Nick as someone who enjoyed television and movies rather indiscriminately. His wife Roberta was recognized as the family member who hated television and many movies and who was actually far more particular about the media her children consumed than Nick was. Because Roberta was absent from the story about renting videos, Nick had offered himself as the watchdog of his children's media use, a role he did not ordinarily take. His family would not let him get away with this, however, and their disbelieving laughter undermined the well-intentioned claim he was eventually forced to abandon.

Similar exchanges occurred when other families gathered to talk about their family's media practices in the study that forms the basis for this book. Parents sometimes presented themselves as more in control of media use in the home than they actually were; when they talked about this in family groups, inconsistencies became clear, sometimes in humorous ways. We begin the book with this example not so much to question whether the Kandinsky family or any other family we interviewed was consistent in their beliefs and behaviors regarding the media, but to explore and analyze what this exchange can tell us about what they attempted to present about themselves as a *family,* and how their media practices related to this presentation. Why was it important for Nick to present himself to a researcher as a parent who was more vigilant about mediated violence and sex than he actually was? What do such claims tell us about how parents view their job as parents in relation to media? How do such claims relate to family media practices, particularly in the increasingly common scenario of the two-household, divorced or blended homes in which children are raised? Moreover, how do children interpret such claims in relation to what they understand about their families, their parents, and their household media practices? It is important to note that many children recognize their parents' *intentions* even if their practices were inconsistent with the parents' accounts of the media. This book explores how parents and children in different families deal with the gap between their practices and their accounts of the media.

The scene with the Kandinskys is an example of an important way families in our study dealt with media in their daily lives: They did so as part of their work as a family, constructing and negotiating what we have come to call "accounts of the media" by which they located their families in U.S. society and in modern life. Our use of the term "accounts of the media" references two different yet complementary meanings of the word "accounts." First, the nature of interviews means that parents were called upon to offer stories, or *accounts,* of how their family operated in relation to media. They often also described having told similar stories to friends, relatives, co-workers, and parents of children's friends. Second, the term "accounts" refers to a related phenomenon that structured how the parents told the stories about the media: Parents were self-consciously aware of the importance of parenting, a task for which they felt *accountable.* The accounts of the media that parents gave in our study were always inflected with their assumptions about proper and desirable parental behavior in relation to the media.

In these accounts of the media, interviewees also constructed a family identity through a process of negotiating with media and culture in modern life. While much has been written about the role of the media in the individual identity formation of children, this book is rooted in our sense that it is necessary to explore how families negotiated a sense of identity collectively and how the media, in turn, played a role in this process. As the exchange among the Kandinskys indicates, we found that families did this collective identity construction in practical ways, around accessible topics such as television and video watching. Negotiation of family identity around media engagement was a significant, ongoing project in these families, as parents reflected on their parenting, as children reflected on their experiences and their parents' wishes, and as they all attempted to explain themselves with reference to certain widely held beliefs about media in the United States. Sometimes the accounts incorporated family members' religious beliefs—an aspect of American life that is not often fully recognized in media studies research (Hoover and Venturelli 1996). In response to our questions about religion and belief, interviewees cited a variety of frameworks and sensibilities, some of which we discuss in case-study contexts in Chapters Five through Eight. Overall, the accounts created in the interview context brought symbolic resources of the media into a negotiation that located people on larger maps of morality, religion, gender, social location, individual purpose, and other parameters of modern life.

Moreover, as researchers we also took part in the negotiation of family identity, in that we approached people and talked to them as members of families. We defined *family* broadly, including families that were blended, single-parent families, parents of the same gender, unmarried parents who were living together, unrelated people who considered themselves family, and others. This does not mean that we ignored individual identity, but that we focused on various individuals' processes of constructing family identity together, in specific contexts, in their homes. The fact that we conducted almost all of the interviews in the homes of those interviewed was central to the study. We were mindful of David Morley's interest in visiting domestic settings to see what people "are up to" and what they do and say about the media (Morley 1996, 319). By focusing on a social grouping in a particular location, the family in the home, we hope to provide some insights into the complexities of American culture in mediated modernity.

PUBLIC SCRIPTS

Almost all of the families we interviewed seemed to draw upon relatively consistent assumptions about media, embracing what Ellen Seiter (1999, 58) has called "lay theories of media effects." Among these "lay theories" is the assumption that heavy use of mass media can cause young people to become violent, insensitive, unproductive, or something worse. The question of whether media can be said to have such effects is a controversial subject in academic circles, but not necessarily in family living rooms.[2] Families' responses to what they believed were effects of the media were quite complex, as we will discuss, but, to a family, everyone in our study believed that the media affected their children in some way.

Such concerns about media effects have long pervaded public-policy discussions about media use among families in the United States. A key example is from Alfred R. Schneider, the longtime head of ABC Television's standards and practices division—its chief "censor"—who used family as his criterion for "the public interest," the standard mandated by the U.S. Congress under which television and radio stations must operate in order to be licensed. The mandate "at the very least, requires the exercise of due care where children are concerned. This amorphous concept of 'public interest' retains some sense of respect for family and order in society and support for institutional values" (Schneider 2001, 132). From 1960 to 1990, Schneider applied his definition when he and his department reviewed program content "for questions of taste, acceptability, language, violent portrayals, and sexual innuendos" (Schneider 133), objections that were frequently cited by our interview parents as well.

Policy debates at the Federal Communications Commission have similarly been concerned with the impact of television on children, and much regulatory debate about the Internet has to do with fears that children can access pornography. Nongovernmental organizations, such as those in the media literacy movement, urge parents to take control of media use in the home.[3] On the Christian right, the American Family Association and other groups move concerns from living rooms to the streets and marketplaces, calling for boycotts of advertisers that sponsor shows with violence, sex, and profanity. In these and in other ways, the notions of family standards for television have been embraced if not enacted throughout U.S. society, providing an important context for the daily struggles over media that took place in the homes of the people we interviewed.

From such debates and actions, in concert with parental experience and belief frameworks, come what we term the "public scripts" about the media that each family in our study wrestled with. We argue that these public scripts are part of what James Carey (1989, 28–29) has described as a "publicly available stock" of phrases, ideas, words, and other symbols that construct a map of a society. In this book, we describe instances in which people constructed these maps by positioning themselves in terms of certain society-wide beliefs about the media.

There are many overlapping public scripts about the media, and most are negative in tone (Ang 1995; Seiter 1999). For instance, the people we interviewed readily talked about problems they associated with excessively violent and sexually explicit television programming, drawing upon public scripts deeply embedded in public-policy debates and some academic studies as well as in more informal venues. To a lesser extent, some commented on how the media reflect misunderstandings based on sexism, racism, or prejudices based in class status or sexual preference. Regardless of the particular position embraced, most parents seemed to believe implicitly that how they dealt with the media, and especially television, defined how well they were doing as parents and as a family.

To summarize, then, we note four public scripts in particular that emerged repeatedly in interviews, often all at once. They were: (1) There is too much violence in the media, and children must be protected from it. (2) There is too much sex in the media, and children must be protected from it. (3) Children are affected in some ways by media. (4) How we deal with media, especially television, helps define us as parents and as a family; therefore, we parents must be especially diligent.[4] All the families we interviewed acknowledged these public scripts.

We did not set out to uncover these public scripts of the media. Nevertheless, we gradually came to see that it was impossible to completely separate public scripts of the media from families' statements about their own media practices, and ultimately their identity as a family. Creating accounts of the media offered an appealing narrative of how a family wished to be perceived in relation to media. Even more important, parents built upon widely accepted public scripts of the media and offered through these accounts an explanation and justification of themselves as "good" parents and, by extension, creators of healthy families.

Although sex and violence in the media tended to dominate discussions in our interviews, the depiction of bad behavior also worried many parents. A television show that came under repeated fire in this regard was *The Simpsons,* the animated situation comedy on Fox Television that depicts a nuclear but dysfunctional family. One father, Jim Mills, said he did not want his children to behave like the Simpson children, particularly in their name calling and use of bad language.[5] "It's not that *The Simpsons* teach those particular things, but there are things I don't agree with that the kids might have a tendency to imitate," Mills said. His role as a parent, he said, was to address such behavior when it occurred. Another parent, Gary Carter, similarly worried about the "disrespect and silliness, the constant need for being funny and loud" that erupted in his children (boys 11, 10, and 7, and a girl, 5) after watching cable television, an intruder that the family eventually rejected by canceling the cable subscription.[6] This was "Bart-Simpsonitis" to Carter, a mode of behavior in which "everything had to be a one-liner crackoff, or disrespectful, 'ha-ha' kind of thing." Sharon Hartman, another concerned parent, pointedly noted her feeling that *The Simpsons* was not suitable fare for her children, 14, 9, and 8.[7] With prompting from her children, however, she cheerfully admitted that she and the rest of her family sometimes watched the show because they thought it was funny. In this, Hartman voiced her belief that television depicted behavior she disliked, and that her role as a parent was to make sure her children did not behave in the ways these television shows depict. She was also voicing a "should" in a common public script about *The Simpsons,* perhaps in part for the interviewer's benefit: She felt that she *should* object to *The Simpsons* because it depicts rude behavior and is unsuitable for children. Jim Mills, Gary Carter, and Sharon Hartman all presented themselves as parents whose role was to intervene and to help ensure that their children were not negatively influenced by television. They had drawn upon their own experiences to interpret a public script that television had effects on children, and in so doing they created their own accounts of the media.

REFLEXIVE PARENTING

To talk about parenting in the contemporary age is to describe a delicate balancing act. Parenting consists of lofty intentions regarding the ever-changing demands that emerge in relation to neighborhood, national, and even international events, along with the daily struggles over finances, custody, and more mundane matters. In a certain sense, such pressures on family life in the United States have always existed. What is different now, some scholars contend, is a greater self-consciousness *about* parenting. Since the 1960s, parents have become increasingly uneasy about raising children in light of increases in drug use, delinquency, teen pregnancy, and suicides among children and adolescents. Indeed, the structure of family life, particularly in the middle classes, has changed dramatically since World War II, as women have entered the workforce in ever-increasing numbers, as divorces rates have risen, and as new family forms have emerged. As the historians Steven Mintz and Susan Kellogg note, "parents have become more self-conscious, anxious, and guilt-ridden about childrearing" (Mintz and Kellogg 1988, 220).

We regard this parental sense of accountability as an important theme today, and we understand this as part of a process of "reflexive parenting." This concept is our extension of Anthony Giddens's notion that in modernity a person is reflexive about how he or she relates to the social world, in that an individual continuously incorporates experiences, including mediated ones, into daily life (Giddens 1991, 1–9, 181–208). The parental reflexivity discussed in this book often emerged in discussions of family as well as of media, particularly when family members gathered as a group to talk with an interviewer. This reflexivity meant that parents in the study were especially mindful of the presumed influences that came between them and their children, particularly those influences over which they felt they had little control. In this context, peers, schools, and especially the media become lightning rods for parental anxieties.

Most of the parents we interviewed were self-conscious about parenthood; they thought and worried about what their children watched on television or saw in the movies. Unlike their own parents, some said, they felt responsible for their children's media engagement and tried to limit what their children watched and how much time they spent watching. In the Garcia family, for example, the parents tried to limit their children's watching to an hour and a half a day.[8] In many families, this attempt to control television was directly related to the act of reading. In the Ahmed family, for example, for every hour of reading, the children were allowed an hour of computer games or television.[9] Most parents also said they tried to police content, to try to make sure that their children did not watch bad behavior or hear bad language, such as many parents found in *The Simpsons.* Some also worried about television shows that were scary, such as *Goosebumps,* or movies that were violent, such as *Terminator.* Some families said they held family conferences to talk about television, and some only wished they talked more about television and other media. Several parents recalled—sometimes fondly—watching far more television as children than they allowed their own children to watch. Their own parents, they concluded, were not so worried about television because it had been an uncomplicated part of life, something a child did after school, before dinner, and then perhaps into the evening. Repeatedly, then, we saw a process of definition unfolding as people discussed family, media, and parenting and cited public scripts about them. This process of definition, an aspect of reflexive parenting, is an important part of the overall project of meaning making in the home.

The rise in self-conscious, reflexive parenting is related to an emergent awareness of "expert" advice. In the decades immediately following World War II, one such expert, Dr. Benjamin Spock, stood out, as his *Baby and Child Care* became the "bible" for a whole generation of U.S. parents. Today, a wide variety of experts inundate parents with often-conflicting theories about child development and parenting, in a dizzying variety of ways. Parents can read parenting magazines, visit parenting Web sites, attend workshops and classes, and go to children's resource centers, in addition to the more traditional information sharing that happens at playgrounds, in religious settings, and at neighborhood barbeques and birthday parties. In these ways, parents try to figure out ways to guard against what they believe are negative outside influences that can derail their own intentions.

Examples of reflexive parenting emerged frequently in families' accounts of the media. We noted that all the interview parents in some way seemed to think it was important to stipulate an ability to be independent from media, yet media were so embedded in their lives that most of them shared stories of being uncomfortably exposed to something they disliked. In interviews, these stories of discomfort often emerged early in the discussion, then were later negotiated away as they described actual practice. Mark and Kristen Franz, for example, said they had not been comfortable with what they had heard about the sexual content of the movie *Titanic* and had not wanted their 11-year-old daughter to see it.[10] Eventually, however, they decided that because the movie was so popular their daughter would not feel normal if she did not see it. Kirsten Franz said they finally recognized the "social appropriateness" of their daughter viewing *Titanic,* and Kirsten took her to see it.

With the concept of reflexive parenting in mind, we ask the following questions in this book: Why do parents make the decisions they do about regulating children's media use, and how do such decisions relate to other aspects of contemporary life? How do parents talk about such matters among their family members and to an interviewer? Moreover, how do their children understand such parental decisions? Finally, how can we think about parenting and media in terms of their social, historical, and cultural contexts?

THE STUDY: COLLABORATION AND DEFINITION

The research reported in this book was conducted following models of ethnographic audience research articulated in the work of Ang (1995), Bird (1992b), Stacey (1990), and Morley and Silverstone (1991). Over a five-year period, the coauthors individually conducted in-depth interviews with 269 individuals in 62 families. Most family members were interviewed in their homes more than once: An initial interview involved the entire family, and a second visit consisted of separate and confidential interviews with each member of the family.

Although the research is rooted in assumptions of interview-based audience research, the distinguishing feature of this work is its collaborative design, analysis, and writing, which will be discussed in detail in Chapter Three. The collaborative process through which we studied these families played an important role in the definition of the project. The five authors met weekly for nearly three years. Our three- to four-hour sessions were lively struggles, sometimes contentious but more often energetic and enthusiastic, as we tried to make sense of what people told us. We discussed interview contexts—the setting, how people seemed to react to us, how we felt about the people we interviewed, what they did, and what they seemed to convey nonverbally—as well as the transcripts that we prepared from our long and open-ended interviews in people's homes. Our meetings became an important part of what we learned in this project, as will be discussed in Chapter Three.

Our collaborative approach helped us make sense of our in-depth, qualitative, semistructured interviews. We recognized that the resulting accounts were a kind of talk, which we view as examples of how people engage with social and cultural resources and processes in the making of meaning. One might ask, "What is the point of this talk?" The talk ranged across the contexts, conditions, and contradictions inherent in family, work, gender, relationships, beliefs, and values in modern life. Media present—and present themselves as the embodiment of—a range of resources and solutions to these life projects. We cannot know everything about people's responses, but we can try to understand how people deal with this range of resources and solutions by crafting meaningful accounts of themselves and their families.

THIS BOOK

This book is divided into two main parts. The first part, "The Study: Symbolism, Media, and the Lifecourse," describes and explains the project, our experiential and theoretical roots, and the methods that we developed. Chapter Two explains our research methods and how they evolved from a postpositivist perspective to a constructivist one. This journey was aided by our informants, who helped us understand the importance of the contradictions and constructions in their discussions of media. The process of building theory to guide us and with which we struggled throughout the project is described in Chapter Three.

Following the chapter on theory, Chapter Four explores the topic of the family. The location of our research in the home helped bring about the description of our project as being in part about family. Parents in particular worried about the media's penetration of the home, the role of media in children's lives, and the embedding of media in daily life, and we realized they were drawing on certain public scripts that emphasized these worries. The concept of reflexive parenting came from our discussions about these worries, and the term is further explored in this chapter, which also places these notions in the context of historical notions of family in the United States and its images in mediated popular culture.

The second part of the book, "The Families: Case Studies," is its narrative heart. We introduce Part II with a discussion of the systematic way we found people talking about the media. They did so through what we call "modes of engagement" with media, descriptive categories that we developed to think about the interviews. We argue that one of these categories, "accounts of the media," is new to media-audience research and deserves further development.[11] We first identified this category as we encountered what seemed to be contradictions between what people said they did and what they seemed to have done with media. We realized that more than contradiction was at issue, and that people self-consciously positioned themselves in relation to media when they talked with us. "Accounts of the media" are found in each family's discussions of how their family related to public scripts of the media. We argue that "accounts of the media" helped people make meaning, individually and as families. Our interpretation of these accounts of the media led us to view this category as an important source of insight into the overall project of meaning making in the media age.

Chapters Five through Eight are case studies of eight families. These four chapters explore the ways vastly different families make meaning. These cases are information rich and are not necessarily representative of a larger population. In them, we address public discourses of media and media policy, and the public scripts we and our informants brought to bear in our contemplation of these discourses. Every family we interviewed shared at least some accounts of the media that reveal conflict and contradiction, an indication that media are not unproblematically naturalized in the home.

Major differences in the way families account for media can be traced to the frameworks that guide what they do and think. This process is apparent in Chapter Five, which discusses the Ahmeds and the Paytons, whose cultural positions are at some distance from the U.S. mainstream and each other: one is a Muslim family with concerns about maintaining their own cultural traditions, and one is an ecofeminist, atheist family with Protestant roots. Their particular accounts of media were consistent with particular frameworks that guided their day-to-day existence. At the same time, these accounts often indicated contradictions in practice. For example, the Ahmeds' differences from the predominantly Protestant U.S. society guided them in their judgment of topics like sex and violence on television. When the interviewer asked about their use of television, they related accounts that fit the way they wanted to live as Muslims outside mainstream U.S. culture, although even they described viewing practices that did not necessarily fit that framework. In contrast, the Paytons did not own a television, a decision consistent with their view that their family should live simply, outside the mainstream, with a commitment to ecological responsibility.

Chapter Six discusses two families closer to the heart of U.S. culture, the Hartmans and the Roelofs. They were lower-middle-class, white Protestant families with contrasting religious beliefs and practices, providing an excellent opportunity to further explore the contribution of religious frameworks to meaning making in relation to the media. The Hartmans used their evangelical framework—a collection of values, ideas, beliefs, and practices—to guide them in their daily lives, including their media use. They saw little or nothing in media that came close to their religious framework. The Roelofs, on the other hand, did not have as practical a religious foundation—they did not attend church and were not affiliated with a church, although they considered themselves Christians. In contrast to the Hartmans, the Roelofs found religious lessons in some television shows, and at the same time they wanted to distance themselves from media. As a result, the Roelofs seemed less consistent in describing media and what media meant in their daily family life. In both families, the children seemed to understand their parents' wishes about media engagement, although both sets of children sometimes challenged them. In this chapter, we discuss the differences in the two families and note that it is difficult, if not impossible, for us to make normative arguments about either family's approach.

Chapter Seven is about two white, middle-class families: the Franzes, a nuclear family, and the Price-Benoits, a family headed by two gay men. Through the Franzes and the Price-Benoits, we explore notions of "normal" and how the media might play a part in the definition of family. Chapter Eight includes two multicultural families, the Vogels and the Carsons, that are deeply and intensively engaged in media, although in very different ways. The chapter considers the term "couch potato" as a public script and what it might mean. Through the Vogels who are relatively well off, and the Carsons who have a low income, we explore media practices in families of heavy users of media in relation to culturally informed assumptions.

LOCATING THE STUDY

Finally, a word about the location and context for the interviews, which were conducted in several localities in the state of Colorado. To retain anonymity of the informants, we have not offered many specific details about their particular locations. However, we would like to offer some general information about Colorado and what was happening economically and socially during the interviewing, from 1996 to 2000. During that time, Colorado's economy boomed. The unemployment rate steadily dropped over the decade of the 1990s, and in January 1999 it was 2.9 percent, the lowest it had ever been, and lower than the comparable national rate of 4 percent. Relatively high-paying jobs in telecommunications and in high-technology companies fueled the boom, but it did not last much past 2000. Two years later, by mid-2002, the boom had bust. Colorado had a net job loss of 56,000 jobs, or 2.6 percent of the workforce, a far bigger rate of loss than in the United States as a whole, which suffered a 1.1 percent job loss in the recession following the terrorist attacks of September 11, 2001. State tax revenues were down, homebuilding dropped greatly, and income growth declined, much of it due to the precipitous shrinking of the telecommunications industry, which had been a strong presence in Colorado in the 1990s. Our interviewing ended before September 11, 2001, and thus any concomitant shifts in news coverage, in politics, and in public scripts in general are not reflected in this book.

Instead, interviewees talked to us during the boom years, when statisticians and journalists alike reported growth and optimism: the population grew, employment grew, and average annual wages outstripped the consumer price index in metropolitan areas like the Denver-Boulder-Greeley area, for example. Construction boomed—the number of construction jobs more than doubled from a low of about 60,000 in 1989 to a high of 146,810 in 1999. Over that decade, the state's population grew by more than 1 million people, to 4.3 million as of April 2000, making it the third fastest-growing state in the nation, behind Nevada and Arizona (Westkott 2002.) That growth gave Colorado a seventh seat in the U.S. House of Representatives. In fact, four of Colorado's counties were among the nation's five fastest-growing counties, including Douglas County, the richest in the country with a median annual household income of $77,513. Some of our informants lived in Douglas County, where sprawling suburbs have been carved out of plains and pasture land south of Denver, bringing at the same time congestion and stress to the state's infrastructure. Overall, the median household income in Colorado, adjusted for inflation, grew from $30,140 in 1990 to $45,738 in 2000 (Florio 2001). However, the average income in the top 20 percent of families grew faster (39 percent) than in the bottom 20 percent of families (17.7 percent), though the gap was greater in most other states, with Colorado ranking 41 in the rate at which that gap widened (Aguilar 2002). The growing income gap and the population increase, along with declines in tax revenue due to a tax-limitation measure at the beginning of the decade, put increasing pressure on the state's schools. Some study parents worried about some aspect of that pressure, whether it was general discomfort with their children's education or frustration at what they perceived to be the uncertain status of the schools due to those pressures. In a few cases, for these and other reasons, parents chose to home-school their children, hoping to control, as one father said, the kind of education his children received.

A growth in wages, high-technology jobs, and population contributed to a steep climb in housing prices, boosting Colorado's median home value in 2000 to $169,070, more than double the value of $82,400 at the beginning of the 1990s. The boom did not extend to everyone, as housing-price increases and soaring rents squeezed those earning lower wages, a problem alluded to by some informants. By mid-decade, African American and Hispanic workers were doing worse than average, with unemployment among African Americans at 14.8 percent and among Hispanics, at 5.8 percent, compared to total unemployment of

4.2 percent. By the end of the decade, wealth was distributed less evenly than at the beginning of the decade. While the Denver metropolitan area and other cities along the Front Range of the Rockies boomed, in outlying towns and rural areas significant poverty remained (Olinger 2002). In fact, some of the poorest families in our study lived in such small, rural areas.

The boom in Colorado brought a major shift in the composition of the population, as the state's Hispanic population nearly doubled, to 735,000 people, or more than 17 percent of the total. The Asian population increased to about 100,000, or a 67 percent increase. The number of non-Hispanic whites also grew, but their proportion of the population shrank, from 81 percent in 1999 to about 75 percent in 2000. The numbers of African Americans also increased, but their percentage of the population was 3.8 percent at the end of the decade, down slightly from 4 percent at the beginning (*Denver Post* 2001). The boom also brought a shift in political orientation; early in the decade, Republican and Democratic registration remained about even, making Colorado a key swing state in national elections. By 2002, however, Republicans outnumbered Democrats by about 176,000. This change was attributed by some political analysts to an influx of residents from other, conservative western states, including a significant number from very conservative areas of southern California (Seibert 2002).

One well-reported influx from southern California came about as a result of efforts by the city of Colorado Springs, the state's second-largest city, to lure religiously affiliated business to the area. That resulted most notably in the relocation of the media conglomerate Focus on the Family, which originated from a syndicated radio program of the same name. Even before the 1990s, Colorado Springs had been home to significant numbers of Protestant evangelical organizations, giving it a kinship to Wheaton, Illinois, and Orange County, California, both areas with a large evangelical presence. Colorado's mountains also host numerous Christian camps, conference headquarters, and retreat centers. Somewhat ironically, despite the presence of religiously affiliated groups in Colorado, the southwestern part of the United States has had a lower level of religious affiliation compared to other parts of the country (Finke and Stark 1992). Protestantism and Catholicism dominate the religious landscape in Colorado as they do elsewhere in the country. In Colorado's urban communities, as is true throughout the United States, the growth in immigration, particularly as fueled by the high-tech boom of the 1990s, meant a growth in attendance at area mosques and Buddhist temples. Although these communities are still small relative to the dominant religious traditions, they experienced growth even as some of the more established urban religious communities continued a decade-long period of declining membership. In addition, more people in Colorado than elsewhere in the country claim interests in mysticism and alternative spirituality, as evidenced in national surveys and in the booming natural healing and health-foods industries located in the state (Kosmin and Lachman 1993). While some people view these practices as an alternative to more traditional religious affiliation, others take part in these alternative religious practices as a supplement to their religious traditions.

In summary, Colorado's profile during the study was in some ways unique, and some particulars are recounted in case studies in this book. But in general ways the state was not extremely different from the United States as a whole in the late 1990s. We saw the study's location in Colorado as an opportunity to explore the global in the local, as they are intertwined in Colorado and in U.S. society as a whole.

All in all, this book stands in a tradition of work that attempts to interpret the experiences of human beings as they inhabit the technologies, artifacts, and practices of the media age. Media experience is a subtle, interactive, and embedded aspect of modern life. It is not easily studied, theorized, or interpreted. We share with many other scholars a desire to go to the field and see what people actually do and say. This book is about what we found when we did, and how we learned from and interpreted the accounts people gave us.

2

The Journey from Postpositivist to Constructivist Methods

Lynn Schofield Clark

"So, how does all of this tie into the media?" asked Sam Grill, a father and computer professional. He posed the question as one of the project's researchers concluded an open-ended interview with the Grill family about their media and family practices. The interviewer explained, "Well, a lot of what we are looking at is how the media ties into, intersects with, other things that happen in your life." Sam Grill, however, was not satisfied with this explanation, which led to the following exchange:

Sam:	Ties into?
Interviewer:	Family habits, interchanges, changes in the family history, the family structure, that sort of thing.
Sam:	Tell us what you conclude from this conversation.
Interviewer:	*[laughs uncomfortably]* Ah, way too soon to tell, really. That's why we take the time to transcribe.
Sam:	So let me see if I can understand or repeat back to you what you've just told me. It is to see how the media impacts major structural changes in families?
Interviewer:	Not so much how it impacts but how it relates to the family as a structure, the family as a sort of dynamic.
Sam:	Are you trying to make links between certain types of media use and certain types of family structures?
Interviewer:	No. That might be something that would come out, but since we're at the very early stage of it we have no way of

knowing what the correlations are. There are a lot of people who think there should be very strong correlations between certain types of families and certain types of media use and so on and we're questioning that, trying to find out what type of experience bears this out.

Sam: So is that, what is the question?

Interviewer: That is a good question. I don't think there is one question out there. I think to tell you the truth—and I know this will sound a little funny—it's trying to find out what the question is first of all. How can we talk about media use and media consumption in the family and make sense of it as an embedded practice. A lot of people in the field of media studies believe that the media is something that is foreign to the family structure, it is something that imposes itself upon the family rather than being sort of part and parcel of everyday life. And that is what we are trying to find out, to what extent that is actually true.

Sam: Well, I don't have a real good feel for what you are doing. It sounds pretty esoteric to me.[1]

We begin this chapter with an excerpt from one of our first interviews to highlight some challenges involved in conducting qualitative audience research. First, this excerpt demonstrates our approach to knowledge gathering, as will be described in this chapter: While specific questions were asked, much of the interview was devoted to following up on issues that arose in the research situation. On rare occasions like this one, the conversation included an ad-hoc description of our research goals. Most often, however, the research evolved as the researcher learned more about the specific family being interviewed. Second, the excerpt also demonstrates something about the status of qualitative audience research itself in the United States. While qualitative audience research emerged in response to the large-scale survey to better account for issues of context, as will be discussed in this chapter, Sam Grill's assumptions about his participation in a research project are still largely formed by expectations of a survey.

Survey-oriented or quantitative audience research remains an important tradition within studies of media use today. However, all methodologies are limited in certain ways. It is difficult for survey-based studies to grasp the dynamic nature of how families make decisions regarding media use, for example, and even more difficult to come to understand how parents justify those decisions for their children, and what children come to understand about both their parents' media practices and the justifications offered for media use in the family. Because of these difficulties, our research builds upon a long tradition of qualitative research into how people make meaning in their lives, and how, in the words of fellow media ethnographer Rob Drew (2001), we might view the role of popular culture in family life as "a way of feeling and experiencing, an apparatus for organizing desire and finessing everyday life" (p. 29).

In our research, we were interested not only in describing the stories of families as they negotiated media practices in their homes, but also in analyzing these stories in relation to what we have come to believe are the larger structures of late capitalist social organization. Thus, we sought to generate a "map" of sorts; a map of how parents and children negotiate media rules, to be sure, but also one that took account of the reflexive parenting that we came to see as emblematic of parental identity and practice at this point in U.S. history. Our aim was similar to that outlined by media researcher Timothy Gibson (1999): to develop "an adequate notion of the totality of a particular society and a detailed understanding of how that totality patterns, constrains, and becomes reproduced within the realms of everyday life" (p. 254). To do this, we looked to the traditions of media audience research developed both in the U.S. and in other parts of the world, and also considered developments in the sister fields of interpersonal communication, anthropology, and sociology. We therefore see our methodology as standing in the important tradition of feminist media research methodologies identified with Ellen Seiter (1999), Radhika Parameswaran (1999), S. Elizabeth Bird (1992), Meenakshi Gigi Durham (2003), Lizbet Van Zoonen (1994), and Ien Ang (1996), among others.

FROM SYMBOLIC INTERACTION TO CULTURAL STUDIES

The U.S. qualitative media research tradition predates the field of mass communication itself. Models for its current form can be traced in part to the early-twentieth-century Chicago-school sociology and the development of symbolic interactionism. This paradigm, associated in its beginnings with John Dewey, William James, George Herbert Mead, Robert Park, and Charles Horton Cooley, and later with Erving Goffman, Anselm Strauss, and Herbert Blumer, examined the interaction between subject and object relations in conversation and the ways in which people come to know the self through interactions with others (Blumer 1969; Cooley 1902; Glaser and Strauss 1959; Goffman 1959; Mead 1910). With its emphasis on human relationships, this tradition advocated the full immersion of the researcher into the context of research; in this sense, it generally developed its theories of "interaction" to a much greater extent than its theories of the "symbolic"(Denzin 1992; Hammersley 1989). Consistent with the goals of the Enlightenment project and American pragmatism, research was pursued with the intent of finding solutions for the problems that had emerged as a result of industrialization and urbanization. Current debates concerning the "political" agenda and role of research and its practical outcomes, therefore, have deep roots (Grossberg 1989).

While qualitative research fell out of favor on this side of the Atlantic for several decades with the emergence of survey methods, the tradition began to thrive again in the 1970s with the work of the Birmingham School in Great Britain, following Stuart Hall. This influence has been central to the reconceptualization of qualitative research into what is more broadly known as cultural studies, foregrounding culture as a site of analysis. The cultural studies tradition of E.P. Thompson, Richard Hoggart, and Raymond Williams emphasized the roles of both historical context and social/structural critiques, introducing new concerns into the research agenda.

Current methodological approaches employed in studies of the media build upon various combinations of these preceding traditions. Egon Guba and Yvonna Lincoln organize the field along a continuum that is helpful here: They argue that research tends to be conducted within the paradigms of positivism, postpositivism, critical theory, or constructivism, and they note that each of these paradigms offers a differing perspective on the nature of the research inquiry itself (Guba and Lincoln 1994, 105–117). Thus while some researchers today aim for descriptive narratives such as those of the symbolic interactionists and E.P. Thompson, others build upon the categories of social science inherited from the U.S. positivist tradition and are more concerned with developing narratives within certain standards of validity and reliability. Some writings take the form of sweeping historical narratives, while others are narrow stories of the researcher's own process of knowledge discovery. In other words, the paradigms sparring to replace (or supplement) survey-based empirical research encompass many different traditions and assumptions.

AN INTRODUCTION TO CONSTRUCTIVIST AUDIENCE METHODOLOGY

We refer to the methodology we developed in this project as constructivist, borrowing that term from Guba and Lincoln's (1994) typology. They employ the term to acknowledge the social construction of knowledge, recognizing that knowledge is always generated in relation to the context—or series of contexts—in which it is created.

In the research that served as the foundation for this book, knowledge about family media practices has been socially constructed in five steps, all of which involved different people bringing a range of perspectives within differing contexts. The first step toward knowledge took place as we constructed our interview guides and formulated the research project's design, as we inevitably coded our assumptions into the questions we chose to ask and the material we aimed to generate through interview-based conversations. The second step occurred in the interview situation itself, and emerged as the result of the interaction between one researcher and a set of family members who had agreed to be interviewed. The third step occurred as our team of five co-researchers analyzed and re-analyzed the interview transcripts over a period of several years as we sought to interpret the learnings from the original interviews in relation to other knowledge we brought individually and collectively to the interpretation. A fourth step in the knowledge-construction process occurred as each of the co-researchers took the original transcripts and wrote up an analysis that detailed interesting patterns that seemed to be emerging as we considered all of the interviews in relation to one another (each of these, in turn, became rough drafts for the chapters that follow). A fifth and final step in the knowledge-construction process occurs as readers review the material presented here, assimilating or challenging it with respect to other theories, both latent and acknowledged, of parenthood, media use, and domestic life in the U.S., among other things. Because we understand knowledge to be socially constructed, therefore, we view ourselves as co-constructors of knowledge who work to create understandings in the sum of the relationships between researcher and research participant, researcher and fellow members of the research team, and finally, researchers and the wider public.

The knowledge that emerges from interview-based constructivist methodology is therefore at least in part created, not discovered, by the researcher. Moreover, we recognize that there are many possible interpretations of the same interview transcripts, all of which are potentially meaningful. As Geertz (1980) reminds us, interpretation is not so much a science as an art. Interpretations, or constructions of knowledge, are therefore not separate from those who make the constructions; they "are not part of some 'objective' world that exists apart from their constructors," as Guba and Lincoln (1989) write (p. 143). This does not mean that all knowledge is individualistic, however, for as Guba and Lincoln (1989) note, it is possible for researchers to create what they term a "malconstruction:" an analysis that is judged by others to be "incomplete, simplistic, uninformed," or one that simply does not make sense given the overall data generated (p. 143). We sought to ensure that the knowledge we constructed was not a "malconstruction" through presentations we made to each other and to professional colleagues, friends, family members, and other research participants. However, we are also aware that the "map" of media, home, and the family that we create is far from a definitive, conclusive story, and we welcome further refinements to the analysis we present here.

INITIAL DESIGN ISSUES

Prior to the 1990s, the bulk of qualitative research produced in media studies both here and abroad was in the postpositivist vein. As our Symbolism, Media, and the Lifecourse project had its beginnings in 1996, it is therefore not surprising that our initial research design was informed by many of the assumptions of postpositivism.

Research in the postpositivist tradition developed out of a dissatisfaction with large-scale survey based research and its tendency to assume that there is a stable, knowable reality. Audience researchers such as Elihu Katz and Karl Erik Rosengren argued instead that research should aspire to describe a reality that is dynamic and can be known only imperfectly (Blumler and Katz, 1974; Rosengren, Wenner, & Palmgreen, 1985). Researchers who wrote in the then-groundbreaking postpositivist tradition noted that survey research often assumes a standardized instrument that can be interpreted differently by various subgroups of a society. In response, researchers in the then "new" paradigm of audience research sought to get as close as possible to the meanings ascribed to various words and motivations of members of the groups in which they were interested, through analysis of group discussions rather than survey methodologies (Liebes and Katz, 1984). Recognizing that no research can be completely free of biases, those in the postpositivist tradition nevertheless aimed for objectivity as an ideal stance toward research, arguing for cross-study comparisons so as to verify findings with qualitative research's smaller sizes.[2]

The Symbolism, Media, and the Lifecourse project began as a multi-methodological qualitative study whose end result would lay the groundwork for a large-scale survey, a fairly typical way of conceptualizing research in the postpositivist tradition. Such a survey could verify our findings and also provide the basis for generalization to the population at large. Our goals were quite general: We were interested in exploring the relationship between individual media meaning constructions and the cultural trends encompassing the decline of both membership in and cultural authority of the historical institutions. Still, we began with a latent hypothesis: that major moments of passage in the life course are important sites of personal reflection and transformation. As such, these moments are the key points in life through which the cultural-symbolic realm avails itself to the individual as a resource for identity construction, transformation, or development. With this in mind, we developed a research instrument that would query people about their media use during (and surrounding) those moments of significant change. What emerged from the fieldwork was inconclusive, and we did not pursue this line of inquiry.

Methodologically, we started with an ambitious goal, even by qualitative measures: We would begin with a small number of household-level observations, patterning our efforts after Silverstone and Hirsh (1992), Lull (1990), and Lindlof (1995). Next, we would add more households to the sample in order to form qualitative interview panels (Hoover 1996, 5). These panels would consist of several households, each of which would be revisited over a period of six to nine months. We anticipated employing the same interview instrument each time so as to maintain standardization across time, hoping that in this way we could observe the encounters with life passages or crises and how these might change the family's approach to media (Hoover 1996, 2). In the third and final stage of the research, we would develop a series of focus groups using representative demographic groups. This ambitious goal changed significantly, as discussed in this chapter and the next chapter.

Like other postpositivist researchers, we sought to distinguish ourselves from the traditions of survey research, and we assumed that our findings might contradict earlier findings based on surveys. As the original prospectus stated:

> Most research is discontinuous with daily life, i.e., it attempts a "slice of time" and therefore misses the ways cultural symbols contribute to consciousness and the "flow" of life. People are not passive receivers of knowledge and information. They actively decode and use knowledge and information they encounter in the public, symbolic environment. (Hoover 1996, 2)

THE "TYPICAL" RESPONDENT

Frustrated with the limitations of standardized survey instruments, postpositivists aimed toward a better understanding of the meanings people assign to their responses to a researcher's questions. In the oft-cited turn of phrase, they sacrificed breadth for depth, choosing to limit the sample size of their inquiry while continually adjusting a relatively standardized interview guide so as to best capture similarities of responses.

Of course, this approach is not without its problems. Seeking to meet the quantitative researcher's standards, the postpositivist is left in the untenable position of having to argue that his or her set of respondents is "typical" and that they therefore serve as a basis for generalization to the larger population (or a subgroup of the population). This is usually done by comparing the demographics of the research participants with those of the broader public. Of course, there is no "scientific" method by which to determine how many people are needed for a generalizable sample in qualitative research. Does sixty sound adequate? What about thirty? What about twelve? Furthermore, how might we boil down the various combinations of race, gender, age, class, education, religious affiliation, or geographic locale so that we might claim that the collection of people we have interviewed comprises a "representative" sample of the population at large? Is one person over the age of fifty enough? What if that person is a wealthy Asian female—can her experiences be generalized? Of what, or whom, might her comments be "typical"? The problem is only intensified when one attempts to make in-group comparisons. To make claims that a particular response is "typical" of the group sampled, how many need to voice it—a majority? More than half (which, in a sample of twelve, is only six people)? More than one? If the wealthy Asian American woman and the 15-year-old African American male agree on a certain point, might we then argue that such responses are "typical" of others, as well?

These questions and others beg a reexamination of the notion of the "typical" research participant. The model itself borrows from the work of Talcott Parsons, who in the mid-twentieth century assumed that the empirical world revealed fundamental properties that could be isolated, classified, and studied. To study a society, Parsons believed it was most useful to assume that society is stable so that its various functions—in other words, what worked to hold it together—might be carefully and independently analyzed. In this model, one might imagine that a "core" of society would include an aggregate of persons with similar attributes and similar affiliations who might act in similar ways, thus contributing to a stable society. The further one was from that core, the less "typical" of the whole that person was.

In the decades following Parsons's writings, media studies, along with a host of other fields competing for entrance into the respected realm of scientific inquiry, strove to perfect the description of the role of media in society and in particular how it functioned in a stable society. Researchers tested media use and its effects across the variables of race, gender, age, and other demographic identifiers. Yet with the rise of increased awareness of difference along these lines, media studies, like other fields, began to call into question the assumptions of generalization. How could one generalize across the entire population when the sample contained so few members of minority groups, for example? Thus, researchers began isolating the variables, to use quantitative terms: A study would look at only one racial/ethnic group, or one age group, for example, so that claims of typicality could be limited by particular demographic identifiers. Still there were problems, not the least of which was the subtle reinstituting of stereotypes through the assignment of an assumed "core" to particular subgroups. Another practical problem involved writing up the data: Aiming for the "typical" responses often meant eliminating the most unusual, richest, and most illustrative stories, making the potential strength of qualitative inquiry its most serious casualty.

We can trace some of the problems back to the disconnect between theoretical goals and the methods used to explore them in our foundational paradigm of symbolic interactionism. This approach, as stated earlier, aspired to address itself to social concerns while focusing on the interaction between the researcher and the research participant. While the goal of this research was to explore the role and possible solution to social problems, therefore, the method itself could lead in a different direction, to explore the meaning systems of individuals. In order for us to return the focus to the social rather than individual level, we can, as noted earlier, look to cultural studies as it was imported from Great Britain. In our own study, our purpose in constructivist research was then reframed in this way: We are not interested in generalizing our findings across people; instead, we are interested in generalizing to the culture.[3]

What did this shift mean? We believe it enabled us to move away from a position in which we sought to explore how individuals are relatively close or distant from an imagined "core" of society. We could approach each person as a "universal singular," to use Jean-Paul Sartre's term (Collins 1980). Each person's story becomes important, for it is simultaneously the story of a unique individual and the embodiment of the social world that has produced her or him. Furthermore, in this move we acknowledge an important learning from postcolonial critiques: that often people at the margins of societal groups can tell us the most about boundaries that help to construct what is accepted as the "typical" or "core" of society (Tsing 1993). Thus the very notion of the "typical" is problematized and implicitly recognized as a historically created category. Our analysis could then move from needing to claim how "typical" one is to identifying how the informant sees himself or herself in relation to some received notion of "typicality." In looking at received notions, we were forced to interrogate our own ideas of "typicality" as well. These received notions are in the public scripts that interview families drew upon to construct their accounts of the media and family.

TELLING THE NATIVE'S STORY

Symbolic interactionism was not the only influence on the current post-positivist approaches to qualitative media studies, of course. With the rise of interdisciplinary inquiry in the 1970s and 1980s, media studies increasingly looked to cultural anthropology for methodological clues. Borrowing the term and spirit behind ethnography, media scholars strove to move away from standardization so as to better capture the stories of everyday life. They embraced the tradition of Bronislaw Malinowski, who wrote:

> The goal is, briefly, to grasp the native's point of view, his relation to life, to realise his vision of his world. . . . To study the institutions, customs, and codes or to study the behaviour and mentality without the subjective desire of feeling by what these people live, of realising the substance of their happiness—is, in my opinion, to miss the greatest reward which we can hope to obtain from the study of man. (Malinowski 1922, 25)

The humanistic and romantic impulse of early-twentieth-century ethnography is evident in Malinowski's aim for "the subjective desire of feeling" and his wish that ethnography would be about "realising the substance of their happiness," and indeed this impulse remains largely intact in contemporary qualitative media research. In her germinal study of women reading romance novels, for example, Janice Radway was particularly interested in "taking the women's self-understanding seriously," which she argues was a missing element in the feminist critiques of literary texts up until that point (Radway 1984, 14). James Lull, another early qualitative media researcher, rather directly pits the benefits of ethnography's humanism against the presumed antihumanism of critical (i.e., mass society) approaches:

> Giving the audience a "voice" has produced tangible, positive results. It has tempered the often pretentious and opaque writing associated with cultural studies, the frequent imposition of privileged interpretations of texts, a reliance on fashionable literature, and the dogmatic refusal to cite "scientific" studies. Still, there are problems in the development of audience research in cultural studies. Most troubling is that we often hear too clearly the theorist's voice presented as if it were the audience's voice. (Lull 1990, 16)

Lull, Radway, and others have seemed to celebrate "giving voice" to research participants, thus validating the subjective experiences of media use among those studied. This humanism has been disparaged by those critical theorists convinced that, by highlighting subjective experience, we lose our focus on structural constraints (Garnham 1995). Yet it has also been increasingly denounced by researchers who embrace ethnographic methods, particularly as a result of feminist critiques. Feminists, while wishing to "give voice" to women's experience, have also advocated placing analyses of subjective experience within larger frameworks of social constraint, usually those determined by gender (Cirksena and Cuklanz 1992; McRobbie and Gerber 1976; Press 1991). The act of "giving voice" does not mean interpretation is removed, these critics argue; indeed, it is all too easy to hide the researcher's views in the voices of research participants, as Lull had suggested.

A constructivist approach retains the political impulse behind the desire to "give voice," to acknowledge the history that made some persons "voiceless" to begin with. It calls into question the notion that the experience of any one group might be assumed to be of universal significance (Nagar 1997, 7–8). In writing, therefore, the researcher must be aware of the constraints under which research participants tell their stories, for this shapes both what is told and how we must contextualize the telling for a larger audience. We must not forget that, as communication scholars Balmurli Natrajan and Radhika Parameswaran point out, the researcher ultimately exercises power simply by writing the qualitative research narrative itself, and this power must be acknowledged (Natrajan and Parameswaran 1997).

THE ROLE OF THE RESEARCHER

Postpositivism assumes, as noted earlier, that the best findings will result if researchers try to approximate what would happen, in terms of media consumption, were a researcher not there to observe these practices (Lincoln and Guba 1985). Thus to some extent researchers are assumed to be interchangeable; someone else entering the field would come to similar conclusions. It is not surprising, then, that those committed to the postpositivist approach tend to resist arguments for reflexivity on the part of the researcher. Expressing the concern that self-reflexive researchers who are themselves acknowledged fans might not maintain the distance required to "develop any kind of criticism," Shaun Moores, for instance, argues that such researchers risk a "populist acceptance or celebration" of the audience practices they observe (Moores 1993, 69). Feminist media critic Tania Modleski (1986) has made a similar charge regarding the need for "critical distance" between a researcher and his or her subject of study. Yet a researcher embracing a constructivist perspective would ask, does "distance" between oneself as a researcher and the practices one observes truly guarantee an objective position from which such criticism can be made? Researchers of such common practices as media consumption should be particularly wary of this claim, for who among us is not a television or film viewer? And by extension, then, how do we know when we have enough distance from our own experiences and practices to warrant a sufficiently critical interpretation (Nightingale, 1996)? As Robert Drew (2001) has asserted in his study of and participation in Karaoke, critical distance is less crucial than the need for all researchers to resist the impulse to treat their own emotional responses to their data as something that can be "cordoned off somewhere in isolation of [our] social selves." He notes instead that "a full theoretical accounting of such processes (of engagement between researcher and his/her subjects) *requires* some attention to feelings" (p. 30). In our own project, we took a middle course on this issue: We sought out as our informants those with whom we had no previous connection, yet we paid attention to how the interviewer and the context of the interview itself might have affected the interview situation and the interpretations that were created.

Because sense making on the part of the researcher must always rely on the knowledge we bring to the research context from either reading or personal experience, a constructivist perspective argues that our awareness of our own relation to what we observe and analyze is particularly important. There is a danger that the story emerging in constructivist research becomes the story of the researcher's self-discovery, yet this is not the only alternative to emerge from this paradigm, nor is it the most common. Instead, while the researcher's acknowledgment of the context and conditions within which the dialogues of research take place might lead to new insights, whether and how they are written about depend upon other factors, as will be discussed later in our discussion of "truth-telling" below.

First, we want to extend the argument for a self-reflexive project a bit further in the particular case of our research, which has foregrounded issues of identity. From the writings on representation, critical theory, and poststructuralism, we learn that identity is never a fixed category (or sum of categories) that may be unproblematically interrogated, but rather it exists as it is enacted.[4] In qualitative research, identity is enacted in the behaviors observed and the narratives constructed for the audience of the researcher. Constructivists do not approach the research participant's statements as "raw data" that might be unproblematically analyzed so as to get us close to "the truth," but as conditional statements made in a particular context and which of necessity require interpretation. Behaviors and narratives emerging in the research context are contingent on how the research participant reads the situation, the researcher's intent, and the researcher's position vis à vis both the subject and the larger culture. In an important sense, then, any analysis of identity construction cannot be separated from the specificity of the researcher/researched relationship. The more insight afforded into the factors shaping that situation, the more likely we are to understand the knowledge produced. This does not require an academic's "life history," but it does underscore the fact that all knowledge is contingent, that all experience is interpreted from a subject position, and that the specific knowledge constructed in the interview process is, as Kamala Visweswaran argues, "itself determined by the relationship of the knower to the known" (Visweswaran 1994, 48). Reflexivity, therefore, subverts normative understandings of knowledge gathering and information processing. As Barbara Babcock argues:

> By confounding subject and object, seer and seen, self and other, art and life—in short, by playing back and forth across terminal and categorical boundaries and playing with the very nature of human understanding—reflexive processes redirect thoughtful attention to the faulty or limited structures of thought, language, and society. (Babcock 1980)

A constructivist approach that encourages reflexivity on the part of the researcher therefore challenges the "givenness" of data interpretation and the ontological and epistemological assumptions undergirding positivist research.[5]

TELLING THE "TRUTH"

Assumptions of knowledge and truth are fundamental to the differences discussed here between postpositivist and constructivist research. Understanding that the goal of reflexivity is to provide the reader with better tools by which to evaluate the "truthfulness" of the presentation, Moores, a postpositivist, claims that reflexivity is not needed due to the "active critical capacities of readers" of audience ethnographies (Moores 1993, 64). Yet while critiquing any researcher's report is a widely accepted professional practice, this in itself does not address the basic ontological challenge of a constructivist approach. The constructivist argument for reflexivity does not concern merely the "accuracy" of the particular reported research, as Moores seems to assume, but the status of that knowledge itself.

At this point, postpositivists are to be excused if they wish to throw up their hands and sigh, "If all is relative and we can't say anything definitive, then why do the research to begin with?" Yet constructivists believe that this pessimism is unwarranted. The point of research in our pragmatist American tradition, a constructivist would argue, is not to reveal "the truth," after all, but to provide insight that can possibly change understandings. While the goals might be shared, the constructivist's approach to analysis and writing is quite different than that of the postpositivist. Rather than seeking to establish objectively defined categories that "emerge" from the "raw data," constructivists evaluate what has been learned from research participants in light of other insights they bring to the field. Constructivists realize that the "truth" that emerges is indeed a "truth" for them; the challenge, then, becomes how to present this viewpoint in a way that is enlightening and convincing to others. In other words, one must establish "ethnographic authority," to use the words of James Clifford (Clifford 1988, 21–54). Erasing the researcher from the writing, as postpositivists do, assumes rather than establishes such authority; the absent writer stands behind the veil of "objectivity" and scientific inquiry. Ien Ang makes a similar critique:

> The comfortable assumption that it is the reliability and accuracy of the methodologies being used that will ascertain the validity of the outcomes of research, thereby reducing the researcher's responsibility to a technical matter, is rejected . . . the empirical is not the privileged domain where the answers should be sought. Answers—partial ones, to be sure, that is, both provisional and committed—are to be constructed, in the form of interpretation. (Ang 1996, 47)

The interpretation itself, we would add, must be presented in the form of an argument. This argument must include a recognition of how the current interpretation relates to the ideas that shaped and framed it. In other words, it must be lodged in an intellectual history of some sort and must carefully relate the transcripts excerpted to the overall interpretive framework, as we have tried to do in the case-study chapters. Our argument, briefly is this: In order to understand family identity construction and parenting practices in the contemporary period, we need to see the media as an aspect of domestic, everyday life that must be negotiated. We believe that this is the case not because people think the media are important or even meaningful. It is because talk about the media—in terms of regulations parents attempt to put in place, sensitive content that parents feel they must address with their children, and simply the everyday negotiations around when, what, with whom, and how much can be consumed—serves as an important and concrete expression of the more general project of self-aware parenting demanded of most adults today. Thus, we present the stories in this book as a way to help our readers evaluate parenting practices around the media, while also considering how these fit within and reflect broader concerns of how parents attempt to guide their children in the world of late modernity which is increasingly defined by risk and change. As this argument is found persuasive by its intended audience, the researcher's authority is established. Thus, in a parallel to poststructuralist "active audience" research that locates "meaning making" at the site of the audience, so too does ethnographic authority emerge in constructivist research as its written arguments are found to be convincing.

The form of the argument turned out to be quite different from that which we expected at the project's outset due to our move from postpositivism to constructivism. Indeed, we believe that one of the benefits of constructivist research is that researchers allow themselves to be surprised by the directions in which the research takes them. The resulting argument that is put forth in this book is truly the result of a collaborative process that takes place between the research team members, the research participants, and those who read, hear, and evaluate its claims. The change in our research paradigm enabled us to reframe our analytic goals so that, rather than focusing only on meanings made, we were able to see those meanings within larger contexts of what we called the "public scripts" and "accounts of the media." Acknowledging their contingency on other cultural narratives was an important step in a constructivist approach.

REFRAMING QUESTIONS

The research approach detailed in this chapter represents one effort in a much larger trend in media research. How families incorporate the media into their daily domestic lives has been a subject long indebted to feminist and critical thought, as will be discussed in chapter three. We set out to define our approach as constructivist in order to situate it in relation to both these developments and the continuing strands of postpositivist research that have undergirded assumptions about research design and conduct regarding media and the family. We have argued that this recent turn in media studies toward what we are calling constructivist research reflects developments in anthropology, post-colonial thought, feminist methodologies and critical theory. In this sense, we hope that we have been able to reframe questions of typicality, generalizability, research aims, researcher roles, and truth-telling that often seem to confound qualitative research in the postpositivist tradition.

If knowledge is something that is constructed, then it makes sense that this knowledge evolves gradually: first within the context of interviews, then as our entire group mulled things over in our weekly analysis meetings, and then finally as we corralled our conversations into a particular form for writing. In this final stage, our writings became an argument rather than a set of findings; an argument that through its sophistication and elegance must establish our ethnographic authority.

Our argument aims to view family life in light of changes in the postindustrial society of late modernity that have encouraged parents to be increasingly reflexive about their parenting choices. Because of this increase in self-awareness, we found that parents tended to approach discussions about media use in the home as a specific and concrete way in which they could express what they value to their children. This argument will be fleshed out in the chapters that follow. To this end, the next chapter addresses more specifically the variety of theory related to culture and media upon which we drew.

3

Developing a Theory of Media, Home, and Family

Lynn Schofield Clark
Diane F. Alters

Scene: the office of Stewart Hoover, Director of the Symbolism, Media, and the Lifecourse project, fall 1998. Around a battered table sit Hoover, Lynn Schofield Clark, Diane Alters, Joseph Champ, and Lee Hood. The last three are graduate students, all perhaps somewhat older than the norm as they range in age from the mid-30s to late-40s. Also remarkable is a sixth person: Jonathan Clark, age 6 weeks, the son of Associate Director Clark, a postdoctoral fellow. Clark, Hoover, and the students take turns holding Jonathan, comforting him or just talking to him, as they do for the next several months of research meetings. His presence has a hard-to-define effect on this group, which has gathered to study families and media. He is more than a diversion, and certainly not an unpleasant disruption. Rather, he is to become a reminder to the group of the constant back-and-forth nature of life in a family, in which people at work think about their families, and people at home use their experiences there to reflect on their work.

In retrospect, the members of the research group realized that Jonathan's presence represented an overlapping of home and work boundaries, and it helped each member of the team to be reflexive about the experiences of interacting with children and about our work together. We saw that, like the people we interviewed, we brought to our work a collection of family-related concerns and experiences that informed our analysis. Jonathan's presence helped bring our own children and others into the room metaphorically, giving all of us permission to bring our own experiences to bear on our research in ways that we had not previously done. This enabled us to consider anew how children are integrated into the life of a group and how ideas and understandings develop collaboratively over time.

THEORETICAL FOUNDATIONS

Like Jonathan, the theoretical foundations for this research project grew gradually and in ways that were sometimes difficult to perceive for those most closely involved. Books often present theories as if they are set in stone or decided upon before any research is conducted, but this was not our experience as we collaboratively developed the theory that became foundational to this book. This chapter, therefore, takes the approach that ideas, like children, evolve over time and in relation to the many other ideas and experiences that occur in a specific historical context.

In our initial discussions about this book, the authors struggled to clarify where we stood in relation to each other and in relation to recent works on the audience. We had learned from the pioneering work of audience scholars, including those in British cultural studies and in the European reception studies tradition, as they sought to understand the role of the media in culture through the interpretation of actual cultural practices. At the same time, we were aware that some U.S. media researchers had encouraged greater attention to the relationship of media to the self and the individual.[1] During our weekly meetings, we recognized that our work specifically addressed longstanding conversations about audiences within various approaches to the study of culture.[2]

A book by feminist audience ethnographer Ellen Seiter, *Television and New Media Audiences* (1999), was particularly prominent in our discussions. Sharing our inclinations, Seiter also uses case studies and engages with social theory far more than most U.S. audience-research efforts. She writes that she focuses on "the role of language, the othering of the subject, the foundational work on media consumption in the domestic sphere, the influence of French sociologist Pierre Bourdieu's work on concepts of class, and the postmodern critique of ethnography" (Seiter 1999, 5). Seiter's book was especially helpful in our discussions of what she calls "lay theories of media effects." These "theories," popular among parents, articulate the concern that the media have various negative effects on children. In contrast to early audience research, Seiter is particularly sensitive to children's interests, noting that children's views and experiences of media might differ from their parents' views. Seiter is also interested in audience strategies of decoding text, as meaning making has been described in the British cultural studies tradition. Yet she also highlights some of the complexities of audience work, such as balancing parents' and teachers' self-descriptions of media use with her own understandings of underlying structural arrangements that privilege certain descriptions over others. As Seiter summarizes her own work:

> What I have presented here are some of the ways in which attitudes towards television viewing emerge from particular material conditions and family configurations, and the ways in which statements about television are produced under particular types of constraint by individuals with a range of investments and defenses at work (56).

In addition to Seiter's work, we were influenced by David Morley's pioneering audience research. Like Morley, we have emphasized the "constitutive role of the contexts and settings of media use" (Morley 1992). Morley notes in *Television, Audiences and Cultural Studies* that he understands media readings as part of a social process that connects people to the larger culture, in contrast to uses and gratifications theory, which understands the audience as a mass made up of individuals with individual, privatized readings of the media.

Also of interest to our project was a second edition of Sonia Livingstone's *Making Sense of Television: The Psychology of Audience Interpretation* (1998), although ultimately it explores the psychology of informants more than we chose to. We particularly related to a central question of Livingstone's that she felt had still not been answered in social psychology or media studies: "how the study of the meaning-making practices of audiences can be put together with the study of the meaning-making practices of people in their everyday lives" (Livingstone 1998, x).

Perhaps most important to the development of our theory in joint discussion was the early encouragement of anthropologist Elizabeth Bird, who studies media practice. She responded enthusiastically to our collaborative approach when we met with her during the third year of the project.[3] In addition to providing us with insights into the analysis of our material,[4] Bird noted that our process of group interpretation was in fact a startlingly different approach from the single-interviewer and single-interpreter approach that dominates the field of media studies.[5] She urged us to write about it, and this chapter—indeed, the entire book—is in part a response to her encouragement.

Our first attempts at developing an understanding of our data were broad and unfocused, as is often the case with ethnographic material. As noted in Chapter Two, we jointly discussed the transcripts of interviews in our weekly meetings, which sometimes lasted for three hours or longer. We initially spent a great deal of time thinking about the families whom we viewed as "outliers" to the overall study.[6] Stewart Hoover challenged us to think about what made these particular case studies so appealing to us. For instance, he asked whether Jake Carson, a heavy user of media who is discussed in Chapter Eight, was an "ideal type" of some kind. Hoover also drafted several versions of what he termed at the time an "Analytical Model (or Typology) for Media Positionality." This model included a typology that he called "three discourses of the media," which later became important to our evolving frameworks of analysis. In these documents, he attempted to map the various ways in which individuals in our sample seemed to be approaching the media and to provide a structure for our interpretations. Drawing largely on work by Tamar Liebes and Elihu Katz (1990) and Karl Erik Rosengren (1994) on the various ways in which media gratify certain needs of individual television viewers, Hoover posited that we were witnessing how media fulfilled needs, such as a need for a sense of self-competence and self-identity, a need to participate in social relations with others, and a need for social and cultural grounding.[7]

While some members of the research team were interested in the ways in which symbolic interactionists focused on the agency of individuals and therefore on what could be said about individuals and their actions, others on the team frequently pressed for an approach that would take into account structural constraints on individual agency. Diane Alters noted that postmodern and other theories had largely extended those of Erving Goffman and offered challenges to the idea that people need to view themselves as coherent and centered. Bringing up the concept of bricolage, she argued that we do not need to assume that people are holding a "core belief" that then dictates their actions. Instead, she argued, we need to recognize, with Anthony Giddens, that identity is always under construction and is related to the specific situation in which it is enacted. She noted that people in our study often expressed inconsistent views that made sense in one part of their story but not in another, a point also made early in the study by Alf Linderman.

As Alters noted in what each team member would come to view as a central aspect of our project, Giddens (1991, 192–202) provides a helpful reading of the prospects of the self in contemporary, mediated life. He argues that contemporary life—high modernity—has drastically changed the nature of daily social life, affecting the most personal aspects of experience. Every day, the individual confronts a dizzying variety of choices, and his or her world is filtered through a wide array of abstract systems in which the local and the global are in constant interplay. As a result, new mechanisms of self-identity have emerged. The self establishes a trajectory that can be coherent only through the reflexive use of the larger environment. This "reflexive project of the self" is one in which the individual continuously incorporates experiences, including mediated experiences, into daily conduct. This is a way of imposing order on the diversity of modernity, Giddens argues. To some extent, the appropriation of mediated information comes from habit, but it is also a way of avoiding cognitive dissonance. Thus the individual's appropriations from media can help form part of the "protective cocoon" that helps her maintain ontological security, a necessary part of living in modernity. Appropriating from media, then, is an integral part of the project of the self, according to Giddens (1991, 188). Compared with previous eras, the complexities of social life are more transparent to us, due in part to the media. This means that the person, in the context of everyday lived experience, will be increasingly aware of a range of claims, discourses, and positions that impinge on herself, a point also raised by Hoover. This self-reflexivity suggests that the constructions and negotiations we encounter at the household level are in some ways directed at the project of the construction of the self and identity in modernity (Alters 1998, 2002a). That project, Alters later argued, was as much a family as an individual project.

The implications of moving theoretically beyond the study of individual agency became clearer as we revisited some of our early research interests, in particular an early focus on typologies of behavior. Lynn Schofield Clark argued that the question was not so much whether or not we could identify "ideal types" or typologies of individual behavior. Instead, we needed to ask how we could describe the processes of meaning construction in which different people engaged, recognizing that these processes were dissimilar due to differing contexts that shaped their experiences, and that our understanding of them was limited to what we could interpret based on our interviews with them. With the help of sociologist Alf Linderman, we began to recognize that, as Linderman stated at one of our meetings, the important symbol set is the one that the family brings with them to their media consumption, not the symbols that they encounter at a particular moment in the media.[8] Moreover, as Linderman noted, the explanations that people give of the symbols that are meaningful to them are not simply a measure of meaning; they *are*, to a great extent, meaning. The kind of reception analysis in which we were engaged was "not a description of how individuals perceived something per se, but rather, a description of how meaning is formed as meaning is expressed" (Linderman 1997, 276).

Over time, the team negotiated, struggled over, and debated the ways in which the differing theoretical traditions of symbolic interactionism, social psychology, cultural studies, and critical social theory might be related to and in conflict with one another. Our weekly meetings were characterized by a tone of respect and collegiality despite these differences. Still, it was clear that the model of "grounded theory," which argues that theories "emerge" as one interacts closely with data in relation to existing theories, was difficult to apply in such a collaborative environment of rich and different theoretical traditions. What would be the ultimate theoretical model amid the sea of interesting possibilities? Although it would make for a tidy narrative to have done so, we did not reach our decision by rational discussion alone; in fact, we did not even recognize our contrasting theoretical commitments as anything other than an obstacle at the time. Yet, as is often the case in the development of such projects, sometimes the intrusion of practical concerns enables a project to move forward in a certain direction.

EMERGING IDEAS

The team had been in the field for just over a year when, in the fall of 1998, Lynn Schofield Clark was about to take a few months off for maternity leave. This prompted discussion about how to continue to include Clark in conversations via email during her absence. Stewart Hoover asked Joseph Champ to take minutes at the weekly meetings so these could be sent to Clark, who could then offer responses at a future point. Hoover also hoped that the meeting minutes could eventually be posted on the project's Web pages, which at that point were in their earliest stages, so that a wider network of colleagues might have access to them.

Champ's title for his notes, "Emerging Ideas," offered a prescient description of how important the process of note taking would become for our analysis. After several months of note taking, it became clear that the meeting minutes were a way for us to keep track of the various discussions that occurred over the course of this project's evolution, and we began to have more focused conversations on the most promising of those ideas. By reviewing the notes, we came to realize that moving from the analysis of transcripts to the development of a larger theoretical framework for the project was going to take a concerted effort. As had been the case with the initial decision to take minutes, practicalities took the analysis in a particular direction. Clark proposed a day-long retreat for analysis at the end of that fall semester so as to catch up on what she had missed during her leave. The goal of the day would be to go through all of the transcripts and attempt to "map" the families along a continuum, using categories that had been discussed throughout the fall. Each pole of the continuum was identified by categories that, at the time, we labeled "suffused" and "differentiated" in their approach to media, an approach that Joseph Champ (Champ, 1999b, c) originally introduced.

Initially, we defined households as "suffused" when family members said their media usage was high, while those we defined as "differentiated" indicated that they used the media much less than others they knew. When we had separated the families along this continuum according to their self-reports, we noticed an interesting tendency: The distinctions between "suffused" and "differentiated" families did not seem to offer a picture of actual differences in the amount of television viewed, computer games played, or music listened to, as we had anticipated. Instead, what characterized the differences in the families was their level of comfort with the way in which media had become a part of their everyday family lives. The "suffused" families were simply more comfortable with media, while the "differentiated" families were much more concerned about the possible negative impact of the media. The families we defined as "differentiated," therefore, were much more interested in presenting themselves to us, and to each other, as holding values that were distinct from the mediated environment as they perceived it.

We also found that it was easier to talk about the families at the poles than those in the middle. Hoover noted that the families at some distance from either pole had three characteristics: The family members did not articulate their beliefs about the media clearly or consistently; the family did not seem particularly interested in engaging in conversations with us about what they believed about the media; and, what we came to see as the most common response, members of the family had differences in terms of how they viewed the media in their family life. This led us to examine a little more closely the connecting point between presentation of self and what might motivate certain families to articulate certain views of the media over others. We recognized that the people in our study were not relating some statement of actual "truth" about their behaviors so much as they were providing a story about their media use that they believed was consistent with what they envisioned about their family's collective life and practices in their homes. What they were giving us, therefore, were not data about their usage so much as what we came to call "accounts of the media," introduced in Chapter One.

Almost as soon as we had used the rubric of the suffused/differentiated continuum, therefore, we found reasons to modify and reconsider it. By early 1999, we had replaced "suffused" with "constructive," as we believed that this term better echoed the active, rather than passive, ways in which families attempted to interpret and explain the media use in their own families.[9] We believed the term "constructive" helped us to recognize that families we identified as "suffused" were engaged in critical approaches to the media, as were the "differentiated" families.

The term "constructive" was to prove problematic also, however, for two key reasons. First, we had begun to refer to our method as "constructivist," in reference to the theories of the social construction of reality as articulated by Peter Berger and Thomas Luckmann (1967). Thus, we were concerned about using two terms that were so similar in different settings. A related issue arose from the emphasis in our methodology on the recognition of the socially constructed nature of all knowledge. We were aware that all families, not just those at the "constructivist" or the formerly "suffused" ends of the continuum, participated in this approach to reality. The challenge then became: How do we describe the ways in which those "differentiated" families socially construct their accounts of media use out of differing assumptions of reality? We decided that it would be more fruitful to offer a more fulsome discussion of these differing accounts of the media, rather than to attempt to "map" them along a continuum that might unconsciously echo some of our own preconceived notions of which accounts of the media might be more or less appropriate. As Alters argued, the problems with a continuum were numerous: Class, race, and religion did not map easily onto either end of the continuum. She was concerned that we could lose our ability to talk about the economic, political, racial/ethnic, and religious contexts in which families operated if we chose to focus on the extent to which we viewed them as suffused or differentiated.[10] Thus, we aimed to be both more attentive to each family's account and more reflexive about our own approaches to those accounts. This led to our presentation of families in the form of case studies in which families could be considered more fully in their social and cultural contexts. With this move, we were poised to explore further our notion of "accounts of the media."

There were several theoretical points of background to the emergence of "accounts of the media" as a category to examine. At this point in the project, Hoover discussed the work of symbolic interactionists such as George Herbert Mead (1910), Erving Goffman (1959), and Norman Denzin (1992).[11] He felt that it was important to focus, as those scholars had, on the constructed nature of self-accounts, drawing on Goffman's insight that it is important to recognize that people always act and speak in response to how they perceive that they will be interpreted by others. Hoover was therefore interested in linking Goffman's insights with more recent poststructuralist recognitions of the relationship between the narrative statements of individuals and the limits of language itself to express meaning. As a social-psychological theory, interactionism focuses on the intersection between the individual and broader contexts of meaning and action, and on how the individual comes to be an expression of his or her culture.[12]

At the same time, Hoover was intrigued by work in the field of "positive psychology," from those psychologists who had decided to stray from that field's long historical emphasis on deviance in favor of an exploration of what makes people centered and happy. Mihalyi Csikszentmihalyi (1990, 1997) was particularly influential to Hoover, for Csikszentmihalyi explored how artifacts ground people culturally, locating them in relation to the rest of the world, giving a sense of self as a positive, healthy human being.[13] If artifacts can be said to play such a key role in providing a personal sense of security and being, as Hoover argued in one meeting, then the way that people select certain symbolic inventories over others from the media says a great deal about us, as well. As Champ summarized for the team, "In other words, [accounts of the media] that say, 'I am a person who thinks this way about media' reveal positioning statements about ourselves. Notions about what we think the media are doing, all the anxiety over effectivity and noneffectivity, tell us more about those we interview than they do about the media."

Art historian David Morgan has also been particularly influential. He has written about the ways in which religious organizations, consistent with modern, Enlightenment approaches to visual images, have attempted to make visual representations stable by claiming the right to define their meanings for others. Morgan is interested in why and how visual images become meaningful to people, apart from the efforts by organizations to fix their meanings. He theorizes that this meaning making occurs in relation to what he believes is a human desire for stability. In this sense, therefore, his theories build upon those of Csikszentmihalyi.

Other, less psychologically oriented theoretical underpinnings also provided a foundation for what was to become the notion of "accounts of the media" as it is articulated in this book. At about this time, Clark had begun to explore issues of hegemony and legitimation, looking to Max Weber's classic theories on the relationship between institutions of power in society and the propagation of certain ways of seeing the world as "legitimate." She was interested in how ideas that become legitimated were similar to what audience members said about themselves related to differing class, racial/ethnic, religious, and gendered positions. She was therefore attempting to bring together Pierre Bourdieu's theory of distinction and the ways in which Antonio Gramsci's theory of hegemony has been related to the media, as articulated by Stuart Hall and others within critical/cultural studies. This approach gave attention to the question of *where* the accounts *come from* and what role they play in relation to the maintenance of certain power relations in society. She drew attention to the un-self-conscious ways in which parents in our sample equated certain media rules and practices as "good" or "preferable," noting that these often seemed to echo norms of the white middle class. She therefore wondered how the accounts given to us by our informants could be analyzed in relation to views legitimized elsewhere in mainstream institutions and organizations of society. Media literacy programs in the United States, some of which also unconsciously emphasized white middle-class norms in relation to media, were therefore a topic of discussion for many of the team meetings. What was being overlooked or obfuscated by the ways in which these accounts were focused, the team wondered? In a similar vein, Alters had become especially interested in class and in the ways in which class differences are articulated in reference to the media. Alters, who was becoming the project's expert on the social theories of Pierre Bourdieu, noted that the rules that parents make about the media tell us something about a family's taste. She pointed out that people who are particularly worried about their class position might have greater motivation than others to police their tastes according to these naturalized middle-class norms (Alters, 1999a, b, 2003).[14] With Bourdieu in mind, then, we began to look at "accounts of the media" as including normative claims for oneself and one's family, not just an informant's notion of what the media should or should not do. This point, as Champ later noted, broadened the notion of "accounts of the media" from a convenient label for normative claims about media practice at the individual level to a broader, more significant theoretical category that would help us understand the society in which these accounts emerged.[15]

It was Lee Hood who first drew connections between our evolving notion of "accounts of the media" and existing theories in American cultural studies. Hoover had identified three levels of engagement with media in his early analytical documents: experiences in, interactions about, and accounts of the media. At that point he had suggested that we call these "three discourses" of media. He noted that, as our informants talked about their relationship to media, these seemed to emerge as distinct categories. He argued that these might serve as a way of structuring our interpretations, and with his encouragement the three categories began to regularly enter our consideration of the interviews. Hood suggested the term we ultimately adopted for these categories, "modes of engagement." She pointed out that the first of these, *experiences in* the media, seemed to echo John Fiske and John Hartley's (1978) emphasis upon paying attention to which media experiences respondents found to be pleasurable. Moreover, she noted that Horace Newcomb and Paul

Hirsch's (1983) notion of a "cultural forum" could be related to our idea of *interactions about* the media, the second level of engagement. Hood recognized that interactions about the media function as a sort of social currency: Talking about the media gives people a way to talk about something they care about. Thus, such talk can be self-revelatory while also allowing a person to address issues of concern in the wider culture. Citing some disadvantages of limiting in particular the first category to Fiske's thinking, Champ added the important point that "experiences in" and "interactions about" the media were means to consider the third category, the ultimately more subtle and important *"accounts of the media"* that frame this book.

These interventions would later lead Clark to reexamine how James Carey's notion of "public scripts" might be applied in order to theorize what it is that people draw upon in the culture when discussing their own personal views and approaches to media use in their homes. Clark cited an essay by Carey, "A Cultural Approach to Communication," in which he discusses his notion of a "publicly available stock of symbols" on which people draw in a culture. Carey uses the notion to relate individual meaning to social meaning:

> In our predominantly individualistic tradition, we are accustomed to think of thought as essentially private, an activity that occurs in the head—graphically represented by Rodin's "The Thinker." I wish to suggest, in contradistinction, that thought is predominantly public and social. It occurs primarily on blackboards, in dances, and in recited poems. The capacity of private thought is a derived and secondary talent.... [T]hought is public because it depends on a publicly available stock of symbols. It is public in a second and stronger sense. Thinking consists of building maps of environments.... Thought is the construction and utilization of such maps. (Carey 1989, 28–29)

This "publicly available stock of symbols" was frequently cited, in different terms, in our interviews. Parents talked about what they thought most people in the United States felt about television, for example, or how their own media rules reflected a stricter (or more lenient) approach to media than their neighbors' rules. These reflections and constructions, Clark argued, are part of what we call *accounts of the media*. All of this theoretical work helped us to recognize that accounts of the media might be articulated differently by members of differing class, racial/ethnic, gender, and other social groups, and that such accounts articulated the economic, cultural, and "post-" or anti-modern concerns inherent within a particular historical moment.

Our interest in accounts of the media was based initially on parents' views of the media. Indeed, our theory is that parents largely viewed themselves as responsible for creating a cohesive family identity, and they sought to maintain an approach to the media that was consistent with that desired family identity. However, we also were increasingly aware of the occasions during interviews when children rejected or subverted their parents' attempts to establish and maintain a certain set of rules regarding the media. Drawing on the theories of media and family communication that had been articulated by James Lull (1990) and David Morley (1986, 1992), we discussed relationships of power as they were enacted within differing familial circles, particularly those in which children identified with two different households due to separation, divorce, or remarriage. In this process, we in essence rejected a common assumption that adults are critical media consumers while children are uncritical absorbers of media, and we realized that we needed to pay attention to how children are aware of and reflect upon the media, even as they do so in ways that are distinct from their parents' practices.

This attention to intrafamily dynamics was yet another example of our exploration of tensions between the individual and the social, between symbolic interactionism and critical/cultural studies, between a poststructuralist "decentered" self and a postmodernist "recentered" self, tensions that shaped much of the team's discussions over the years. These discussions helped build on the notion of accounts of the media. Hoover affirmed the value of focusing on accounts of the media, which he viewed as a concept that could improve on the symbolic interactionist project by providing what he called a "much-needed cultural landscape of the household." Alters added that our project also offered a social emphasis that went beyond symbolic interactionism by recognizing the notion of intersubjectivity—that subjective responses are not strictly individual but are shared by members of a culture, drawing on connotations and myths operating in the culture, in particular in media texts discussed in the interviews.

FINAL REFLECTIONS

The decisions that brought this book to its completed form came about, again, largely out of practical concerns. They were also the result of reflections on interactions with scholarly colleagues from inside and outside our own institution. One of the earliest of these reflections was rather painful for us, and it came in response to the first article on the project's research submitted for publication, written by Hoover, Clark, and Alters. Two anonymous reviewers requested that we provide major revisions to the manuscript before resubmitting it for publication. The primary critique was that, as one reviewer commented, although the article was "bursting with ideas," it lacked focus and cohesion; we seemed to be trying to move in too many directions at once. The critique was well taken. At that point in the process, we had assumed that a single, coherent approach would eventually emerge—but it had not. It would take another two years of interviewing, joint interpretation, and singular writing before we were able to settle on a balance between establishing enough coherence so that this book would hold together while maintaining the individual intellectual contributions of each author, specifically symbolized through the signing of chapters by their authors. But like so much of this project's evolution, this move to a balance came not as a result of planning but out of practical considerations: those stemming from time constraints as we faced the task of moving from analysis to the final writing phase of the project.

In the spring of 1999, Stewart Hoover agreed to serve as Interim Dean for the School of Journalism and Mass Communication at the University of Colorado at Boulder, a post he was to hold from that time until January 2001 (He later served as Interim Dean again, from March 2002 to July 2003). During that time, team members continued to interview families and to work on book chapters, jointly discussing those drafts at day-long meetings. Because of the time commitment of serving as dean, Hoover asked Alters to take on the task of establishing a unified "voice" for the project, a job that would entail rewriting each chapter and considering which ideas should be emphasized for maximum coherence between chapters. With Clark's ongoing help, and with input from Champ, Hood, and Hoover, Alters worked on this effort for the better part of a year, until she turned over a draft of the manuscript to Hoover and Clark in January 2002. The manuscript was not in fact written in a unified voice—a goal Alters found impossible to meet. Each author's essays reflected different intellectual commitments and emphases, despite the joint discussions of each interview. It seemed obvious, in retrospect, that the joint discussions had stimulated individual thinking as much as they had clarified certain shared commitments (to the interview process, to the value of recognizing meaning making), as the authors were challenged to pursue their own, separate interests in the project. It was impossible to impose a unified voice because one did not exist, as many of our issues reflected the differing commitments of the authors, as reflected in their doctoral dissertations (Alters 2002a, Champ 2001, Clark 1998b, Hood 2001). Each essay in the book reflected each author's own intellectual interests, and as a result we agreed to sign each chapter with the names of the individuals most responsible for the work involved. Chapter Two, written by Clark, is based on her own writing and research on methodology and on the role she played in the project. Chapter Four, written by Alters, is based on her writing and research and reflects her interest in the history and social context of our work on families.

The case studies are similarly reflective of each author's interests. Chapter Five, on the Ahmeds and the Paytons, and Chapter Six, on the Hartmans and the Roelofs, reflect Clark's and Alters' interest in placing the study families in social context and exploring what they bring to their media engagement. Chapter Seven, on the Price-Benoits and Franzes, reflects Hood's interest in how families view themselves and how they engage in media as a result. Chapter Eight, on the Vogels and the Carsons, reflects Champ's interest in examining and questioning labels assigned to families in the United States—in these cases, the epithet "couch potato."

With our increased emphasis on the family context, Clark became interested in how some parents in the study seemed to view themselves as participants in a culture that is not the "mainstream." This adherence to a different culture, whether defined by religion, racial/ethnic background, immigration, or some other category of identification, could serve as a way in which parents and children could share a common view of themselves as different from what they viewed in the media. Inculcating their children into an alternative culture, therefore, could allow parents to sidestep the intellectualism implied in sorting through what is good and bad on television—a task that in any case might be overwhelming for many families with young children. Clark noted that American evangelicals seem to have taken this approach to heart, creating many popular cultural products that together can provide the resources for the construction of a family culture that is defined by its distinction from mainstream, mediated culture. Alters noted that products like the *Veggie Tales* series of videotapes exactly express this desire for alternative cultural products that emphasize what some parents view as "moral" approaches to the world in packaging that is quite sophisticated and appealing to children.[16] These considerations of alternative cultures contributed to our thinking about the case studies, as reflected particularly in Chapters Five and Six.

With this increasing emphasis in our work on family culture, and at the same time our interest in the project of the self in modernity, we began to talk about how we could think of identity in terms of a joint, family project, as individual informants seemed to interact in their families to construct a joint identity. Like individuals, families do not construct identities as part of a conscious project. Yet identities emerged as families struggled with the everyday issues that faced them: how to guide children; how to understand parents in relation to other sources of authority like teachers and peers; how to establish or maintain a position in a culture that some family members find overly permissive, violent, and so on. To think about the collective nature of the family suggests the need to think more fully about definitions and terms under which contemporary families operate *as* families. This is discussed at greater length in the next chapter.

4

The Family in U.S. History and Culture

Diane F. Alters

When 12-year-old Bobbi Ann Mills volunteered to be the first in her family to offer her views on the meaning of "family," she withstood a barrage of good-natured, television-centered joking about her romantic notion of the term.

Bobbi Ann:	I have thoughts about how a family could be like, you know, you see on TV, a perfect family is. Sometimes you sit down and go, "You know what? Our family is not normal." I want it to be normal, as in happy. Well, love, and everybody has a well-paying job, and the kids go to a pretty good school and stuff.
Spencer [her 9-year-old brother]:	Pretty good.
Jim [their father, ironically]:	We're that way, aren't we? For the most part?
Bobbi Ann [seriously]:	For the most part. So, I think a family is what—
Connie [their mother]:	Is that the Cosbys you're talking about? *[laughing]*
Jim:	Tim Allen?
Connie:	Yeah! Which show is this?

Bobbi Ann:	Well, you just see it on TV. I used to think that—
Jim:	Dr Quinn?
Bobbi Ann:	—like our family should be happier. Our family should go out camping and be happy. Like my brother and I get—*[Connie laughs]* my brother and I get into fights a lot. You see on TV, oh, brothers and sisters are perfect little angels, and together they're—
Jim:	It's called "acting." *[All, including Bobbi Ann, laugh.]*
Bobbi Ann:	Okay. Move on from me.[1]

Bobbi Ann's opinionated, talkative real-life family did not see themselves in her vision, and in many ways they were not the family she longed for. "Everybody" did not have a well-paying job, and money was often tight in this white, middle-class family. The schools the children attended were not always "pretty good." And family harmony was often elusive as they struggled to blend the remnants of two former marriages into a cohesive new one, with three of eight children still at home. They were not "normal" in the television sense that Bobbi Ann offered. Her mother, Connie, tried to illustrate their differences from this norm by describing their family Christmas Eve at a local café, where they shot pool and turned their backs on an expensive, traditional luxury-hotel event that her ex-husband and some of the children attended. Still, in the interview they recognized Bobbi Ann's cultural vision, and they flung it back to her in the television-family names they laughingly shouted out until she retreated. Later, they returned to her vision, indirectly, as they described many experiences and adventures they had as a family: a house fire and its aftermath, children's illnesses, Fourth of July celebrations, weddings, playing Scrabble with Grandma during a long visit with Jim's family in another state. Like the vivid personalities that made up their large family, the narratives they drew upon to construct "family" were numerous and varied. Like the Millses, other interviewed families also drew on television programs and other forms of mediated popular culture, where public scripts about family often reside, to define their families and their beliefs about what a family should be.

This chapter explores the sociohistorical context of the family narratives that emerged from the interviews we conducted. The family stories were often part of families' visions for themselves, and they often appeared in interviewees' accounts of the media. The families we talked with made meaning from a complex variety of resources, including various media products and the public scripts in them. The family identities they constructed were dependent on social, historical, economic, and cultural circumstances in which media played an important role. In this context, this chapter explores some historical roots of contemporary notions of family and the relationship of media to those notions of family.

The family stories amount to a profusion of intersecting cultural narratives that include those embedded in the study itself. The term "family" was used in the study in a number of different but related ways. "Family" describes almost every group of people we interviewed. One of the researchers would say, for example, "I'm going to interview a Mormon family," or, "I talked with a single-parent family." The interview guide for the project is entitled "Family Interview," and the term appears several times in the consent forms people signed before the interviews. In other words, we asked for families and we got them. Not only did we seek entities called "families," but we also asked what the term meant to each group we interviewed. In response, almost invariably, the members of the group recognized the term as hailing them, and they discussed what "family" meant to them. We sought, then, to treat family as a social, rather than individual, identity. We came to understand that both individual and social identity are related; it is through the social identity of the family that individual family members think of themselves in social terms.

Furthermore, in seeing "family" as a social identity we also saw it, in many ways, as a public identity, although much social theory has viewed the family as an essentially private entity (Bourdieu 1996). Instead, "family" in this study has both private and public connotations. In fact, we came to believe that public/private was a false distinction, in that both meanings are contained in the term "family" and both work together to construct what the term has come to mean in public scripts in the United States.[2] This project of understanding meaning making in families as they engage with media comes at a time when scholarship in several fields has been increasingly attentive to the changing definitions of family in the United States, particularly in history, anthropology, and sociology as well as in media studies. Outside academia, too, assumptions about the nature of family have come under increasingly scrutiny in the years since World War II, as the term has emerged in political campaigns, public policy debates, and pulpits. A related turn to the audience is also apparent in the work of some media scholars who are interested in interrogating family meanings as they are expressed by people who engage with various media (Morley 1986, 1992). This chapter, then, is situated at the intersection of audience research and studies of the family in U.S. life.

A CHANGING DEFINITION OF THE FAMILY

In the aftermath of World War II, anthropologist George Murdock offered a universal definition of the family, based on his own analysis of 500 societies. The family, he argued, was

> a social group characterized by common residence, economic cooperation and reproduction. It includes adults of both sexes, at least two of whom maintain a socially approved sexual relationship, with one or more children, own or adopted, of the sexually cohabiting adults. (Murdock 1949, 1, quoted in Gerstel 1994)

Murdock's 1949 definition was widely used for many years in scholarly accounts, despite the fact that some historians and anthropologists had noted wide variations in family form, according to Naomi Gerstel (1994). New evidence indicates that since the 1960s Murdock's definition can account for only a minority of households worldwide, Gerstel notes. She offers this fluid definition of family:

> While the modern West has come to emphasize the family's emotional significance, we may have changed the conditions that could sustain such an emphasis. The very concept—the family—then, cannot capture the range and diversity of experience that many now define as their own. A family—really many different families—are 'here to stay'. The family is an ideological and social construct. Any attempts to define it, as a bounded institution with characteristics universal across place or time, will necessarily fail. (Gerstel 1994, 223)

Indeed, we sought out families that belied Murdock's definition and reflected Gerstel's, including single-parent families and families with parents of the same gender. As a result, we found a variety of family forms.

Accordingly, this chapter works with a fluid definition of family. For example, Rachel Albert, the mother in a blended family, offered this definition:

> I think being a blended family...has really shaped our family, and also making the commitment that even though some of the kids have different original parents, that doesn't mean that we're not a family. So speaking to the whole family, there's not your-kid, my-kid kind of segregation. We look at ourselves as a whole unit, and we think that that's significant. Because realizing, too, that lots of blended families these days don't look at it that way. You know, "Well, we've got our core family and we've got our stepfamily" and that whole thing. We don't believe in that. Relations with Terry's first wife are good. Everybody seems to work together so it's not an unhappy thing, and I think that's shaped us as a family, to help us all include everybody.[3]

Cindy Peterson, a mother in a lesbian relationship, described how she and her partner chose to keep a psychological distance from her

biological family because her father's strong objections to her relationship threatened to interfere with the relationship. Instead, their neighbors, also lesbians, became their family. "Oh, we totally love them," she
said. "They're like our best friends, our family. We *call* them family."[4]

Members of a household consisting of a father, his two sons, and three
nephews (ages 11–19) also thought of themselves as a family. In affec-
tionate, teasing terms, all in essence said they thought family consisted
of people they could trust. The patriarch, Rob Carson, noted that his
family helped him define his place in society: "Family is a very fun and
exciting way for me to devote a huge amount of time and energy. It's
also a power trip. It's a way of getting a place in society, in which I have
more prestige and authority than I would if I didn't have a family" (he
laughs).[5]

These examples indicate that the term "family" is not a fixed category,
either across time or contemporaneously. The meaning of family varies
according to sociohistorical circumstances as well as according to the
person using the term. This flexible definition underscores a longstanding but often submerged debate in the latter half of the twentieth century
over the meaning of family. This preoccupation with family meaning has
occurred over roughly the same period as the rise of television, the most
familial of all media.

Television entered U.S. homes in the late 1940s and early 1950s. From
its inception, it has been a family medium: It was and is intended to be
viewed primarily in the home, by families. It is not a coincidence that both
television and family have at various moments been centers of polarized
debates about meanings and effects. At the very least, it is significant that
the U.S. family went through striking changes in the years after World War
II, while at the same time television had an increasingly visible presence
and perceived impact on U.S. life.[6] This is not to argue that one caused the
other. It is to argue, however, that both phenomena are enveloped in—
and act upon—the same culture. Furthermore, television is not the only
home medium; all media have a domestic character, as Shaun Moores
argues (Moores 1993, 78–116). Thus print, radio, the Internet, and the
telephone occupy positions of varying importance in households and in
family sensibilities, and their use often overlaps with television, as the
present study recognizes. Clearly, though, television's domestic character
in the late twentieth century was so strong that television was markedly
present, even when its use was limited by family rules. Even families'
experience of cinema was often through television; many families in the
study rented videos of movies far more often than they ventured into
movie theaters.

In keeping with this presence in the family home, television's imagery
is overtly familial. Situation comedies centered on the family have been

a staple of television since the very beginning. Social historian George Lipsitz argues that early family situation comedies such as *The Goldbergs* and *Mama* began as vehicles for advertisers to lure newly prosperous postwar families into spending their wartime savings on a dazzling variety of consumer goods (Lipsitz 1990, 40–42). Family sitcoms have been through a variety of changes since then, from *Leave It to Beaver* (a middle-class white nuclear family), to *The Cosby Show* (an upper-middle-class African-American nuclear family), to *Married . . . With Children* (a working-class white nuclear family), to the short-lived *The Geena Davis Show* (a wealthy, white family with unmarried parents, with two children living with their father).

Sociologist Ella Taylor has examined the shifts in family form over the lifespan of prime-time television. Television in the 1950s and 1960s depicted the "harmonious, well-oiled building blocks of a benignly conceived American society founded in affluence and consensus," while 1980s television showed a variety of family forms but emphasized the nuclear families of such shows as *Family Ties* and *The Cosby Show* (Taylor 1989). Taylor elaborates her view of television's relationship to society and family life:

> These shifts [in family forms depicted on television] raise interesting questions about the relationship of television to prevailing social concerns in different periods. Television is no more a mirror to (or an escape from) the social world than any other fictional narrative. True, television's naturalism feeds our expectations of verisimilitude. Its mimetic visual form persuades us that Ozzie Nelson (of *Ozzie and Harriet*) lives on, schmoozing the day away with his neighbor across the yard; that the Bunkers (of *All in the Family*) really live in Queens; that the Huxtables (of *The Cosby Show*) frolic day after day in a well-appointed Manhattan town house. But family life never resembled that of the Nelsons, or the Bunkers, or the Huxtables, at least not in any narrow sociological sense. Like all storytelling, television speaks to our collective worries and to our yearning to improve, redeem or repair our individual or collective lives, to complete what is incomplete, as well as to our desire to know what is going on out there in that elusive "reality." Television comments upon and orders, rather than reflects, experience, highlighting public concerns and cultural shifts. (Taylor 1989, 3)

In late 1989, one of the most striking families in American popular culture appeared on television in a half-hour show: the Simpsons. They are striking not just because they are a successful prime-time cartoon family; they are significant in our study because interviewees usually mentioned them in passionate terms. *The Simpsons* was banned in some families, praised in some, and watched guiltily (the guilt was mainly parental) in others. A succinct analysis of *The Simpsons'* place in U.S. culture is contained in this reflection by Mark Price, a gay father who, in contrast to his partner and their 11-year-old daughter, liked the program.[7] "I think *The Simpsons* is insightful," he said. "It makes statements on how American families work. I mean, it's silly, but it really talks about how we work and how we are."

The Simpsons may be silly, and they are emphatically *not* a "traditional" 1950s-style television family in their dysfunctional cartoon antics and fanciful story lines. However, they are more or less 1950s in form, with a breadwinner father, stay-at-home mother, and children. With its success, *The Simpsons* has a place in many stories about families related by interviewees in this study. *The Simpsons* is funny and highly disturbing at the same time as it is a reminder that the family no longer has the fixed identity it once appeared to have. The Simpsons behave in ways a traditional 1950s family ought not to behave, in that they are rude, reckless, and irreverent. Yet they meet cultural ideals of what a traditional family should be: They are nuclear, they resolve their differences, and they are loyal, in a bumbling way, to one another.

The family theme is apparent in television news as well. David Morley saw family themes as central to the news content of *Nationwide*, a British news magazine program. In the United States, evocations of family appear on the very sets some news programs construct. The studio set of ABC's *Good Morning America*, for example, at times has been built to represent a family living room, complete with crackling fire and big color TV, as Cecelia Tichi observes (Tichi 1991, 4). Audiences, then, are seeped in the discourse of family, in their own constructions, and in the representations of family that are evident in the media in which they engage.

THE FAMILY IN U.S. HISTORY

Contemporary notions of family in the U.S. context are a complex amalgam of meanings—including a fair amount of nostalgia. Stephanie Coontz argues that current concepts of the traditional family have roots as recent as the late nineteenth century; what is thought of as traditional has not always existed. The notion of a private family in which morality and personal identity are centered developed in the Gilded Age of the 1870s to the 1890s, a time of "unrestrained wealth-seeking and political ambition" (Coontz 1992, 101–5). There was a corresponding sentimentalization of private life, one basis for current notions of the traditional family, she argues.

The image of the traditional family that today provokes much nostalgia is the family associated with the 1950s: father as breadwinner, mother at home with children, in a private, autonomous unit. Indeed, in the 1950s family life and gender roles in the white middle class became more predictable and settled, in contrast to the decades before and after the 1950s, due to a variety of social changes. During this time, social values shifted to emphasize the immediate nuclear family as the place to put "all one's emotional and financial eggs," Coontz writes. In the present study, the 1950s image and era was held out by some interviewees as the best for domestic life.

For example, in one large family, the Walkers, the mother and father longed for the 1950s when things were more "moral," as they termed it, when "family" meant their white, middle-class family: a salaried father, at-home mother, and children.[8] They sought this model by buying or borrowing children's books from the 1950s for their five children (ages 10, 7, 4, 3, and 2 months) and renting early Disney movies or old cartoons. They were disturbed by certain images they had seen on television, including depictions of gay lifestyles on such programs as *Ellen*, which they felt worked against the grain of the nuclear family they wished to maintain. Over the past decade, they had increasingly limited their children's television viewing, particularly after they noticed that their middle child was keenly interested in any screen display she encountered during shopping trips and other outings. Eventually, the television was banished to the basement, to a cabinet behind closed doors. Mara, the mother, estimated that no one in the family in a normal week watched more than three hours of television. Still, the Walkers were conversant about many television programs, particularly children's, and a variety of movies and videos. The parents felt they could not completely isolate themselves from television because they had to know about it in order to criticize it. Television, then, was important to them as a negative measure, because it helped them define their family by comparing their family to contrasting images depicted on television.

Coontz observes that the nostalgic image of the 1950s family is accurate, but only in very narrow ways in the white middle class. Moreover, the 1950s nuclear family is a "historical fluke" (Coontz 1992, 28). American families before and since the 1950s have not fit this model, although it persists in the form of yearning and nostalgia in popular culture. The 1950s family was possible because of a "unique and temporary conjunction" of economic, social, and political factors. As Coontz states:

> [T]he traditional family of the 1950s was a qualitatively new phenomenon. At the end of the 1940s, all the trends characterizing the rest of the twentieth century suddenly reversed themselves: For the first time in more than one hundred years, the age for marriage and motherhood fell, fertility increased,

divorce rates declined, and women's degree of educational parity with men dropped sharply. In a period of less than ten years, the proportion of never-married persons declined by as much as it had during the entire previous half century. (Coontz 1992, 24)

Furthermore, most people at the time understood that the 1950s family was new. The Great Depression in the 1930s had exacerbated family tensions as economic destitution forced extended families to live together. Family members were separated during World War II, but they crowded together once again due to the housing shortages of the war's immediate aftermath. Coontz notes that family counselors warned of marital crises caused by extended families being forced to live together. Sociologists such as Talcott Parsons urged a move to the nuclear family that was centered on raising children, nurturing emotions, and shaping the modern personality. With postwar prosperity and favorable government mortgage policies that often excluded non-whites, white nuclear families did indeed reassemble in their new, separate houses in suburbia. Women left their war time jobs and returned to the home and housework. Men were also affected and were expected to change. "For the first time, men as well as women were encouraged to root their identity and self-image in familial and parental roles," Coontz writes (1992, 27). In addition, she notes that a general optimism influenced people's views and experience of family life in the 1950s (Coontz 1997, 41).

The 1950s family carried the seeds of its own destruction, Coontz argues. Advertisers created a youth market for products, effectively bypassing parents, and promoted sex as a key part of life, working against the grain of the traditional family definition. Other "time bombs" were set, in the form of increased debt and weakened labor unions, conditions that helped destroy the family-wage system of the 1950s, in which the father was expected to earn enough to support a stay-at-home wife and children. Since World War II, changes in child-rearing values and parents' behavior "reflect realignments in the way families articulate with larger social, economic, and political institutions, as well as changes in environmental demands on adults and children," Coontz writes (1992, 215).

Such changes in child-rearing values and parental behavior include "a radical new self-consciousness about child rearing," according to the historians Steven Mintz and Susan Kellogg (Mintz and Kellogg 1988, 217). Since the 1960s, parents have become uneasy about how to raise children in light of increases in drug use, delinquency, pregnancy, and suicides among children and adolescents, worries that were also reflected in our interviews. At the same time, the circumstances of marriage and family have changed dramatically. For example, the proportion of children growing up in nuclear families has declined, while the number growing up with single-parent or two-worker, two-parent families has increased, as has the divorce rate. The rapid movement of mothers into the work force since 1960 has prompted debate about who cares for children and how they are cared for outside the family. Mintz and Kellogg describe this anxiety:

> Each of these changes has evoked anxiety for the well being of children. Many adults worry that a high divorce rate undermines the psychological and financial security of children. Others fear that children who live with a single female parent will have no father figure with whom to identify or to emulate and no firm source of guidance. Many are concerned that two-career parents with demanding jobs substitute money for affection, freedom for supervision, and abdicate their parental roles to surrogates. Still others fret that teenage jobs undermine school attendance and involvement and leave young people with too much money to spend on clothing, records, a car, or drugs. Today's children and adolescents, many believe, are caught between two difficult trends—decreasing parental commitment to child nurture and an increasingly perilous social environment saturated with sex, addictive drugs, and alcohol—that make it more difficult to achieve a well-adjusted adulthood. (Mintz and Kellogg 1988, 218)

These changes frighten parents, and as a result "parents have become progressively more self-conscious, anxious, and guilt-ridden about child rearing," Mintz and Kellogg write (1988, 220). These emotions were apparent in our interviews, as parents repeatedly described their fears for their children. As Mintz and Kellogg note, parents were mindful of many barriers that seemed to come between a parent and his or her child. Chief among these perceived barriers is television, and, as our study suggests, television is a lightning rod for parental worries about how they are raising their children.

Contemporary television, and to a lesser extent other media, were seen by study parents as barriers to worry about and to try somehow to change. This is why television and other media are at the center of our concept of reflexive parenting, as described in Chapter One. In our study, parents worried a great deal about the time their children spent watching television, the content of the shows they watched, and the impossibility of watching everything with their children. If parents could not control history, perhaps they could try to control television, a tangible symbol of postwar change.

As we shall see in the following chapters, parental approaches vary tremendously. The Hartman parents, who watched a great deal of television with their children, seemed to be constantly asking, "What do we think of this?" when they watched. The Roelofs, who watched less often with their children, seemed to be asking, "How does this square with what we believe, or want to believe?" Other parents sometimes added this question: "What kind of parent am I to let my child watch this?" The Ahmeds in effect asked, "How does this help or hinder our faith?" And the Paytons often measured media by how they contributed to waste—of their time as well as by encouraging more consumer goods, consumption, and landfill waste. Television, especially, was always available for parents as a way to locate themselves and their families in society.

Sometimes parents criticized other families' media practices and raised questions about their community. The Goldmans, for example, who had just moved from a suburban town to a city neighborhood, said they had been particularly concerned about the movies and television their 12-year-old son Don had seen with friends in their new location.[9] "One of the things I notice is how much more difficult it is for me when I feel like other families around me don't have similar rules," Ruth Goldman said. Her husband, Harvey, saw the problem as a lack of "common sense" on the part of other parents:

Harvey: I think regulating what they see, and I mean, you have to practice it too. I mean, we don't sit up there in our room and watch *Married… With Children* and tell them they can't. We don't watch the movies that we tell them they can't. Setting down guidelines as far as how much TV to watch a night. And you read about all these stories about, so-and-so went out and killed five people because they watched this movie on TV.

Don [interjecting]:   And a little kid burned down his house because of *Beavis and Butthead.*

Harvey [continuing with his story about the movie that he said prompted murder]:   And then they sued the producers of the show, and I think, we didn't have to watch it to begin with. And I think if there was more parental control—not government control, not censorship, but just common sense.

In a sense, the Goldmans, who were middle class and Jewish, saw television as a negative measure of belonging, a yardstick with which to measure themselves against other parents who were less careful.

Another parent, Sheryl Murphy, a college professor, was dismayed that parents of friends of her children, ages 13 and 10, allowed their own children to watch movies that were banned in her house.[10] Unlike the parents the Goldmans criticized, the parents Sheryl discussed actually watched the movies with the children. "Most of Paul's friends—and these are families with good educations, have very high values, they're concerned about their children, but their kids go to see all these violent films. And they go to see all these sexually explicit films," Sheryl said. Such comparisons emerged frequently in interviews, as parents often contrasted their parenting to that of other parents. As often as they did this, they also looked to the past for differences in approaches.

PARENTS' REFLECTIONS ON THE PAST THROUGH THE MEDIA

Many parents recalled their own childhood experiences with television and movies in a reflexive way, in that they often compared their own parenting practices to their parents' methods. Some parents said their elders had been far less worried than they about television and other media. Some noted that they had watched television freely as children, but they thought it important to limit their own children's viewing because television content had changed. For example, a mother in the study, Vicki Stevens, remembered very different content on television when she was a child.

> I think it's hugely different from when I was a kid. When I was a kid, the shows were, there was hardly any violence on shows. A lot of family-related shows, that's what we saw all the time. I mean, even things like *Bonanza*, where there were people getting shot once in awhile, it wasn't this continual blood and—you never saw anything, it wasn't just people going after each other with machine guns.[11]

Perhaps it was the general optimism of the 1950s and early 1960s, mentioned earlier, that prompted some parents in the study to prefer movies and television shows from that era to those made at the end of the twentieth century. Although many of these parents remembered television fondly, they said the content of contemporary television convinced them that they should regulate television far more than their own parents did. For example, Ray and Lydia Montoya, Hispanic parents in an upper-middle-class, dual-income suburban family, encouraged their children, 9 and 5, to watch reruns of *I Love Lucy* rather than contemporary sitcoms.[12]

Lydia: The thing about *I Love Lucy,* I think it's just nice, clean—
Ray: See, we grew up with *I Love Lucy,* though.
Lydia: It's just fun. It's funny. What I don't like about the new sitcoms is I think they're just *[she almost whispers, as if not wanting her children to hear]*, I mean even the family, I don't even know which

ones, but it seems like the ones coming out today are just—they refer to sex a lot or the kids are smart-mouthy to their parents. That's supposed to be funny? I don't think that's funny. You know, *I Love Lucy* is just nice, clean humor. It's just funny. The kids really like it a lot. We laugh because it's funny. Silly is what it is. It's not really smart-mouthy stuff. Just corny, is what it is.

Likewise, Jim Mills, introduced at the beginning of this chapter, was firmly convinced that television was better when he was a child.[13] Programs like *The Andy Griffith Show* contained many stories of goodness and demonstrated values that Mills felt had been important for his own moral growth.[14]

In contrast, a single, African American parent, Paula Pearson-Hall, did not think much had changed in media from her childhood to the present, and that people's responses to movies also remained the same.[15] Paula, mother of 2-year-old twins and teenagers Tammy, 19, and Michael, 15, believed that a child's understanding of a particular show depended on how and where the child was raised in the first place, a key to her own reflexive parenting. In fact, she maintained that clear messages were available for children like hers in certain movies with African American characters. As she spoke, she increasingly took on the talking style of the movies she described:

Paula:	Well, my personal opinion is, there's a lot of movies that come out, like *Boyz in the Hood* and stuff like that, that portray the life of living in a neighborhood that's gang-ridden, that was pretty factual. Because there were people who were writing them that had lived it themselves, so they were not only doing the action—And it's no different than when I was growing up. We had *Superfly,* early black movies that came out, that was trying to show the community, the wrongs that was going on, but showing you how to get out. But the people that were like me, who did think past the nose on their face, seen the message in the movie, and the folks that was into pimpin, because you know that was the main thing when I was growing up, the drugs *[dealers]* were pimps, and they had TVs in their car, and they would lean in with the gangsta lean, that was the thing that was going on when I was growing up.
Michael:	And they lived in the projects. *[This brings laughter, as Paula had said earlier that she grew up in an apartment, not the projects, in Chicago.]*

Paula:	Yeah, you got it. Anyway, so they wasn't gettin it. All they could see was that Superfly had this bad hat, and this fur coat, and this big car, and he had the women. See? So they only seen that, the surface. But they didn't see that the movie tellin them that this brother was sick of this life, he hated it, and the whole movie was about him gettin fed up with it and finally making that decision to get out of that life. And all the trouble he had to go through just to change his life, because he had put himself in that position before. Do you see what I'm sayin? And it's the same with these movies nowadays, because *Boyz in the Hood* had a wonderful message. But all the ones, only they thinking about is being strapped, sellin their crack, you know makin a wad of money in they pocket, drivin that biz, you know having that gangsta—a coupla gansta broads by they side. All they gonna see is the end of the movie, because that's all they want to see. You see what I'm sayin? And the Tammys and the Michaels [*her kids*], and the kids that are lookin for better things, then they look at the movie and they see the story. And that's the problem with the John Singletons and stuff that make these movies. They try to give a story, but ain't nobody seein it, except for the ones out there already not doin the bad things. Cause I remember when *Superfly* came out, we were all just so infuriated, that here was this great movie, showing this struggle this man was goin through, and all these fools—and excuse me, I hate to call em that, but that's what we felt at the time—all these idiots is comin out the show, wantin to be pimps and wear fur coats.
Interviewer:	They just didn't get it, huh?
Paula [*laughs*]:	Yeah! And that's frustrating. Because folks is dyin while *you* ain't gettin the message.[16]

In this way, Paula clearly took account of the social context of both the movie story and the viewers, and lamented what she saw as the failure of many viewers to understand "the message" of these films, both in her own childhood and currently.

For other parents, recalling the act of watching with someone else brought richer memories of conviviality than of content. Barb Norton, from a white middle-class family, recalled watching the soap operas *As the*

World Turns, Days of Our Lives, and *Guiding Light* with her grandmother during summer vacations, over the objections of her own mother.[17] "It was like I was doing something naughty," she recalled. She and her grandmother would discuss characters and plots, giving rise to her fascination for similar stories and companionship, as she described watching soap operas with friends throughout high school and college.

Indeed, memories of watching television with her mother and father seemed to help Cathy Swenson, a white, single mother of two teenaged daughters, to reaffirm her role in a troubled family that consisted of her sister, an alcoholic father, and a distant mother.[18] She had somewhat conflicted memories of watching television with her parents:

> My dad was really into sports, so we watched a lot of sports, and I learned all about baseball, football, basketball, because you know, *[laughs]* I always kind of felt like my dad wanted to have sons. Although one time I asked him and he said no, he was glad he didn't have sons. My parents were older and he had been in World War II and he was glad he didn't have a son because he was afraid he'd be drafted and have to go to war. So I remember watching a lot of sports with him. I don't remember many things from my childhood. My sister always teases me, "You don't remember that?" But I very vividly remember my mom, and I can't remember what night it was, but every week when *The Dick Van Dyke* show was on, my dad was away teaching a class on those nights so he wasn't around. I can remember my mom popping popcorn, and we would sit down and watch *The Dick Van Dyke Show.* That was one of the few memories I have of my childhood. I remember looking forward to that as much as my mom did. My mom really enjoyed that program, but I remember looking forward to that, too.

Whether a child watches with parents or alone, Jim Mills argued, television is not a child's plaything. In contrast to the kind of television he remembered as a child, he felt that late-twentieth-century television was too complex, and too many programs on television could push a child into adulthood more rapidly than Jim could have been pushed by the milder programs of his childhood.

Mills's view is somewhat ironic when we consider the passage that began this chapter. In it, he amiably mocked his 12-year-old daughter's romantic notion of an ideal family as happy, prosperous, and peaceful, a notion she based on contemporary television programs such as *The Cosby Show* and *Home Improvement.* It's just acting, he had told his daughter. *The Cosby Show* and *Home Improvement* were shows his children were allowed to watch freely, perhaps much as he had watched *The Andy Griffith Show* when he was their age. By mocking the lessons his daughter had drawn from these approved shows, however, he seemed to be

II
The Families: Case Studies

5

The Case Studies: An Introduction

Lee Hood
Lynn Schofield Clark
Joseph G. Champ
Diane F. Alters

The chapters that follow tell the stories of eight families who engaged in media in various ways, with sometimes widely divergent reflections on media. They are presented in case-study fashion to indicate as best we can the context in which each family spoke with us. This introduction discusses the concepts we developed to try to make sense of what families told us, and we illustrate those concepts with examples from families that for the most part do not appear in the case studies.

Because we realized we needed some way to organize the various ways people talked about the media, we conceptualized a three-part scheme we call the three "modes of engagement" to sort the interviews into three different kinds of stories, all related. The first mode, "experiences in the media," included straightforward descriptions of media experience such as "I like it!" The second, "interactions about the media," described times when people told us they had talked to other people about media. In these interactions, media were treated as a kind of social currency that enabled them to communicate with others, even about things that extended beyond media. The third kind of story, "accounts of the media," is emphasized in this book as it describes complex narratives that join experience and belief as people reflected on their media engagement. These accounts included comments such as "I know I shouldn't watch this, but I do." In the following sections, we elaborate on each of these categories.

EXPERIENCES IN THE MEDIA

What we came to call "experiences in the media," quite simply describes the diverse ways in which people said they experienced actual media texts—programs, plots, characters, visuals, and the like. These are the interviewees' fairly straightforward reports of media engagement. From the beginning, the notion of experiences in the media pointedly focused our attention on the perspective of the audience rather than on the views of an outside critic. We assumed that audience members saw, understood, and made judgments about media texts based on their own life experiences and belief frameworks and that they decided whether to return to these texts based on their experiences and beliefs.

The focus on audience members and what they said about their media experiences is fundamental to the research approach in this study. How much control over meaning audience members really have is a subject that has been debated throughout the history of audience research. A range of audience researchers has noted that the meanings audiences draw from the media they consume are not completely determined by the producers of media or the economic positions of audiences—but that they are not completely individualistic, either.[1] We began by paying attention to these "experiences in the media," which required listening to audience members and using the categories they employed as a starting point of analysis. In this, we agree with Janice Radway, whose approach "focuses on the various ways human beings actively *make* sense of their surrounding world" (Radway 1984, 8; emphasis in original). Radway argued that meaning not only is found in texts, but is also produced by a reader as a result of her specific social and historical circumstances.

"Experiences in the media" were perhaps the most common responses from children who were anxious to let us know that they not only enjoyed, but also understood, programs they saw. They were eager to demonstrate what John Fiske (1987) has referred to as "cultural competence." He describes this as follows:

> Cultural competence involves a critical understanding of the text and the conventions by which it is constructed, it involves the bringing of both textual and social experiences to bear upon the program at the moment of reading, and it involves a constant and subtle negotiation and renegotiation of the relationship between the textual and the social.[2] (Fiske 1987, 19)

For example, Angela Montoya, 5, explained how she believed her favorite television program, Disney's *So Weird*, got its name. With this, she demonstrated that she had enough knowledge to interpret the program in a way that was close to the one offered in the text itself: "It has real people in it, and they don't have a house. Like, they go in a bus thing. Well, like a camper thing. The girl, she's a teenager and she has a computer and it shows pictures, like her bus crashes into a car. That's why it's called *So Weird*."[3] Like some of the adults' stories, Angela's "experiences in the media" indicated a basic competence that enabled her not only to interpret a program but also to offer back an interpretation that conformed to producers' intentions regarding basic plots lines, characters, and narratives.

The range and diversity of these "experiences in the media" were striking. Even families that did not own a television set and avoided many other forms of media, such as the Internet, had a working knowledge of some media products, including popular television shows and Internet terms. The category of "experiences in the media" helped us understand that media are important sources of symbols and meaning from which every family could draw.

Within the concept of "experiences in the media," we identified three major ways people seemed to discuss these experiences: with pleasure, with ambivalence, and by differentiating themselves from media. People often told us they just liked a program, with little or no explanation as to why they did. A number of scholars have associated the notion of pleasure with audience practices, including Ien Ang (1985), Dorothy Hobson (1982) and Janice Radway (1984).[4] It is also a recurring theme in Fiske's work (1987), for which he has been criticized. Fiske asserts that the pleasure of using media is greatest when one has a sense of control over meanings and feels as if he or she is actively participating in the cultural process, a point that has drawn accusations that Fiske is romantic and blind to material and structural processes of culture.[5] Nevertheless, we found Fiske helpful in a limited way by pointing out the importance of pleasure as we puzzled over the pleasure the interviewees reported deriving from media, and how their reactions often seemed connected to a family's habits, values, and attitudes. The Hansens, for example, enjoyed watching videotapes of the movie *Rudy* (the story of an underdog college football player who perseveres) and *Hoosiers* (a movie about the unlikely triumph of a small-town basketball team).[6] Blair, the father, said he watched videos of the two movies several times a year. His 15-year-old daughter, Sara, liked the films because they provided "good entertainment and a cool story, like dreams come true or something like that." The upper-middle-class, white, suburban family was deeply involved in sports and regularly attended an evangelical Christian church. It seemed self-evident to the Hansens that they "just liked" the movies and found them pleasurable; the movies were as immersed in sports and Protestant ethos as the Hansens were.

Sometimes people's "experiences in the media" were ambivalent. That is, a person might enjoy something in the media but feel distant from it. Fiske (1987) describes this as a kind of negotiation, a process we also noticed in the interviews. For example, Jan Van Gelder, a lesbian who lived with her partner and 9-year-old son, described her enjoyment of the "coming-out" episode of the television show *Ellen,* whose title character is also a lesbian.[7] In this, she was negotiating her own position outside of television, and, not incidentally, negotiating meaning with the interviewer:

Jan:	I thought the episode was very good. I think it really showed her struggle in terms of coming out, and it was just nice to have something like that on TV, because so often we're not portrayed. So it was really nice to have something. I was disappointed that it got canceled and that the producers got a lot of flak for it. I've heard different things about why that is—that there was too much of a focus on her romantic life and it got too focused in that way. I also think that just like *Murphy Brown* got a lot of flak about being pregnant (and single), I think, you know, some religious organizations really went after the producers.
Interviewer:	Did you relate to Ellen's character at all in the episodes that you saw?
Jan [after a long pause]:	I thought that she was very funny. Do you mean, related personally?
Interviewer:	Yes, like was there anything she was portraying that reminded you of what you had gone through?
Jan:	Well, certainly in her coming out, the awkwardness of her doing that initially was kind of portrayed, but not other than that.

Another family, the Carters, liked the sitcom *Home Improvement* because of its humor and what they called the "family values" that they also found in their Mormon beliefs.[8] When Tommy Carter, 10, observed that his father and the show's main character were both clumsy, his mother admonished him for being disrespectful to his father. Unfazed by his son's comparison, Gary Carter explained that he was self-conscious in his appreciation of the character. He identified with certain aspects of the character but rejected others: "I'm into things like electronics, and I'm not so much into cars like he is, but, you know, tools and fix-it repairs and stuff like that. And sports and stuff like that. So, I mean, I wouldn't make myself exactly him, but there's a lot of elements in him that we have here." These pleasures were not blind or unexamined, but they were negotiated within the context of a family, contingent on the show's message being acceptable to their moral framework.

Other "experiences in the media" reflected some differentiation from media. For example, the South-Schultzes, a white, middle-class family who lived in cooperative housing and shared property and communal duties with neighbors, believed that television was a time-waster that promoted consumption.[9] They watched videos on a monitor that did not pick up broadcast signals, and they did not subscribe to cable television. Their experiences in the media mostly revolved around radio, as the parents said they often listened to news on a National Public Radio affiliate.

The Cains, a white, working-class family with more conservative political views, also differentiated themselves from media in their stories of "experiences in the media."[10] They watched television but often found it hard to reconcile television with their conservative Baptist beliefs. As a result, the Cain parents instituted a number of prohibitions on what their children could see. The children's "experiences in the media" therefore reflected some differentiation from television. Nevertheless, Kelli, 10, and Patrick, 8, described listening to episodes of the Christian children's radio program *Adventures in Odyssey* in the way that other children might watch television. "We sit in front of the radio and I color or we sit there and do nothing," Kelli said.

Even though many people described their pleasure in media and demonstrated their ability to construct meaning based on their cultural competence—the sense they made of texts—we also wanted to better understand the way media texts were integrated into family life. So we turned to stories in which people described talking with others about the media.

INTERACTIONS ABOUT THE MEDIA

We described stories about discussing media with other people as "interactions about the media." As other scholars have noted, meanings and ideas derived from media can become a form of social currency and can contribute to social and cultural interaction as they are brought into conversation. Previous studies focusing on some aspects of "interactions about the media" (without using the term we have chosen) include James Lull's analyses of family television practices (Lull 1980, 1991). Lull points out that television becomes both a resource for conversations in family social interactions and a means by which families structure their time together.[11] Building on this and other work on audiences, Elihu Katz and Tamar Liebes (1985) argue that television is a social process. They note that viewing often takes place in the presence of family and friends, and that "people discuss what they have seen and come to collective understandings" (Katz and Liebes 1985, 187). Characterizing viewers as actively participating in meaning making from specific media texts, they also argue that *what* a viewer sees is important. They write:

> We are suggesting ... that viewers see programs, not wallpaper, that pro-
> grams do not impose themselves unequivocally on passive viewers; that the
> reading of a program is a process of negotiation between the story on the
> screen and the culture of the viewers; and that it takes place in interaction
> among the viewers themselves. (Katz and Liebes 1985, 187)

Like Lull, Morley, Katz and Liebes, and other audience researchers, we found that study families' "interactions about the media" sometimes seemed to serve a clear purpose, such as reinforcing a particular family's values. The Stevens–Van Gelder family, for example, described watching a Disney program for families every Sunday night because the program felt safe to them. "It's a time that you can generally assume that it's going to be appropriate for a kid to watch," Jan Van Gelder said.[12] Sometimes, however, Jan and her partner Vicky Stevens noted lapses into sexism in the program, and they discussed these with their son, Brett, 9. Vicky said:

> Actually, we sort of laugh about that. Brett really picks up on it, because he's
> really been raised, this is a pretty conscious household in terms of sexuality,
> racism, all that kind of stuff. And those are things we talk about all the time.
> So he's really aware of it, and he'll laugh about it. He'll see it on a TV show
> and he'll say, "Oh, my God. All of a sudden the guy's here, now the woman
> acts like she can't do anything." And we'll laugh about that and how, "Isn't
> that silly?" and that kind of thing. So we just talk about it.

These interactions about the media also illustrate the ways in which families use the media to structure family time. The Stevens–Van Gelders' Sunday night tradition was "a cozy family time" that drew the family together. Some combination of reactions—here, a pleasure-negotiation-opposition process—appeared repeatedly in interviews, and we came to see that such complex readings were the norm, not the exception, in each family.

The point of "interactions about the media" is that media are a re-source for how families talk with each other and with people outside their families, even about what it means to have a "cozy" family gathering, or what it means to be a family that tries to combat racism and sexism. It is important to note that these families were not talking about media pleasure in the same sense we saw with "experiences in the media." They might derive pleasure from the media, but social interaction is the key experience. Among the study families, the media helped make social interaction possible, whether by providing specific points for a discussion of media texts or by providing an inexpensive form of entertainment that a family enjoyed together and recognized as an important part of their family life.

Next, drawing on the concepts of "experiences in the media" and "interactions about the media," we turn to our attempts to explain the role of media in contemporary usage with the concept of "accounts of the media." While the first two concepts are not new to media research, we believe that our notion of "accounts of the media" is new. We look at how these accounts are related to family narratives of identity, and we also place the accounts in the specific context of contemporary U.S. family life and the rise of what we call "reflexive parenting."

ACCOUNTS OF THE MEDIA

As our research project unfolded, we became particularly interested in the changing nature of the U.S. family and the attendant relationships between parents and their children; relationships between children and their siblings; and relationships with extended, blended, or chosen (i.e., not related by biology or marriage) families. One of our starting points concerned parental intentions surrounding the media. We frequently noticed inconsistencies between what parents said about their media engagement and the actual practices they described. To put it simply, what parents *said* to us about the media did not always match what they said they *did*. This, of course, would not be terribly surprising to anyone who is or ever has been a member of a family. Yet it took some time before we realized that exploring the inconsistencies themselves might be quite revealing about the nature of family life and its relation to wider discussions of both the media and religion in contemporary U.S. culture.

The public scripts upon which families drew to discuss the media played a large part in our thinking about the inconsistencies. For instance, in the United States there seems to be substantial agreement that the media can be a negative influence in a family's life. Most of the parents with whom we spoke voiced some concerns about the media and their children. They worried that their children spent too much time in front of the computer or television instead of interacting with one another, or that there might be consequences if their children consumed too much violent (or sex-filled) media, or a host of other objections. Their fears fell into two distinct categories: a fear that children would reproduce the behavior they saw, and a fear that media would desensitize their children to the problems of modern life. An example of a parent's fear that a child would reproduce televised behavior appeared in an observation by Tammy Jarrett, who connected her son Justin's viewing of professional wrestling on television with his new habit of pushing around his brother and sister.[13] She made him stop watching the shows, and his behavior improved, she said. In another family, desensitization was the prime worry in this comment from Lanny Gordon, the father of two children, 13 and 10: "What really worries me is people who grow up and think, 'That's the world, and I don't have to make any choices about that. If somebody gets in my way, I kill em, I don't have to make a choice about that.'"[14]

As these two examples suggest, some parents felt less able to guard against desensitization than behavioral consequences. They seemed to recognize that their fears of desensitization were not necessarily based on direct experience but involved more abstract hopes and fears for their children's futures. Overall, most parents feared both kinds of consequences, depending on the media product and their observations of children.

Parents in the study also seemed to believe that any regulation of media should begin in the home. Thus when asked what they did with regard to the media, their "accounts of the media" were inevitably inflected by what they thought they should be doing. Parents drew upon public scripts about the media when even the most lenient said they believed that too much media consumption was bad, and that it was up to them as parents to provide restrictions. These statements tended to reflect two important reactions: how parents *accounted* for or described media use in their own home, and the sense in which parents felt *accountable* for such media use due to societal expectations. Furthermore, "accounts of the media" indicate an important relationship between media and family identity, as they deal with how people integrated their media experiences and their identities, and how they integrated themselves and their families into public culture.

With these "accounts of the media" in mind, we went on to explore a secondary question involving the relationship of these accounts to family behavior: Does it matter what parents say about the media—even (or perhaps especially) if it is disregarded in practice? If the expression of distaste or a fear of consequences does not result in consistently regulated behavior, do the expressions themselves serve some other purpose or hold some perhaps unrecognized value? We came to believe that they do.

THE CASE STUDIES

To explore these questions, we needed to understand the context that each family brought to their media experience. This is why we presented the following chapters as a series of case studies. We wanted to help the reader to understand not only the three modes of media engagement but also how each of these modes operated within specific contexts of contemporary family life. The first chapter in this section contains case studies of two families who are culturally at some distance from the North American mainstream and each other. They are the Ahmeds, a Muslim family with restrictive rules about media use, and the Paytons, an ecofeminist family with Protestant roots that has few ties to the media as they do not own a television set and seldom engage in other types of media. The second chapter presents case studies of two families, the Hartmans and the Roelofs, which are closer to the heart of U.S. culture. The two white, Protestant families help illustrate the relationship of media engagement to religious frameworks and meaning making. The third case-study chapter highlights the Price-Benoits, a family headed by two gay men, and the Franzes, a 1950s-style nuclear family. The final case-study chapter presents two families, the Vogels and the Carsons, which are deeply engaged in media but in very different ways. Each case study is designed to indicate the contexts in which families engaged in the media and the interrelationships among the three modes of engagement with the media.

6

Being Distinctive in a Mediated Environment: The Ahmeds and the Paytons

Lynn Schofield Clark

What does it take to construct a family identity that is significantly distinct from what people see and hear in the media? In this chapter, we look at two families that seemed to be quite successful in creating a distinctive family identity: the Ahmeds and the Paytons. The Ahmeds were a biracial family highly committed to maintaining Muslim practices in their home. The Paytons were committed to ecology, not a particular religion (they were atheists), and sought to get the most out of consumable goods so as to contribute minimal waste to the environment. These two families distanced themselves from the media by certain rules and practices, detailed later in this chapter. This distancing helped separate them from larger North American culture and norms, which tend to be reflected in media.

We emphasize these families' "accounts of the media," the phrase we use to describe how people reflect public scripts and their family's media use. These operate in the rules governing media practices in the home and the families' commitment to instilling a distinctive or (in the case of the Ahmeds) a "two worlds" perspective in their children. We conclude with questions that arise from these case studies: Does it matter what parents say about the media—even (or perhaps especially) if what they say is often disregarded in practice? If expressions of distaste or fears of consequences do not result in consistently regulated behavior, do the expressions themselves serve some other purpose or hold some other value? We have come to believe that they do.

This chapter first explores these questions through a case study of the Ahmeds, who had very restrictive rules about media use. Because their religious background is so important to an understanding of the Ahmeds, we begin with a discussion of Islamic identification in North America.

Coming from a Western cultural background, we researchers write about Islamic identity with some reservations, mindful of Edward Said's concern that people of the Eastern (and, one might add, the Southern) hemispheres have been too frequently represented in academic literature by those from the West (Said 1978). This means, as Gayatri Chakravorti Spivak and others have noted, that Western writers have tended to collapse differences and overlook agencies, assuming essential distinctions between "us" and "them" (Spivak 1988). "We" in the West have tended to see—and depict—Islam as a religion that is unitary, static, and antiwoman (Mir-Hosseini 1988). Some scholars have observed that such monolithic approaches to Islam and Middle Eastern cultures have served political ends: It was, after all, the European sense of superiority over cultures of the "Orient" that provided ideological support for colonization (Djait 1985). More recently, such prejudices may have been marshalled to fuel interventionist efforts in support of U.S. economic interests, as was the case in Iraq in 1991 and 2003.

Like all religions, Islam is fraught with inherent contradictions. In recent decades, literature on Middle Eastern cultures has sought to tease out these contradictions and the way that this religious system has played itself out in various nation-states (Mir-Hosseini 1996, Ramazani 1993). This has offered a contrast to earlier research in the West, in which sociologists studied (and often assumed) the erosion of minority Islamic values and traditions as individuals assimilate into the culture of the majority. These assimilationist studies have underestimated the roles of tradition, values, institutions, and communities of shared belief that shape responses to the majority culture, as more recent scholarship points out (Ross-Sheriff and Nanji 1991). One example is the view of the role of women in Islam. Despite the stereotypes of Islam as a patriarchal system that restricts women's progress, which might suggest that any egalitarianism is the result of assimilation into Western European values, Muslim feminist scholars point out that egalitarianism has always been at the heart of Islam. This, they note, is evident in ancient laws protecting inheritance rights, property rights, divorce, dowry, and child custody, among other things (Abu-Laban 1991). One historian notes that Egyptian Muslim women frequently had more power before European colonization than after (Tucker 1985). Like all religions, therefore, Islam can be employed in support of increased freedoms or increased restrictions. Cultural context is an important consideration, and much evidence suggests that Islamic values have not been "watered down" so much as they have taken new and frequently vibrant forms in Western contexts. Islam is, after all, the third largest religious group in North America, and the fastest growing (Waugh, McIrvin Abu-Laban, and Qureshi 1991). While still a minority in the United States, then, the religious identity of Muslims in North America is informed by the tremendous spread of the faith and its dominance, both culturally and in several cases politically, in many parts of the world.

This is a tremendously brief introduction to a complex faith and its attendant practices, but it is intended to provide a context for discussing the Ahmed family in terms of religion and its emergence in (and mediation of) accounts of the media.

INTRODUCING THE AHMEDS

Just hours after the interviewer received Jemila Ahmed's name from the local Muslim Society, and before the interviewer had had a chance to call, Jemila telephoned to say she was ready to schedule a time for interviews.[1] As any qualitative researcher can attest, such enthusiasm is rare; the norm (in our study at least) seemed to be almost endless rescheduling to accommodate different family scheduling conflicts. In contrast, Jemila seemed to welcome the opportunity to answer questions about their Muslim faith and how it related to their family's media use.

As we were to learn, her enthusiasm was part of a larger commitment to promote increased understanding about Islam. Jemila also spoke about the faith at her children's schools, wrote editorials to provide a Muslim perspective on various current events, and, on a more symbolic level, wore a hijab (head-covering scarf) when in public. Although perhaps more intentional than others, such public demonstrations of religious beliefs are not rare among what McIrvin Abu-Laban calls "differentiated" Muslim families, those composed of the most recent cohort of immigrants. These families, McIrvin Abu-Laban argues, often eschew the assimilationist or accommodationist stances of earlier Muslim immigrants, choosing instead to differentiate themselves from the broader U.S. society due to their commitment toward maintaining and propagating the Muslim faith. McIrvin Abu-Laban also notes that, compared with earlier cohorts, contemporary immigrant Muslims find it much easier to provide their children with a "two world" perspective, as technology has facilitated contact between old and new homelands. Telephone, fax, and email contact allow frequent exchanges of news and perspectives, and trans-Atlantic trips have also become a more feasible option for many.

Although the largest population of Sunni Muslims in the United States and Canada are immigrant couples with children, the Ahmeds are biracial and bicultural. Jemila, of European descent, was raised in Utah as a United Methodist and converted to Islam upon her marriage to Umar Ahmed, a then-recent immigrant from Libya.[2] Together, they have four children: Hasan, Saleem, Aziz, and Sakinah, who at the time of the interviews were ages 14, 13, 11, and 9.

Discussing Media Representations of Islam

Although many research participants who identified themselves as Christian had expressed incredulity at the idea that religion and the media might be intersecting topics of interest, the Ahmeds—parents and children alike—were eager to discuss misinformation and bias in representations of Islam in popular and news media. In addition to Edward Said's well-known indictment of Western media bias concerning Islam, other research endeavors have noted the media misrepresentations that both influence and reflect prejudices and stereotypes in North American culture (Said 1981). This pattern of bias led the local Muslim society, of which the Ahmeds were a part, to take a proactive stance. Among other things, they called the local media whenever there was a national or international story on the Muslim world, offering to provide contacts to "localize" the story. Jemila observed that the family was pleased when friends and acquaintances from their local mosque were interviewed on television, and they took note when any Muslim was portrayed positively. More often, however, she saw stereotypes in media:

> Unfortunately, what usually happens is if it's a story or if it's a fantasy, the Arab's the terrorist, the bad guy, and of course an Arab is a Muslim *[said sarcastically]*. You know people don't get that Muslims are from all over the world, and so they always put it in that way. And then it's a double whammy for my kids, because you know, they are part Arab. So it's hard.

As other scholars have noted, individual Muslims often suffer prejudice when tensions heat up between the United States and predominantly Muslim countries (Awass 1996). This prejudice factors into peoples' responses to Hasan Ahmed, as he noted:

> Most of the time I'm not [discriminated against], but sometimes kids, they just, like, tease you, because they know you have to pray five times a day, or they tease you because the Israeli prime minister just died, and they're like, "Did you kill him? Do you know Yasser Arafat?" And then they call you Aladdin, and camel jockey, and stuff like that. My friends do that, but they're just joking around. But some other people, they tease you for what's going on in the media and the news and stuff like that.

Most previous research on Western biases toward Islam has dealt with the news media almost exclusively. However, as pre and early teens, the Ahmed children undoubtedly were more interested in entertainment media. Jemila noted, for instance, the family's excitement when Disney's *Aladdin* was first announced. As a rare representation of an Arabic tale, *Aladdin* had become a staple in their home video collection. Nevertheless, their feelings about the movie were ambivalent:

Interviewer: Did you see that movie?

Jemila: We did, and we saw it—I think I saw it in the theater. Because I saw it with the first song, and it was before people came out in the media and were offended by it, and I went, "Oh, my goodness!" You know, because they were talking about cutting off the hands, and how things are—and I was [*she mimics a gasp.*] Again, even this story that's supposed to be—they never came out and said this was about Arabs, but it's pretty obvious, *Aladdin* is an Arabic story. [*She laughs.*] But again, they couldn't find the positive things, it's sad. So I think it was in the theater, because I think the tape toned it down a little bit.

Interviewer: Oh.

Jemila: And we did get the videotape, and it wasn't as offensive, but it was still like, oh, that's sad that that's what they pick up on.

Interviewer: Yeah, I remember when that song came out, and many Arabs protested that visualization. Of course, I think that's par for the course for Disney in terms of racial/ethnic representations.

Jemila: Yeah. There was also, I hadn't seen it before, but my mother had the movie, and my kids had seen it, now I can't remember—*Ducktails? Treasure of the Lost Lamp*, or something like that. And oh my, again, I just saw that and it was just—! The Arab that was portrayed there, they were at the Pyramids, so it was obviously Egyptian Arabs, and he was called a dirty thief and dog. And the character was a dog. And again I just thought, you know? He had an Arab accent. But then the genie that came with the lamp that was one of the heroes, didn't have that accent, even though he came from the Arab lamp. And I thought, isn't that interesting how they made sure it was an Arab accent for this dirty thief and dog that was a character of a dog, but they didn't keep that in the genie. It really, like you said, all the different races are portrayed not so fairly, and I think the Arabs are the ones to be picked on now. It's safe, is the best way to put it.

The interviewer watched *Aladdin* one evening with the Ahmeds. The interviewer heard the many objections raised by Hasan and his mother, but she was struck by how much 9-year-old Sakinah seemed to enjoy the film. Given the family's intention to develop a distinct Muslim identity, we might guess that Sakinah will eventually learn to approach the film with ambivalence. For the moment, however, the enjoyment of seeing someone that looked a little like her and referenced her racial/ethnic background seemed to override any discomfort. This was one of the interviewer's first clues as to the tensions of fostering a "two worlds" identity in the Ahmed children in the context of Western media.

The Household Rules for Media Use

The Ahmeds kept two charts: one for household chores, and the other for media use. The latter chart had the names of each family member in a column, with a row for each day of the week, so that family members could keep track of their allotted media use. The chart stated the rules governing media use as follows:

> There is only one hour of TV or video watching daily and two hours daily on the weekend. TV/video may be watched 3–5 P.M. or after taleem [a 10–15 minute daily educational session on Islam to be conducted with the whole family present] daily. On Saturdays, the TV/video may be watched until 10 A.M. and then again at 3 P.M. We will rent only one video a month. There is one-half hour video/computer game playing daily and two one-half hours of video computer game playing on both Saturday and Sunday. Everyone is given two hours of video/computer playing or TV/video watching a week free. The rest needs to be earned by leisure reading of novels, magazines or newspapers. To earn these above mentioned times, reading needs to be completed $\frac{1}{2}$ hour for $\frac{1}{2}$ hour of watching or playing. Fill out the chart below to keep track of reading time. Reading time cannot be carried over to the next week.

The children acknowledged, however, that while they knew the rules for media use, they did not always follow them. The interviewer asked them about this:

Interviewer: What makes it hard to follow the rules?
Hasan [14]: Well—
Sakinah [9]: We like TV!
Saleem [13] [in a stage whisper]: Temptation.
Interviewer: Like, what? What are you tempted to do?

Saleem:	Actually, I think it's addictive.
Interviewer:	Television, or video games?
Saleem:	Both.
Interviewer:	So you would like to watch television more, or you think it's a good rule, or?
Saleem:	I would like to. And I do.
Interviewer:	What about you guys?
Aziz:	Well, the chores? Our dad gets to watch TV and he doesn't have to do chores, so we're kinda mad at him.
Jemila:	*[laughs]* But what about TV?
Aziz:	But when we get home from school, there's some shows we like—
Sakinah:	—like *Batman*—
Aziz:	—so we watch it—
Hasan:	—so we don't change our clothes—
Aziz:	—so we don't follow the rules and then we watch it, and there's some more shows that we kind of like and we don't get to watch them.
Sakinah:	And then Dad comes home.
Aziz:	And then we quickly turn off the TV— *[We laugh]*
Sakinah:	—and run to our rooms.

They all laughed as they talked about this not-too-secret transgression. Yet while they presented themselves as not always keeping the rules about television, the siblings seemed to have a vested interest in holding each other to the 30-minute limit on computer games. As there was only one terminal and often more than one person wanted to play the games, someone (usually the second or third in line) would set an egg timer and watch until the first person's time was up.[3]

While Jemila joined in the good-natured laughter at the bent rules surrounding television practices, it seemed that she had effectively communicated her views about the media to her children. This was evident in the following exchange:

Interviewer:	So why do you have the rules?
Hasan [joking]:	So we don't have to get grounded? *[We all laugh.]*
Aziz:	So my mom doesn't have to remind us.
Interviewer:	Okay. But why do you think you have the rules to begin with? Do your parents have a reason?
Aziz:	So—

Saleem:	Because the TV can take over our lives, and she doesn't want that to happen. And she doesn't like the influence of the Budweiser frogs. *[We laugh.]*
Hasan:	And—
Sakinah:	—and, and—
Hasan:	And also, it's not always appropriate.
Sakinah:	Yeah.
Interviewer:	What's not appropriate?
Hasan:	The content.
Interviewer:	So do you make choices based on content as well as the hours?
Sakinah:	Yeah.
Interviewer:	And do you make that choice yourself? Like if you watched a program would you pretty much know if your parents thought it was a good idea to watch it or not?
Hasan [interrupting]:	The whole family knows. The whole family knows what they're supposed to watch; it doesn't mean they follow it.
Aziz:	No, we follow it. It's just—
Hasan:	Most of the time.
Aziz:	Sometimes.
Jemila:	Pretty much what happens is we'll watch videos because we can control that, or even TV because we can switch the channels. And usually for Mom it's violence. When there's violence I get uncomfortable, [and I'll say] "Okay, let's switch for just a little bit," and then we go back, and for Dad it's seeing kissing or anything that looks like they're gonna kiss, or *[laughs]* anything like that. And the kids have lived with that all their lives, with our discomforts, and so they know what to expect.
Hasan:	On cable, you have more temptations, so we don't have cable anymore.

In individual interviews, 11-year-old Aziz and even 9-year-old Sakinah said there were television programs and music that made them "uncomfortable." Sakinah cited the prohibition against casual dating in Muslim practices as a reason for disliking programs with sexual content. So while there were stated rules, the Ahmeds also relied on the exhibition of their discomfort with certain programming that they considered objectionable. These views, Jemila explained, were related to their interpretations of the Qur'an. Obviously, there is nothing in the Qur'an about media, but there are implications for moral living:

Jemila: There are things like, lower your gaze, which means don't go ogling over men's and women's bodies, and all that, so that would carry through to TV, you know you wouldn't watch the *Playboy* show. So that's just a logical thing; what are you doing, what's your purpose here.

Interviewer: And so how does that relate to what you're trying to teach your children?

Jemila: Yeah. Morals, and think about what you're doing, and what is your purpose. I think my biggest thing—not just with the media, but with all of everything they do, is what are your intentions, and why are you doing this and how will it help you as an individual, and how will it—you know, something like last time, Hasan mentioned dating. Again, what is the purpose of dating? Is it just to—just to be with each other, and eventually, you get to kiss each other, and eventually, and eventually? Is this something, really—I mean, what are your intentions and goals? What really do you want to do with this? So that's the same with TV. It's just—are we wasting our life here in front of the TV, in front of Nintendo? Or are we really doing something? And then at the same time, very realistically, it'd be nice if we were much more strict, but—. We have leisure time too, and we're, I guess, of the lesser perfect humans! *[She laughs.]* You know, we do just go ahead and waste some time, but we try to say, let's limit it a little bit.

As Jemila noted, the restrictions on both time and content for media use had to do with what she described as the Muslim commitment to living a purposeful and moral life.

Other restrictions were on viewing options. As Hasan said, they had canceled their cable television subscription to eliminate some program possibilities. MTV and *The Simpsons* were off limits, but the children were familiar with these and other objectionable programs, having watched them as recently as two months earlier when the family still subscribed to cable. The boys had seen the programs at friends' homes and had heard about them in conversations at school.

Like other families, the Ahmeds inconsistently applied their rules against sexual and violent programming and parental practices—

inconsistencies that the Ahmed children were glad to point out:

Interviewer: So you say that you watch *ER* as a family?
Hasan: Yeah.
Interviewer: All of you do?
Aziz: Even though, even though it's like people who are cut open, my mom doesn't care.
Interviewer: So, that doesn't count as violent?
Saleem: And she watches those corny, not soap opera movies, but based on true stories where husbands beat their wives and then they beat their wives again and then the sisters get mad and the husband gets on steroids and kills everybody.
Aziz: Yeah, that's what I was thinking. That steroids one.
Jemila: You guys aren't supposed to be watching it.

Yet, as noted earlier, the children had incorporated at least some of their parents' objections into their own approaches to the media. In fact, in an individual interview Hasan said he believed that a part of his role as the oldest son in the family was to help enforce household rules, including those concerning the media.[4] Just how he enforced the rules provoked rebellion from his siblings one evening when the interviewer and the children watched the Laurence Olivier version of the movie *Robin Hood* on video. Hasan asked Aziz to fast-forward through a section of the tape, but Aziz protested that he had not seen the part. Hasan was growing somewhat agitated, directing all of the kids' attention to himself as Sakinah asked excitedly if "they're gonna do it." Aziz replied with relish, "Four times!" as Hasan got up and took the remote control out of his hand. Then Sakinah said (to no one in particular) that the film was not rated.

Hasan: It would've been PG.
Jemila: Not G?
Sakinah: PG, yeah.

As Sakinah returned to her homework, Hasan, who now held the remote control, fast-forwarded as soon as Robin Hood said to Maid Marian, "That's why I'm in love with you." During the silence as the tape fast-forwarded, Aziz said, "There's the first kiss." Hasan looked irritated, and Saleem commented with some irony, "We've seen it before anyway."

"There they go again!" Sakinah exclaimed as they kissed again. When the kissing scene ended, Hasan stopped fast-forwarding and they resumed watching. Saleem turned back to the computer game he had been playing in the corner of the room.

Hasan's enforcer role had less to do with enforcing family rules than it did with a larger frame of reference, their Muslim beliefs. Their account of media, while perhaps not consistent with their rules and practices, was consistent with what it meant to embrace a Muslim identity. This was clear in 9-year-old Sakinah's comment about her religious and racial/ethnic background:

Interviewer: How about if you weren't Arab-African/American. If you were from a different racial background, how would your life be different?

Sakinah: I would like eat pork, and it wouldn't really matter if I eated any kind of meat. And, I could listen to music. And, I could probably watch MTV if we had cable. And—that's it.

Thirteen-year-old Saleem also equated media rules with his family's religious guidelines:

Interviewer: If you were a parent, do you think you'd raise your kids Muslim?

Saleem: Probably.

Interviewer: Would they have the same rules you do?

Saleem: Not the same rules.

Interviewer: What kind of rules would be different?

Saleem: They'd get a bigger allowance, and they could watch as much TV as they want and stuff.

Hasan also drew a relationship between media use and Muslim faith:

Interviewer: Do you think there's a relationship between the rules and Muslim teachings?

Hasan: Mm, kind of. Because you're supposed to follow whatever your parents say and respect your parents, so whatever the parents say, you're supposed to do that, and you're supposed to read the Qu'ran, which is like the Bible to us, so if you stay away from Nintendo, you'll read the Qu'ran more.

Interviewer: Do you wish that your parents enforced the rules more?

Hasan: Yeah.

Interviewer: What do you think they should do?

Hasan: Like, punish us if we don't do it, because we know too well that we're not supposed to do that stuff.

Interviewer: Do you think you'd follow them more if you got punished more?

Hasan: Yeah, like, take half our allowance away, or ground us for half a day, or send us to our room for half an hour or something like that.

For Sakinah as for Hasan, rules regarding media use were all part of the same continuum that encompassed prohibitions on meat and restrictions concerning dating. Rather than seeing media restrictions as punitive, then, they became one aspect of the important family project of maintaining and nurturing a distinct religious identity.

This would seem to make following the strict, stated media rules less consequential. In fact, Jemila had a rationale for their inconsistencies between rules and practice, which she articulated when she noted that it was difficult to keep children sheltered from all media:

Interviewer: And I'm sure if they didn't watch any television here, because of the culture they live in, the American culture, it's impossible to not know anything about movies or television.

Jemila: Oh yeah. And you know, too, that's always been my philosophy, is that if we were going to stay in an environment that was so-called sheltered, and they didn't have to see those things, well, then, that will work, but that's not true, and one of purposes of childhood is to practice, to be able to handle the world in your adulthood. And if you've been sheltered, then all of a sudden it's like *[mimics a gasp]* you're not quite sure what to do when you're an adult. So they need to practice now in making choices that hopefully they can do, in a good way. Hopefully they'll make some mistakes, and hopefully they'll get some consequences from that so that they won't make the huge mistakes adults make.

Thus even the "mistakes" the children might make by engaging in inappropriate (or too much) media were understood within what Jemila explained as the Muslim view of childhood as "practice" for adulthood. This, too, was important, for it framed media transgressions—and other actions considered undesirable—according to Muslim practices. Some transgressions related to media had implications for identity, however.

A "Two World" Identity

During their interviews, the children and even Jemila acknowledged that despite the Muslim objections to music (which translated into a household prohibition on stereos, boom boxes, Walkmans, etc.), they did listen to music occasionally. In the following exchange, it was also clear that the restriction had limited the children's grasp of U.S. popular culture:

Interviewer: So, you don't listen to popular music, or sometimes you do?

Aziz: Sometimes.

Hasan: We know the popular music from MTV, and—

Aziz:	Kids sing it at school.
Hasan:	And sometimes when you're with your friends you sing along.
Interviewer:	Well, so—there's kind of a rule that you're not supposed to listen to music, though, right?
Jemila:	*[laughing]* That's right. There's *kind of* a rule.
Hasan:	Sometimes—they're not that strong on it, though. Because she listens to it, too.
Interviewer:	You listen to jazz sometimes? *[Jemila had indicated a preference for jazz earlier.]*
Jemila:	Yeah.
Aziz:	She listens to the Beatles, and the, um, rocks, or the sandstones—?
Jemila:	*(laughs)* The Sandstones!
Hasan:	The *Rolling* Stones!
Jemila:	I was going to say that the only time any of us listen to it is when we're with somebody else who's listening to it, like at work. That's where I heard it.
Aziz:	Or giving a ride to my soccer coach.
Sakinah:	Your coach likes Mashed Potatoes.
Aziz [correcting her]:	Meat Loaf.
	[We all laugh.]
Jemila:	That's like the Sandstones. I think he means the Rolling Stones.
Aziz:	You like that kind of stuff, the Beach Persons. *[More laughs as he's corrected.]*

Although Aziz's last comment was meant to be funny, both his earlier reference and Sakinah's malapropism seemed to be genuine confusions.[5]

Their lack of knowledge of popular culture and music in particular would presumably reinforce a distinction between their own family and their peers at school or in the neighborhood. Yet an irony was apparent when Hasan talked about the family's visit to his father's homeland of Libya. The visit, which had taken place about a year and a half earlier, was cited as one of the most significant events of their lives. The media had surfaced in new ways for them:

Interviewer:	When you were in Libya, did you think the kids there were like you?
Hasan:	Kind of.
Saleem:	They listened to more music that we do. Except they didn't understand what anything said. It was all American.

Sakinah: "You like Michael Jackson?"

Interviewer: Is that what people asked you? So they listened to American music then?

Sakinah: Yeah, but they didn't understand a word. They asked us to translate.

Hasan: They asked me about *Born in the USA.* They did! And I didn't know what they were talking about, and then they put in a tape and I'm like, "Oh, yeah!"

Aziz: They asked Hasan to translate.

Saleem: Most of the time there's like two shows we could watch, and the rest were gross.

Sakinah: Heidi, and Smurfs.

Hasan: See, and the rest we didn't understand [the language]. But we could understand what they were doing.

Saleem: And most of the time there was just those lines [test patterns]. And then finally like Olympian music. It was funny.

Knowledge of the music industry and its celebrities seemed to take on a different role in the Libyan context. In the United States the Ahmed children were somewhat less knowledgeable about popular culture than their peers, but in Libya their extended family associated them with the very North American popular culture their family eschewed. In fact, the children took some pride in acting as experts on that culture for their relatives. Hasan, for example, said he enjoyed interpreting North American culture. He noted:

> They had these songs, and they would ask me if I ever heard of it, but it was an old song, like a 70s song, and I didn't know what they were talking about because first they would sing it in English, but they were singing in an accent, so I couldn't understand. But then when they put it on the radio—they only had a couple songs—and they put it in the radio, then I'm like, "Oh, I know that one!" And they're like, "You like? You like? You like?" And I just said, "Yes."

Yet while he relished his role as an expert on popular culture, when asked how he felt about being a North American, Hasan offered:

> I don't know why I think like this, but I don't think of myself as American, mostly. I think of myself as Libyan or Muslim. I know I'm American, but I guess I take for granted the running water, that we have water all the time, and the TV, and video games, and the stars and stuff.

Hasan's statements illustrated his sense of a "two-world" identity. His younger brother Saleem, who was more invested in North American popular culture, nevertheless acknowledged that he, too, identified with Arabs.[6] Aziz also seemed aware of the "two world" identity, although he focused on the distance he perceived between his Muslim identity and that of the dominant Western culture of the U.S.:

Interviewer: How do you think that your racial group is perceived by other people?

Aziz: Well, some people, like my friends, when people get to know Muslims, they know that they're good. But some people think we're terrorists or other things, but we're not. And some people, like with the Oklahoma City bombing, they like automatically blamed us. But my friends knew that maybe some people did that, but they knew that I wouldn't do that. Or none of my friends would do that.

Interviewer: Do you ever feel that you have to be a representative of Muslims, or help people to know something about Muslims other than the idea that "they're terrorists"?

Aziz: No. Well, sometimes, I feel like just going up to those people and saying, "We're not bad people, we're just like you are."

Interviewer: So, do you ever do that in school? Like if this came up in social studies class or something?

Aziz: Nobody really cares if I'm Muslim or not. They just think I'm a regular person.

While Aziz's sense of himself as a "regular person" within the U.S. context might seem the antithesis of his older brothers' identification with Arabic culture, it was only the other side of the same coin for this "two worlds" family. The Ahmed children were faced with a challenge: how to appear different and distinct, yet also like a "regular person." In the United States their prohibition on music served to reinforce their identification with Muslim culture, yet in Libya their knowledge of music reinforced their identification with North American culture. This kind of ironic twist is the subject of some reflexive humor in "two worlds" cultures. At the American Place Theater near Times Square in New York City, one could see *Sakina's Restaurant,* a popular play about an Indian family living in the United States. In one scene, the young son who visits India for his grandmother's funeral throws a tantrum. He says while clutching a Nintendo Game Boy: "Everyone in this country is stupid! And they just want all my cool stuff, 'cause they don't have any cool stuff of their own, and they're just jealous, 'cause we get to live in America and they're stuck here in ugly, smelly old India, and I never, ever wanna come back here ever!" (Gourevitch 1999).

A reporter for *The New Yorker,* who related this scene, noted that the audience members near him—two middle-aged Indian couples dressed in tweed suits and saris—shook with the laughter of recognition at the character's outburst (Gourevitch 1999). The play's run was extended for many months, perhaps demonstrating the fact that Indians in New York, at least, feel comfortable enough with the paradoxes of dual citizenship that they are able to laugh at its challenges. As demographics in the United States continue to shift toward increased pluralism and bi- and multiracial identities, such distinctions the Ahmed children experience may indeed become "regular" for the Ahmed children and the generations that follow them. In the meantime, despite discomforts, there are benefits to inculcating such a "two worlds" perspective, as we will discuss in a moment. First, however, we introduce the Paytons.

THE PAYTONS

Soon after the interviewer arrived, Corrine Payton, leader of this single-parent family, took him to a single-car garage behind her house.[7]

Inside, the air was thick with the humidity of decomposing organic matter in row upon row of tiered, five-foot trays. Under pieces of carpet covering each tray were six inches of dark, rich dirt populated by small, reddish worms—a variety Corrine called "Red Wrigglers," tiny cousins to the night crawlers used as fish bait. These worms, working by the tens of thousands, rapidly eat and transform anything once living into worm waste, or "casings," the very richest compost. At fifteen dollars a pound, the worms helped the Paytons pay their bills.

The way these worms survived and thrived mirrored the approach to life that Corrine and her two daughters embraced. Together, they were dedicated to taking even the smallest scrap of material or leftover food and making it into something useful. A seamstress (another source of income for the family), Corrine cut up worn-out jeans and sewed them together to make window coverings. Ratty T shirts were transformed into throw rugs, and old underwear became cleaning rags. Food was made from scratch, with leftovers served to the dog and the family's eight chickens. What the dog and chickens did not eat went to the worms. As a result, in a month's time the Paytons might fill one large flour sack with refuse for which they could find no further use. That was the family's only contribution to the overcrowded landfills of North America, a fact the family—particularly Corrine—related with pride.

The Payton family had begun to live this way five years earlier. A former computer programmer, Corrine had moved the family to their rural home following a divorce that left much less money in the household budget. At one time, Corrine had found pleasure in living a more frugal lifestyle to support her desire to stay at home with her young children. "It was fun to take things off the grocery list. It started as a challenge as far as getting thrifty. Now, after the divorce and everything, it's more of a necessity," she said.

Corrine saw a larger purpose in her commitment to ecological responsibility:

> Businesses are always slammed for looking at their bottom line, but if households would look at their bottom line, if you don't buy a lot of this stuff, it's cheaper! And you know what? Then you don't need to have two jobs, and then you have more time to go do stuff and you don't need money to purchase things to do. So maybe going and doing stuff is going as a family for a walk. You know, as opposed to going to the movie or going to the theme park, or whatever, where you have to pay somebody to get in, there are things to do that don't have to have the exchange of money.

In a separate interview, Connie's younger daughter, 12-year-old Brenna, articulated the philosophy that undergirded her mother's actions:

> She's just generally trying to—her main problem with today is, like, a lot of the overpopulation that's harming the Earth, and people are taking advantage of the Earth and stuff, and the Earth is not going to last forever. And people need to understand that.

Yet Brenna did not plan to be as "careful" as her mother when she became an adult. She explained:

> I think she's doing a good thing, but I think it gets a little frustrating at times. I was cleaning out my room and she was like, "No, that goes in recycling," you know? "You can keep it if it's blank on one side for scratch paper." And I just want to throw it away! I mean the Earth does need people like Mom, taking care of it, making sure that the dumps don't get filled up, and she is helping the Earth. It's just a little frustrating at times, you know?

Clearly, Brenna fully understood both the expected household practices regarding recycling and precycling, and her mother's rationales for these choices. Brenna's frustration with her mother seemed to give voice to the U.S. adolescent desire to appear separate from her, yet it was also clear that Brenna respected her mother and the choices the family made. In fact, the only choice that seemed to be a particularly volatile issue involved the television.

As a part of Corrine's effort to scale down, she had given her ex-husband the television set. Having no television did not seem unusual to Corrine. She had grown up in a household where her own media use had been much more severely restricted than her friends', as she noted:

> Well, with my mom not being all that fond of TV, when we [Corrine and her two sisters] got to high school, you know, what do kids talk about? They don't talk about the weather and the stock exchange or whatever; they talk about what they watched on TV last night. And we ran into, "Did you see—?" whatever show was on last night, and we'd say, "No." And change the subject. I've had some concern about the girls running into that. But my sisters and I, we weren't cast out.

While Corrine said she was happy without television, she often mentioned her concern about her children's peers disapproving. She was aware that her hard-line approach was softened by the fact that girls watched television at their father's house: "We might get a TV at some point, but right now...to have that passive activity is what I object to. And they do get TV on weekends. So as far as the peers say, 'Hey, did you see *ER* last night?' or whatever, you know, they're not totally out of the loop."

In fact, the lack of a television did mark the girls as different from their peers, a situation that made them feel ambivalent. With her mother, Brenna seemed proud of her family's decision:

Brenna: A lot of people know that I don't have a TV and they're like, "How can you manage without a TV?"
Interviewer: What do you say?
Brenna: I say, "It's easy," I mean, I have a lot of other stuff I can do, you know? And I just prefer not to, I mean, there's some good shows but otherwise it's—I don't really like it.

Yet when Brenna was alone with the interviewer, her dislike for television at first became conditional: It was the advertising that she didn't like:

> I don't like television a lot, I don't like all the commercials. But I mean, I would like to see some shows that are on, you know? Because basically all I can watch is on the weekends and there are a lot more different shows on in the week. Like *Home Improvement*, I've seen that a couple of times and I like it because it's funny.

She confessed that she preferred to be at her father's house because she had "more choices" in how to spend her time. She felt her peers singled her out because there was no television in her mom's house:

Brenna: In computer class, there was this guy who was sitting on the other side of the table from me, and he was talking to his friend about me, saying, "And Brenna doesn't have a TV." And he started going on, "And a refrigerator, or a microwave, and anything." And I'm like, "That's like, not true." You know? "I have everything, except TV," you know? And he's like, "Really, I didn't know that." And he thinks just because I don't have a TV I don't have anything else, you know? Like I'm a cave person!

Interviewer: How did you feel when he was doing that?

Brenna: I was, I was offended, I think. Because, I don't mind not having a TV—it would be nice at times, you know? But I don't mind, except if other people bug me about it, like he did.

Interviewer: Did that make you feel like you wanted to get a TV then, because he was doing that?

Brenna: For a little bit, but then I was like, no, I don't, I don't mind not having a TV here, and I wouldn't mind, you know, although in some cases it might be nice having a TV here. And you know, I don't want to get a TV just because somebody's bugging me about it.

Interviewer: When you get older, how do you think you'll, let's say you're in college or even after, you've got your own house, how's your house going to be set up as far as media?

Brenna: Well, I don't—some people have like a whole rec room where they have like the radio, the TV, everything in there, and I don't want to have that. I want to have, like, in my living room I want to have my radio and my TV and all my stuff and not just have a separate room for it, you know?

Interviewer: But you would have that stuff.

Brenna: Yeah.

This story from Brenna seemed to be infused less with pride than with indignation and ambivalence, although the family's lack of a television had seemed to be a point of pride in earlier conversations and indeed had been related to popular criticisms of television's commercial aspects.

Like Brenna, 14-year-old Sally said she enjoyed watching television at her father's house. Her views about the absence of TV at her mother's house were also ambivalent:

Sally: In some ways I like it, but in some ways I don't. Because like, people at school talk about shows and I'm kind of curious.

Interviewer: And how does that make you feel?

Sally: Um [long silence.] Well, I sort of feel, left out because, I'm feel like me and Brenna are the only ones at school that don't have a TV.

Sally added that she would have a television when she grows up.

Like the Ahmeds, the Paytons' lifestyle choices were undergirded by a clear philosophy. In the Ahmed's case it was Islam, in the Payton family ecofeminist spirituality. While Corrine Payton and her daughters all described themselves as atheists, Corrine worked at a local Unitarian church and attended services twice a month. She clarified that while "religion" meant nothing to her, she felt a deep connection to the earth: "If I couldn't go out and get dirt under my fingernails, I would shrivel up and die." She was particularly averse to the idea that religion, as she saw it, might allow people to shirk responsibility to the environment in which they lived:

> I think the most crippling thing that religion has done is this expectation that God, or Goddess, or Gods, or Goddesses, will come in in the last act and save humanity. If you remove that figurehead, and we all had to take responsibility for how the play's going to turn out, I think people would live differently. And so that's where the atheist [beliefs] come from. That, I need to—I personally need to live my life as if there were no God.

Sally, too, made reference to a nature-centered spirituality when asked about her beliefs: "Well, if I were to believe in God, I would believe in something among us, sort of a Mother Nature sort of thing." Still, she noted, she preferred not to think of God in any traditional way, much like her mother: "I've talked with Mom a lot about God and stuff, and I think that has sort of led me to not believing in a God."

On the other hand, rather than embracing a particular nature-centered spirituality, Brenna said she appreciated the fact that both of her parents, as she said, "let us believe what we want to believe. They don't stand in our way." Unlike her mother and sister, Brenna seemed particularly drawn to science fiction and its questioning of the universe. She spoke of a friend at the Unitarian church whose beliefs seemed to be similar to her own: "I think God is who you make him to be, if you make him as a guy in a white beard sitting on a cloud, then that's who he is, all powerful, all knowing. There's this girl at church who, God to her is, like, the unknown. Like, outer space and everything, the unknown."

Brenna said the films *Contact* and *Close Encounters of the Third Kind* depicted ideas that resonated with her beliefs. Like Corrine and Sally, she was particularly troubled by representations of God that seemed closely related to the traditions of Christianity, although, unlike them, she was able to find stories in the media that intrigued her. In contrast, when Corrine was asked for examples of media representations that reminded her of her beliefs, she noted, again, the importance of its absence: "I would define my spirituality while I was out in life. . . . It was the *absence* of media that allowed me to define [my spirituality]."

Like the distinctiveness that came with not owning a television, the Payton daughters saw their religious beliefs as different from those of their friends and other family members. "Pretty much everyone believes in God," Sally explained. In this way, their philosophical commitments undergirded their media choices and further provided the daughters with evidence of how they were distinctive from mainstream North American culture.

INCONSISTENCIES AND UNDERSTANDING

As we have noted elsewhere in this book, the inconsistencies between parental rules and practices surrounding media can sometimes result in confusion among children. Yet despite the inconsistencies in the Ahmed family and between the two households in which the Payton daughters lived, the children in each household were able to articulate accounts of the media that were similar to those of their parents. They also seemed to understand the restrictions and were able to make their own judgments of media as they operated within the religious framework, or philosophy, of the family as a whole. In fact, we believe that this is the key to why the children in these families seemed to understand how to make critical assessments of the media: Despite inevitable variations in practice, the children perceived that the larger frameworks represented a consistent system. In the case of the Ahmeds, the reference was to Islam; in the Payton family, the system was a commitment to environmental awareness. Thus, these children did not have to become "media literate," per se; it was the intentional presentation of the family's values as distinctive and informing that seemed to provide a foundation for a desirable relationship between parental intentions and children's media practices.

These case studies, then, open up theoretical and practical questions regarding the relationships among family accounts of the media, actual family practices, parental intentions regarding the media, and how well children understand and incorporate these intentions. We argue that the Ahmed parents and Corrine Payton succeeded in inculcating in their children the parents' desired approaches to the media not only because they intended to, but also because both families embraced views distinct from the perceived norm of Christianity in the United States. Islam functions within the United States as an "alternative culture," and the parents drew upon this when teaching their children their sense of what it means to be Muslim.[8] Similarly, while atheism comprises a less coherent system (as evidenced even within the small case of the members of the Payton family), it is distinct from the beliefs of the U.S. population in general, a majority of whom claim a belief in God (Gallup and Lindsay 2000).

Although the Payton daughters did not articulate the ecospirituality of their mother, they both said they did not believe in either organized religion or God. This is a significant point, for studies indicate that few people in the United States say they reject all concepts of God, although many voice reservations about organized religion and its attendant beliefs (those of traditional Christianity in particular) (Gallup Institute 1999). Scholars of atheism have noted that people who reject concepts of God often suffer prejudice and mistreatment, as atheism is commonly believed to be associated not with differing values but with a lack of them altogether (Nash, 2002). Moreover, while adherents of religious faiths may bemoan the misrepresentations of their traditions that appear in television and film narratives, atheists rarely appear as central characters at all, and when they do such representations are rarely positive. All of these factors work together to establish atheism as a philosophical system distinct from mainstream North American culture.

In the case of Islam, the distinctiveness is even clearer. Both news and entertainment media continue to represent people of the Ahmeds' religious (as well as racial/ethnic) background as different or in some way outside the norm, thus reinforcing the idea that identification with Islam is distinctive in the U.S. context. In a culture in which prejudice and social alienation often face Muslims and persons of Arabic descent, religion, the religious community, and the immediate and extended family become important sources of support. Moreover, because of their parents' intentional inculcation of Muslim beliefs, the children were already aware of their religious and cultural background as a mediator to their experiences of dominant U.S. culture, including that of the popular media. Using the language of media literacy, one might argue that these children were able to approach popular media critically. Yet again, we believe it is important to note that this has occurred not out of a program of education related to the media content itself, but within the context of the larger framework of Muslim beliefs and practices. As the Ahmed children perceived themselves as inhabiting a "two worlds" identity, they had already attained a sense of distance from popular media and its values. Thus their critical distance from the media was integrally related to their critical distance from North American culture and its values—including its religious values—in general.

Thus we are left with several questions for further exploration. First, we wonder: Is it easier for parents to raise children with their desired values regarding media when those values are set within a religious and cultural framework that is distinct from the dominant culture? What about the children of immigrants who are more interested in assimilation than in differentiation—might we expect that those families would encounter different problems related to practices surrounding popular media? On a related note, the Ahmeds' case has demonstrated the interconnections between religion and cultural context, for we can see that the distinctions of both Arab and Muslim identities reinforce one another. Thus we must recognize the difficulties in expecting a religious system such as Christianity to serve as a basis for distinction within cultures (such as the United States) so infused by that religion's values.

All of these questions and many more are worth further exploration. These case studies have demonstrated, however, that perhaps we should try to understand the development of the frameworks underlying a family's accounts and practices of the media rather than concentrating solely on how parents talk about media with their children. With this in mind, we turn to case studies of two families that view themselves as close to the heart of U.S. culture.

7

At the Heart of the Culture: The Hartmans and the Roelofs

Diane F. Alters

As white, middle-class Protestants, the Hartmans and the Roelofs were firmly ensconced in American culture. What's more, they *thought* of themselves as at the heart of the culture, unlike the Ahmeds and the Paytons of the previous chapter. Like the Ahmeds and the Paytons, however, their "accounts of the media" were lodged within a larger frame of reference. In the Hartman family, this consisted of a set of neoevangelical religious beliefs that were distinct from those suggested in most media in which they enthusiastically engaged. In contrast, the Roelofs' religious frame of reference was made up of their generalized Protestant beliefs, which were not so distinct from the media in which they engaged—and certainly the Roelofs viewed them as inherent in much media. Likewise, the families' rules for watching television and movies were quite different, although both sets of rules were aspects of the important family project of maintaining and nurturing a family identity within their beliefs. These differences were demonstrated in the strikingly divergent daily media practices of the two families. The task of this chapter is to explore the qualities of difference in beliefs and actions of two families close to the heart, not the periphery, of U.S. society.

The Hartmans' framework of belief gave them a well-defined net of constraints within which they engaged in media and daily life. This framework also gave them something of a critical distance from media, as the Ahmeds' and the Payton's frameworks did for them. However, the Hartmans, who were part of the broad and varied neo-Evangelical movement in the United States, did not see themselves as minorities in the culture. They did not take on the Ahmeds' "two worlds" approach, because they saw themselves in a world where most people were like them. Indeed, their religious beliefs in many respects made them part of a new cultural mainstream in U.S. society, as Wade Clark Roof describes (1999).

The Roelofs, on the other hand, saw themselves as sharing the values of a larger, Christian culture. Their views and practices would align them with what Roof describes somewhat ironically as a declining pool of "mainstream believers." They also did not see themselves as minorities in U.S. society, but rather as fully integrated into what they believed were its best aspects.

The Roelofs' and Hartmans' religious frameworks and practices helped them locate their families in U.S. culture; their media practices, inflected by their religious frameworks, confirmed their places in the culture. As we shall see, furthermore, the Roelofs' stated religious framework was much more imprecise than the Hartmans, but when seen in terms of the larger U.S. culture it is in many ways as focused as the Hartmans' framework.

So what is to be learned by comparing these two families? Why were these families different, and what do these differences mean? And can we say that one approach is better than the other? We will explore these questions in case studies of these two families. First, we will consider the social context of their religious beliefs.

NEOEVANGELICALS AND MAINSTREAM BELIEVERS

The Hartmans were evangelical Christians, a broad and complex population in U.S. society. There are many churches, styles, and networks in the broadly defined evangelical movement in the United States, as Roof (1999) writes. The Hartmans best fit into what Roof describes as a new evangelicalism with origins in the 1940s and 1950s. The neo-Evangelical movement "shifted emphasis away from the 'truth-oriented' posturing of an older religious conservatism toward a more 'conversion-oriented' and/or 'spiritually-oriented' faith, one denoting personal transformation, and the second an expressive, joyful, soulful mode of religion" (Roof 1999, 185).

The Hartmans were among the many college students in the 1970s and 1980s who were exposed to this new style. Most important for this analysis, evangelical Christianity underwent "a process of cultural mainstreaming—with consequences for religious styles, social respectability, and claims on the wider culture." Roof explains:

> Gone are much of the narrow-minded exclusivism and even some of the
> rigidly defined moral and symbolic boundaries that persist as stereotypes
> in the minds of many Americans about conservative Christians, charac-
> terizations quite fitting to Fundamentalists, traditionalist, and dogmatists
> but much less so for those espousing more popular-style, experiential faith.
> (Roof 1999, 186)

This experiential faith includes an emphasis on the Bible and personal
salvation through Christ.

Being evangelicals in a U.S. context suggests having conservative politics, although Mark Hulsether (1996) notes a wide variety of political
views. Hulsether writes that among evangelicals is a group that could
be described in the way we would describe the Hartmans, as "moderate
evangelicals of the Billy Graham type" (Hulsether 1996, 383, 5n). Both
Hartman parents admired this evangelical minister and called on his
writings to explain some of their own moderately conservative political
views. Hulsether admonishes scholars to explore the "rich and multi-
faceted" aspects of evangelical culture—an approach we hope we have
applied to all ways of life explored in this book.

The term "evangelical" is not appropriately applied to the Roelofs,
even though the Roelof father, Ryan, was raised in a Pentecostal church.
Ironically, this church was in the same national network of Pentecostal
congregations as one with which the Hartmans were associated for many
years. Ryan moved away from that church in his youth, and he and his
wife, Janet, expressed a generalized Christianity based on the idea of
treating people as they themselves would like to be treated. They could
be classified as what Roof calls "mainstream believers" who on the whole
have only weak ties to religious institutions and who have a "Golden Rule"
religion, a depiction that well describes the Roelofs' beliefs. According
to Roof, these mainstream believers are:

> neither very cold nor very hot religiously, but mostly concerned with pro-
> viding for their families, helping and caring for others, doing good deeds,
> being friendly and civic-minded, and living a good life. Tolerance and re-
> spect for people who are different and treating others as you would like to
> be treated are more honored than either strict adherence to doctrinal creeds
> or unrestrained emotions (Roof 1999, 195–96).

Roof notes that the "mainstream believer" label is something of a mis-
nomer, as these believers are no longer the mainstream in terms of
demographics or institutional vitality. However, the social location of
mainstream believers is not so peripheral as that of neoevangelicals;

mainstream believers are most likely to identify themselves as "in the mainstream of the way Americans live and think." The Roelofs in many respects would fit comfortably into this description of mainstream believers:

> Even if they cannot say why or articulate clearly what they believe or who they are religiously, they see themselves as worthy of core cultural values and ideals closely linked to the American Way of Life. They resonate with a normative set of values, hopes, and dreams even if its religious components are at times blurred in their own minds. Hence their stories differ in significant ways from those of Born-again Christians: they are rooted more in family tradition and cast more in terms of old-style social activities and communal belonging. (Roof 1999, 191)

Indeed, the Roelof parents viewed their religion as very much part of a social process. For example, they said their religious views guided how they thought about society and how they wished to treat other people, a perspective that will be explored further later in this chapter.

In contrast, the Hartmans stressed personal practice in religion and in daily life rather than social processes, and they tended to focus on personal behavior depicted in certain television shows. Also in contrast to the Roelofs, the Hartman children's media use was guided by the strong authority of their parents, a reflection of their evangelical framework. In the next section, we will discuss the Hartmans' rich and multi-faceted relationships with the culture, along with their sense of distance from it.

THE HARTMANS

The Hartmans were decidedly urban.[1] They were surrounded by neighbors in a subdivision close to the center of a medium-sized Rocky Mountain city. John, 43, a former pastor, worked two blue-collar jobs, one as a self-employed construction subcontractor and the other in a Christian organization. Sharon, 42, clerked part time in a large store. These urban jobs gave them a variable family income that was lower to middle class. Both Hartmans had college degrees. The Hartmans's only living pet was a hamster cared for by Laura, 9, and Amy, 8. The girls had pet substitutes: five small electronic "Gigapets" that beeped throughout the day and night "asking" to be fed, taken for a walk, or otherwise attended. John and Sharon were amused by the plastic objects and the effect they seemed to have on the girls. For out-of-the-house recreation, the Hartmans camped and fished in the nearby mountains. Sometimes, Laura said shyly, they visited the malls together, an admission that brought laughter from her parents and siblings.

At home in the small living room was the Hartmans' only television. On shelves below it were a VCR, a stereo, Super Nintendo gear, and some videotapes. A long couch faced the television, and to one side was a rocking chair. On the coffee table was a small Bible. Against another wall was a bookcase with several novels, histories, and two chess sets. Homework was done at a small table in the adjacent kitchen, which could be walled off from the living room by a sliding plastic curtain. In the parents' room was a computer with email that their son, Glen, 14, used daily to communicate with his cousin in another state. Clearly, television and video viewing were done in the living room, and program choices were more limited than the Roelof family's. The television could receive only five channels, not the several dozen available were they to subscribe to the local cable service. Sharon insisted on this limit, and John, who would have liked better reception, agreed with her that more channels could lead to a habit that would distract them from more important pursuits: time with their extended family, their religion, and reading. They subscribed to a daily newspaper and some magazines. Both parents listened to radio news, Sharon to hourly reports on a Christian music station, and John to a National Public Radio broadcast on his way home from work.

The house, in which they had lived for five years, was the latest of several they had rented over the past decade, having relocated many times because of their religion. When John had started a church in another city, the family pulled up stakes and moved. They moved again a few years later so John could pastor a new church in a distant city where Laura was born, but that effort eventually failed. The Hartmans left the church and returned to their current city, and John no longer felt called to be a pastor. They joined a larger, non-Pentecostal church to "stabilize" the children, John said, while they sought a church that better answered their wish for a small community of worship. Still, they were active in the church. John and Sharon taught Sunday school, and the girls went to Awanas, a children's Bible club, during the week. Glen sang in the choir.

John was estranged from his childhood church (which he described as "liberal Presbyterian"), and some intense personal experiences during a wild college life led to his conversion to his current set of beliefs. Sharon, who grew up Catholic, described a conversion after college. These experiences and beliefs characterize the Hartmans as New Evangelicals, in Roof's terms. A key element of the Hartmans' religiosity was daily practice, such as prayer, an important fiber in the net of constraints the Hartmans wove around their media accounts and practices. In contrast, the Roelofs did not attend church or think much about religion, they said, and these differences in religious perspective and practice played a significant part in shaping the contrasting cultures of the Hartmans and the Roelofs, how they regarded media and life, and how they presented their accounts to the interviewers.

For the Hartmans, religion was an integral part of daily life. Each of the Hartmans described having thought, on daily basis, about God, including when they were reminded of the topic by something they encountered in media. They had intertwined media and religious practice in their daily lives. For example, Sharon's favorite movie, *Chariots of Fire,* reminded her of the way she would like to live, with a "strong Christian character." One of the main characters, a devout Christian who refuses to run in an Olympic race because it is on a Sunday, prompted her to say, "I wish I was doing something in my life where I could manifest that." She had bought a copy of the movie and had watched it several times. Clearly, she saw the movie as an example of a way to act in life: "I may not see myself as being a strong Christian or anything, but it brings me back to that point where I'm saying to myself, you know, I've never done anything like what he did, but here I am. Am I doing it like him? It's a good movie for the kids to watch." In this way, Sharon measured her religious practice with a movie, a practical, personal approach to media and religion.

Unlike the Roelofs, the Hartmans distinguished between being religious and being good. The television drama *Touched by an Angel,* for example, was *not* religious to the Hartmans, although it was to the Roelofs. *Touched by an Angel* could even be interpreted as a threat to religious beliefs, John said. Shows like *Touched by an Angel* and *Early Edition* reflected a sense of right and wrong, a notion John carefully distinguished from religion.

John: [These shows portray] morals about what's right and what's wrong. But don't get confused between that and religion, quote unquote. Because there are a lot of people that are not religious that are good people. There are a lot of people of different religions, you know, that are very upright in their behavior and very *[he searches for a word, then concludes]*—but they're not religious. And so, there's a difference between that, having good morals, and what religion is all about.

Interviewer: So you wouldn't call those religious shows?

John: Well, it's, how do I put it? It's sort of a generalization. [Sharon] said something that kind of struck me: She said as long as they're looking for help from God. Well, that's true, *but* that's such a generalization of God. Looking for some higher power, or a New Age thing. To me, that's a dangerous thing, too.

Sharon: It can be.

John:	Because it can be such a generalization. It makes people think, "Oh, but it makes me feel good." And they got to say, "Well, I agree with that." But it's like a Protestant Christian talking to a Mormon or something, where they think they're communicating, and the whole time the Mormon's got a whole, totally different definition of words, even though they use the same words. Totally different thing there. And yet they're never communicating. They think they are. And so there's the same danger when you see those kinds of things. You think, "Oh, cool." But it's really not. I think true religion, if it were broadcast on TV, and it was up-front, not disguised in different ways, I think people would be offended. I think there would be a lot more reaction. There wouldn't be something that people would say, "Oh, that makes me feel good." I think there would be some things that would offend people.
Interviewer:	Because it wouldn't be their particular belief, or just that it's hard to—
John:	Because part of religion is to face the truth that we're all sinners. People in general don't like to hear that.
Interviewer:	It's not a feel-good—
John:	It's not a feel-good thing. I think that the reason you probably won't see it on TV is because it doesn't sell. It won't sell products.

As this conversation illustrates, John did not use television so much to inform his specific religious beliefs as to contemplate his distance from television, including what he saw as the biggest barrier to reflecting his basic beliefs: its commercial nature. The family's specific religious beliefs were bolstered by Bible reading and church, where they studied the concept of sin that John articulated. Television offered specific examples of behavior, and the parents, exercising their authority, constantly made decisions about whether to show the examples or turn them off.

In fact, in many of their stories of television watching, the Hartmans described occasions when the parents or Glen decided to turn off the television because the program was not appropriate for the younger children. There was little immediate discussion of the reasoning behind turning shows off, all the Hartmans said. Instead, the children were expected to learn underlying meanings in church and in other family interactions, and to try to follow parental media practice by imitating it or going along with it—a practical application of belief.

Accordingly, John said he could imagine better television: It would provide a variety of choices, just as he saw the Internet offering a great deal of variety to the alert user. He clearly thought these media offered only a few of many choices available in life. This notion of individual choice was integral to the Hartmans' approach to life, and in fact the Hartman parents believed that one of their main tasks as parents was to encourage their children to make good choices based on their rather specific set of beliefs. The ability to make good choices would increase as the children grew older, with parental authority always looming, at least in the background. Teenager Glen, then, was seen as able to make better choices than his younger sisters, and he sometimes was left to monitor his sisters' television viewing. Their beliefs, and the monitoring help, gave the Hartmans parents a kind of tolerance and calm about television and other media that Janet Roelof did not have, as we will discuss in the next case study.

Sharon's calm was evident in a story she related about the time Glen found pornography in an email message. Relating the story to emphasize Glen's good judgment, Sharon said, matter-of-factly, that he came to her to tell her about it. The interviewer, surprised at her manner, sought to determine if Sharon was more disturbed than she appeared to be by the pornographic message in her son's email.

Sharon: When he was talking to [his cousin], he came in the other day and said, "There's pornography on here." He could tell what it was from the blurb, what it was. *[She's talking about the email header.]* You could tell.

Interviewer: Someone just sent him?

Sharon: Yeah. Before we even knew how to get on, it was on AOL.

Interviewer: Doesn't AOL have any responsibility for that?

Sharon: I don't know. All I know is that Glen recognized it and I said, "You're right!"

Interviewer: Did you register a complaint?

Sharon: *[Indicates she did not.]* I don't know anything about it. I'm in the dark.

Interviewer: Does that worry you, the pornography?

Sharon: Not really. That's rare. But I think if it happens a whole lot more, we would find something to block it, whatever. But he's been pretty good.

Interviewer: It sounds like you can talk about stuff.

Sharon: I'm real proud of him. [If something comes up, it's] just tell Mom or just do something.

Rather than seeking outside regulation, as the questions implied, Sharon relied on her son to make what she felt was the right decision—to come to her with the offensive email.

However, Sharon was not quite so calm about a television show that depicted behavior she found offensive: *The Simpsons*. She saw rudeness and lack of respect for others in the Simpson children's behavior, and she said her children were not allowed to watch most episodes. The show was a prime example of what she as a parent felt she should not let her children watch—a commonly voiced public script in our interviews. The children acknowledged some limits, but they still watched enough of *The Simpsons* to be able to enthusiastically provide detailed plot summaries of some episodes. In particular, one episode, "Homer the Heretic," made fun of God and mocked religion, a point the parents and Laura made in separate interviews. Nevertheless, Sharon found some episodes funny and joined in the laughter when one of the girls recounted a plot.

Television had not always played a major role in the Hartmans' lives. When they were deeply involved in a startup church, they did not own a television set. That was during the first six years or so of Glen's life, and Glen believed that not having television allowed him to use his imagination more than his friends who had always had TV—a public script also cited by other families. His father and mother agreed. "I think it made a big difference," John said. Glen was enrolled in a tough academic program at his high school, and he read a lot, a result of his early lack of television, the parents said. However, John and Sharon also noted that all the Hartmans were "readers," even the girls, who grew up with television. Amy, the youngest, liked to read aloud in her room; one night during an interview with another family member, the interviewer could hear Amy fluently reading from C.S. Lewis's *The Lion, the Witch and the Wardrobe*. Sharon described herself as a dedicated reader, one who even read the girls' library books after they did—for the stories, not to check up on them, she added. They read mystery series together, and she tried to get them to "read the book" before they saw a book-based movie. In both individual and group interviews, the girls and Sharon often recounted a plot or favorite part of a book they had read.[2]

Still, the Hartmans managed to watch a fair amount of television and videos, a practice they readily acknowledged and enthusiastically described. Although the children recounted times when they watched television programs or videos while their parents were otherwise occupied, the entire family often used various media together. For example, they made it a point to see reruns of *Home Improvement* together every afternoon, after Sharon and the girls watched *Jeopardy*. All said they did not regularly watch evening sitcoms, and indeed they did not seem to be familiar with various sitcom characters and story lines. Sometimes, when Laura and Amy had the television to themselves, the parents or Glen would walk by to see what they were watching. This process of monitoring, as John called it, was an integral part of the family approach to media use.

Their family guidelines were fluid, but the limits were practiced frequently, as a parent or Glen often commented on the girls' viewing or turned off offensive shows. This had the effect, we would argue, of making television and other media products just a story in the sense that the Hartmans did not expect these media to accurately depict their religious views. When the parents monitored television, they also monitored behavior. These limits were *not* connected with industry ratings of movies, as they were with the Roelofs. Indeed, Glen seemed genuinely not to have known the rating of a James Bond movie he had just seen, *Tomorrow Never Dies*.

What prompted the parents to turn off the television? Here's what John said:

> If I walk in and it gets sort of gory, and I feel like it's getting gory, or it's getting sicko, I just say, "Turn that off. Find something else." It's not something that I ever tried to make a rule for, I just sense that it's—And then there may be another time, if my mood is different, I say, "Cool, watch it." *[This prompts the girls to giggle.]* I'll be honest with you; sometimes it's kind of a mood-type thing. Sometimes, too, as far as—I've noticed that sometimes if, say we have to leave all three of the kids for an hour or something, do an errand, she's at work or something, I'll say, "Watch TV" or something like that. And so normally, they may have already watched a certain amount of TV, or it's a way for us to keep them occupied, if we're going to do that. So there are times when we are looser than other times. It's kind of flexible.

The terms "gory" and "sicko" were fluid, too. Subsequent elaborations in the interviews also were linked to mood, plot, and the children's ages, not to strict definitions of the words themselves. For example, some *X-Files* episodes were acceptable if they were about aliens. Furthermore, the parents clearly were the final authority in most discussions, although the children were involved.

Parental authority seemed to be a given for Glen, who tried to explain the family's approach during an individual interview. What he said illustrates the creativity-within-constraints nature of the Hartmans' approach, as well as the fact that his parents had the final say:

Interviewer: Do you actually have a set of rules for watching?
Glen: Not really a specific set of rules. Like when my mom's not home, she'll say, "You can watch an hour of TV." And there's like the shows we know we can and can't watch. So we'll watch what we want to.
Interviewer: Are there specific shows you can't watch?
Glen: Umm. Well, I don't think they've set the boundaries what you can and can't. Probably, don't watch the older soap

operas that are on in the afternoon. I get home, and they're
there. So, to an extent we want to watch TV and to an extent
we want to watch something worth watching, too. Mostly,
it's not worth watching.

Interviewer: Sounds like you feel like you have a say in what you can and
can't watch.

Glen: Well, kind of *[laughs]*. Yeah, to an extent. Then Mom and
Dad say, "Okay."

The fact that teenager Glen was also sometimes a surrogate for his parents in monitoring tasks might have underlain his notion that what was acceptable depended on the show or the episode. Even young Laura noted the fluidity of the definitions, however, and seemed quite comfortable with it; she clearly understood the family's underlying belief framework. Laura was happy that her father sometimes liked an episode of *X-Files*, which he would demonstrate by leaving the show on. Conversely, he would turn off a show he did not like. Laura seemed unperturbed by such interruptions.

When Laura's father, mother, or brother acted out family guidelines by turning off the television, it was because they, being older, "know what it is," Laura said. The older family members were thought to have more judgment, a concept connected with age. Parents in particular were viewed as having more authority, consistent with their neoevangelical beliefs. Laura elaborated on the rationale for her elders turning off television:

Laura: Because they know what it is. I don't know what it is, and
they just turn it off, because they know that it's not for me.

Interviewer: Do you get in trouble when you watch it like that?

Laura: [*Shakes her head in a "No."*]

Interviewer: That's not what you get in trouble for?

Laura: Uh-uh. But if I start watching and they told us not to watch
them, like *Millennium* or *X-Files,* they don't want us to
watch all that often, and so if they see us watching them,
they'll say, "Turn off the TV and put on a movie." Or else
just go to bed.

In Laura's stories of monitoring, then, the media choices were clearly demonstrated, and someone older than her decided whether to turn off the TV or leave it on. Although she sometimes disagreed, and otherwise tried to get around the family guidelines, she did not refashion them.

Rather than refashioning the guidelines, Laura sometimes questioned and tested her parents' reservations, as she did in the following conversation about the television version of *Goosebumps* and the series of scary children's books upon which the show is based:

Laura: And also they won't let us watch *Goosebumps* and those scary stories because they have skeletons in there.

Interviewer: Are they worried that you're going to get scared?

Laura: Either we're going to get scared or we're going to get the wrong influence. I know I asked my mom about reading *Goosebumps,* and I asked her why she didn't want me reading them. She said it was like opening a door into a dark, dark room but you can't see where you're going and you might run into the wrong thing. I can see what she's getting into that, because they are scary, and we don't know what they're going to do.

Interviewer: What do you think of that, going into a dark, dark room?

Laura: Well, I can see myself going into a dark, dark room. But I don't see bumping into something that's bad for me. I just can't see that. Because I've read two *Goosebump* books, and they were dumb! *[She laughs.]* And she tells me, "Don't read them because they're scary." But they're dumb! I don't want to read them. They're stupid!

Her mother's reservations were based on their religious beliefs—certain depictions of death, such as skeletons, are images of evil that extend evil into the world. They can be scary or, worse, a bad influence. Laura tested this view and found herself unaffected, or at least not scared. This kind of questioning was expected in the Hartman family. In fact, they had a term for it: *judgment.* It was a process of critical evaluation that develops as one matures, with help from parents. When Sharon warned Laura that reading or watching scary presentations was like "opening a door into a dark, dark room," she seemed to be trying to help her daughter develop judgment in this sense. What she got in return was questioning within the limits of their beliefs.

In short, the Hartmans seemed less conflicted about media than the Roelofs, although their approach also involved nuances and paradoxes. The Hartmans' stories contained fewer accounts of anger and surprise and more enthusiastic recounting of shows they enjoyed and situations they encountered through the media. John and Sharon Hartman had woven a tight, complex net of constraints for themselves and their children, allowing for some creativity within the constraints. As a result, the children and parents had consistent stories about use—and the children seemed to understand clearly their parents' views because they restated them in individual interviews with examples of their own experiences. Underlying meanings were not assumed with the Hartmans, but they were acted out more than they were detailed verbally, just one of many differences from the Roelofs, who will be discussed in the next section.

THE ROELOFS

In contrast to the Hartmans, the Roelofs were emphatically nonurban.[3] They had moved five years earlier from a large West Coast city to a town in the Rocky Mountains, then to a house on sixty acres of rural land on the plains. Their ranch was some ten miles from the nearest small town, on a road that was more dirt than pavement. In fact, the pavement ended some five and a half miles away—the nearest point at which they could take delivery of a daily newspaper, if they subscribed. They were forty miles from the store where they usually rented videos, although their access to movies multiplied severalfold when Ryan Roelof, 35, installed a satellite dish at one point during the three-month interview process. Janet, the 35-year-old mother, raised horses—her passion, along with her children, she said. She was a self-taught, self-employed clerical worker in a technical field and had not graduated from college. Her husband, Ryan, commuted several miles daily to his job as general manager of a company in the television service industry. He had an associate's degree in television engineering. Both Janet and Ryan spent many hours doing ranch work, and their two boys, Michael, 10, and Cary, 9, did chores to help out.

A focal point in Michael and Cary's lives was clearly their house and the room they shared, where they had a television set for video games, a VCR, and a Nintendo 64. Cary loved to roller blade in the yet-to-be-finished basement, where the family also kept an old television set that got a few channels if the aluminum foil on the antennae was positioned just right. In the living room was a big perch for the family's pet birds, along with much of their media equipment: a television set, a new VCR, a stereo, and a satellite-service box. A computer with an Internet connection was in a third bedroom that Janet used as an office. Outside, a few chickens pecked around in the yard.

In this setting, the Roelofs felt better than they had in years; they were unhappy and had felt crowded and in danger in the city. "You have to battle a lot more [in the city]," said Janet, who grew up in a rural area. "It seems like you spend a lot more energy battling bad influences when you're surrounded in a community, versus when you don't." In the country, Janet saw herself as part of a larger community of like-minded people: "You tend to have a lot in common . . . just the same thought, the same basic, good old-fashioned morals and lots of commitment to your family. There's a lot of that out here."

This presentation of herself (and her family) is based in part on a somewhat circular public script that she and her husband drew upon: that their family had certain agreed-upon morals because they were a family. When Janet and Ryan applied this script to media, they voiced another public script: As parents, we are (and should be) especially diligent about media. These assumptions often conflicted with the reality of their own daily lives, as we shall see.

The Roelofs defined themselves as Christians who did not attend church. Unlike her husband, Janet was not raised in a church, and she said that her lack of religious experience sometimes made it hard for her to sort out what was important: "He was raised in a church and I wasn't, and so I'm one of those who goes to church and feels like I have to do everything they tell me to.... Sometimes it's really difficult for me to take what I need from it and leave the rest, whereas he can do that."

Ryan, who as a young man left the Pentecostal church of his childhood, remembered many restrictions his parents imposed in the name of the church. He was not allowed to attend school dances, for example, although he managed to do so despite the prohibition. Although their religious backgrounds were different, both Janet and Ryan said that they wanted to lead their children with "a Christian moral" and to encourage "religion-informed morals" in their children. Ryan elaborated with what Roof would call the Golden Rule religion of mainstream believers: "You know, love-thy-neighbor-as-thyself type of attitude, do-unto-others-as-you-would-have-them-do-unto-you type of situation."

Such attitudes seemed to have had a less-specific connection to religion for the Roelof children than for their parents, although Janet in particular was concerned about presenting to the interviewer a united front about religion. Therefore, she was surprised when Michael claimed not to have thought about religion much when the interviewer asked how important religion was in their lives.

Janet: It depends. Like I say, because we don't go to church. We're very firm believers. I'd say I'm much more an emotionally passionate person, I'd say that that's—it's not the structured religion, but as far as how I feel personally, I'd say it's very important.

Ryan: Fairly important, yeah.

Interviewer: And Michael, can you rate that for yourself?

Michael: I don't know. I haven't thought about it much. *[He sighs.]*

Janet: *[Laughs]* Guess that shows we need to work on that, huh?

Later, Michael expressed surprise when his parents described *Touched by an Angel* as a religious show. "There's religious shows?" Michael asked.

This generalized religion constituted a social ethic to the Roelofs rather than a religion in the Hartmans' sense of a personal journey to God. However, the Roelofs' beliefs, though not structured by a church, were an important part of how they said they regarded media. Ryan said that a movie should be acceptable in a "spiritual sense" that questions "blood and gore," swearing and "perverse" topics. He elaborated with Janet's help:

Ryan: Movies can be very lifelike, real life, and/or perceived lifelike or real-like, versus this is a form of entertainment. And I think children in general have a very difficult time with the separation of, this is a form of entertainment versus real life or lifelike.

Janet: And isn't it funny what we call entertainment? You know, if you think about it, it's called entertainment. It's not entertaining to watch some of this stuff.

Ryan: Yeah, but anyway, from that standpoint, depending upon whether the content, whether it be—

Janet: —sexually or—

Ryan: —morally perverse.

Janet: Yeah, what was it we were watching that seemed to have that—

Ryan: Where we hopefully get most of our morals have been from a spiritual or biblical sense. That's kind of a foundation for everybody, whether they approve of it or disapprove of it, it's always been something that everybody's always turned to say, "Here's our foundation, now which ways are we going?" So that's why I picked the word "spiritual." Whether using that term was right or wrong, but from our standpoint, from our moral standings and how we want our kids to grow up and understand their neighbor and so on, you know, some of these movies, hunh-uh.

In this way, Janet and Ryan expressed some doubts about children's competence to judge media. They also placed their beliefs in a social context: They believed that they shared with other people in the society certain morals that helped them judge media products. They also used a version of a common public script: that parents are supposed to provide a spiritual foundation for their relatively incompetent children so that they can negotiate through life, and parents at the same time are supposed to control media products.

One way the Roelofs said they chose movies was to try to evaluate them before viewing. They looked at ratings, but in a very complex way that will be elaborated later. Ryan sometimes consulted his employees, who went to a lot of movies. Furthermore, Janet added, they considered whether a movie would be scarier on a theater screen or at home on the small screen. During this discussion of content, both parents described themselves as involved in and aware of what their children watched, and as having imposed limits on media. At the same time, Janet, in particular, described herself as a person who did not watch much television. The children, on the other hand, described a fair amount of viewing without their parents. These differences in viewing habits led to some differences in their accounts.

Shortly after Janet described certain limits she placed on radio and television—"We don't want them to have free access to television, especially at night"—she was surprised when 10-year-old Michael said he liked to watch *King of the Hill,* an animated Fox Television sitcom that aired on Sunday nights. Janet reacted emphatically, if contradictorily:

Janet: And you are not allowed to watch that! It is, actually, I watched it once and it is funny. But you know, a lot of times I come down on them for watching stuff and then I watch it. It's actually entertaining. It's just—

Interviewer: So you let them watch it?

Janet: Very rarely.

Michael: It's on every Sunday.

Janet: The only time I really let them watch stuff I have a question about is if I'm sitting there and I get caught up in it, then I approve of it.

Janet was also surprised when Michael said the old television set in the basement got three channels.

Janet: You guys really get TV down there? Do you really?

Michael: Yeah, but it's—

Ryan: If they put the foil on the antenna just right. *[Janet explained that a lot of people give Ryan old equipment but it doesn't always work.]*

Janet: I didn't know they could get TV down there! But you guys don't watch it, do you? *[She turned to the interviewer.]* They've been going down and watching TV and I didn't know it!

Michael: Well no, we only get—we don't watch the TV, it's unhooked, because Dad needed it for something.

As if trying to reassure his mother, Michael added that the set received only two Public Broadcasting Service channels and a "little bit of" a commercial channel. In other words, he knew what worried her about television. Janet was surprised and uncomfortable with this collision, in front of a stranger, between the image she wanted to convey of a parent who knew about her children's media engagement—a public script—and the workings of her family's life.

The parents often worked outside on the ranch when the boys were in the house, and both parents said they did not have time to watch television. Janet maintained that her family did not engage in much television, a picture that did not match the children's accounts of their own viewing, although it probably more accurately described her own media experience. In downplaying her family's viewing, Janet was constructing an image of a family that engaged in media in a way she believed was socially acceptable. Other parents in our interviews attempted to represent their families' media practices in similar ways. To some extent, Sharon Hartman also did this in her initial insistence that viewing *The Simpsons* was tightly controlled in her house, although overall the Hartmans seemed to construct socially acceptable images of their family far less than the Roelofs.

Occasionally, the whole Roelof family watched a program together. This happened when the boys wanted to watch something that the parents suspected would not be good for them. For example, the boys were allowed to see the television program *When Animals Attack* only because the family watched and discussed it together.

Janet: So we did. We actually sat and watched it, and we discussed it a lot.

Ryan: And it was interesting, because we were able to point out all the mistakes made by the people.

Janet: And we didn't necessarily have to.

Ryan: The kids were saying, "Why is that guy being so stupid, doing that with a deer?"

Janet: So, in a way, sometimes when you watch the programs you don't approve of it gives you an opportunity to let the kids use their minds and maybe think through what's right and wrong about what's going on and—

Ryan: —have a discussion with them about it.

Janet: Yeah. Sometimes just saying, "That's wrong," is going to make them want to watch it, but if you're there to discuss it, sometimes it gives you an opportunity to maybe let them learn something.

Unfortunately, Ryan noted, they rarely had time to watch together. Still, Ryan and Janet considered the discussions they had had over the years to be a major reason the boys made "wise choices" about their viewing practices. In recounting practices, then, Ryan and Janet saw competence in their children, although their accounts of the media did not always accommodate that assessment.

The parents said that sometimes the family media discussions had a religious tone to them, based on the content of a particular show as well as the Roelofs' beliefs. Ryan elaborated:

> I mean, the whole idea of, say, *Highway to Heaven* or *Touched by an Angel* is
> based upon Christianity. So that's how we make the tie, you know, working
> forwards and backwards from that point, yes. I would say, yes, they [the
> discussions] would have more of a religious, moral, Christian type of—
> Well, we have to give them [Cary and Michael] reasons for this stuff, you
> know, because they're just going to plain old ask us.

Such discussions were closely tied to the Roelof parents' views of
society and how people should treat one another. For example, Ryan
said some television shows prompted him to discuss racial bigotry with
the boys, relating the topic to an African American woman they knew
and liked. Occasionally, the boys got "talked to," as Michael did when
Janet noticed he had channel-surfed past a scene in which a man was
abusing a woman. When Michael wanted to watched more of the scene,
Janet stepped in, according to Ryan:

> And so she turned back to it for like 10 seconds. And it wasn't a rape situation;
> it was just an abusive situation. And then she turned it off, and she said,
> "Have you ever seen anybody treat someone like that?" "No." "Okay, what
> do you think are the possibilities?" "I have no idea." So Janet went through,
> and I swear, Michael got, not lectured. They had a discussion for like a half
> hour about, Janet touched on spousal abuse and the emergency room and
> stuff like that, how ugly it is in general, how demeaning it is, how that person
> may have been raised. Because typically it can be, you know, a family thing.
> You know, [she] went through all the attributes of that. And she says, "So
> why would you want to sit there and watch that?" "Well, I wouldn't," but
> then looking around the corner type of thing. So I was going to say, Michael
> got talked to about that.

Not all unacceptable moments of television or film were as clear cut. All
the Roelofs acknowledged that violent content was forbidden in their
household, but they all made subtle distinctions in their definition of
violence.

Michael's interpretation of violence was based in part on one of the
times his parents did not consult each other on the choice of movies he
and Cary could watch. While his mother was away, his father and the boys
rented *Alien* and *Carnivores*. With some relish, Michael offered a synopsis
of *Carnivores* that provoked a grimace from the interviewer. "It's sort of
like *Jurassic Park* and *Alien* put together, and you saw a girl's arm socket
getting ripped up, you saw the cords snapping," Michael said. When his
mother returned home, his younger brother regaled her with graphic
tales from the movies. Perhaps predictably, Janet was angry: "She didn't
even know that we rented rated-R movies until my brother goes, 'We

watched *Alien* and *Carnivores*. They're rated-R movies,'" Michael said. "And my mom's all*[he mimes anger]*." However, it wasn't necessarily the rating of the movies that so angered Janet. It was the "blood and gore," according to Michael. Indeed, Michael noted that Janet had encouraged her husband and sons to see "classic" R-rated movies, such as *Psycho*.

But even when made jointly, the Roelofs' decisions about movies were complex and in some ways contradictory. For example, Ryan said an "unspoken rule" for the Roelofs was "no violent TV," and he noted that he agreed with Janet about a prohibition on blood and gore. Janet made many strong and seemingly definitive statements: No horror movies, no daytime TV, no violence, no "garbage TV." However, she amended her no-violence stance, saying that *bloody* violence in movies was what she objected to. And horror movies might be all right if they were viewed at home on the small screen, rather than on a large theater screen. Janet declared that the family had "certain hard and fast rules," but she went on to say that she and Ryan tried to avoid laying down the law, although sometimes they felt they had to. She would "definitely draw the line and set a rule" if the boys watched "too much" television, a circumstance that she said emerged about once a month. Michael acknowledged another rule imposed as a result of the children's practice: the boys were not allowed to watch televised movies unless they asked first, because they accidentally ordered *Dante's Peak* six times from their satellite service. Above all, Janet said she would prefer to discuss her reasons with her sons because she could not supervise them all the time.

If she could not supervise them all the time, she knew that she also could not control their behavior. She explained: "And sometimes if you say, 'No, you can't watch that,' they're going to watch it anyway. But if you discuss why you don't like it and you ask them to watch something else, they usually will. So I almost find that it's better to discuss things. That doesn't work all the time."

Discussion had its limits in more ways than Janet anticipated. In an individual interview, Michael said he was not aware of what his parents said about violence, nudity, and bad language in movies,[4] but he knew how they felt about violence in video games—a medium his parents seldom mentioned in the interviews. In fact, Janet said in an individual interview that her only limit on video games was *time* because she had noticed that the boys "get very cranky and they always end up in a fight"— a different sense of violence than Michael described in this conversation:

Interviewer: You said the R-rated movies have nudity, language, and violence. How do you think your parents feel about those things in movies or TV shows?

Michael: Um. I've never heard their comments about violence, nudity, and language in movies. But like in video games and stuff, they say, "We can do without the blood and gore stuff." But, we don't even pay any attention, and they know that. We don't pay any attention to the blood. It's cheap, anyways.

Interviewer: What do you mean, it's cheap?

Michael: Well, you've seen *Mortal Kombat*, right? *[The interviewer says she has, at least the video game. Michael demonstrates the way the blood squirts out.]*

Michael: Well, on *007*, say like if you shoot someone, you shoot them and it's a flash and it's stained on their clothes. It's like, huh?

Interviewer: So do you mean in video games it doesn't seem as realistic?

Michael: Only in *Mortal Kombat*, well, see, in *Killer Instinct* you can turn the blood on low, medium, high, and off, and when it's on high, once it falls it disappears. In *Mortal Kombat* you can't turn it off. It falls and stays there for like 30 seconds and then it disappears.

The parents did not mention blood as a primary indicator of unacceptable violence in video games, although Janet mentioned that criterion for movies. More often, the parents drew a distinction between unacceptable programs, which were more realistic in depicting violence, and acceptable ones, which were more unrealistic and "so bizarre they're entertaining," like James Bond movies, as Janet noted. Cary echoed his mother's distinction between acceptable fantasy violence and unacceptable reality violence, noting that programs about giant bugs or dinosaurs were acceptable whereas shows closer to reality were not. In these ways, the boys seemed to have understood something about their parents' sensibilities, nuanced though they were.

Michael, for example, was able to articulate the key account of the media expressed by his parents, a lay theory of media effects: "I know for a fact that we shouldn't see R-rated movies when we're children, because it gets an effect on our lives. . . . And even though they know that when they're grown-ups that it's not a game, they still have the urge to do things like that. Like serial killers and just plain old murderers."

The younger boy, Cary, seemed to have wrestled with his parents' exceptions to the no-violence rule as well as to their elaborate parsing of acceptable levels of violence. Ultimately, he was not confused by these seeming contradictions because he had invented his own way of interpreting his parents' restrictions and their relation to actual practice. After several exchanges with Cary, the interviewer realized that Cary had introduced a new category of unacceptability. He assumed that what was considered undesirable by his parents was directly related to on-screen warnings, such as "The following program includes adult content," or "Program edited for content." This surfaced as the interviewer realized Cary mispronounced the word "content" as if it meant "satisfied."

Interviewer: Are there any TV shows that you really dislike?
Cary: Yeah, some rated-R movies and the con-*tent* movies and the mature movies.
Interviewer: Now, are you saying con-*tent*?
Cary: *Con*-tent, or whatever.
Interviewer: Oh, like the ones that say "Adult Content"? Is that what you mean?
Cary: Yeah. And there's this one rated-R movie that has a lot of blood in it that I don't like. I started watching it because my mom and dad started watching it. But my brother and I started playing video games because it was getting real bloody.

Earlier in the conversation, Cary said that he understood that programs featuring con-*tent* had realistic depictions of things deemed undesirable by his parents, but that these were different from the R-rated programs that he was allowed to watch. He explained this difference in his parents' terms: He could watch the *fantasy* versions of certain behavior but not the *real* versions. When he expressed a desire to watch professional wrestling, but at the same time affirmed his parents' stated objections to his viewing such programs, the interviewer attempted to clarify:

Interviewer: And you can or you can't watch that?
Cary: I can't. Well, only if my mom and dad let me, sometimes.
Interviewer: Do they let you sometimes?
Cary: Uh, not yet they don't.
Interviewer: You say they won't let you watch this wrestling stuff?
Cary: No, not yet.
Interviewer: But you've seen it sometimes?
Cary: The acting stuff, but not the con-*tent* stuff.
Interviewer: But how did you know that there's a difference? Did somebody tell you that there's this other kind?
Cary: No. When they're talking in the show and they're acting, they tell you that they're acting so that children can watch it. And on the real stuff it tells you that kids shouldn't watch it, because you know, it's *real.*

Interviewer: But you would like to watch that?
Cary: Maybe. I don't know. I'd rather roller blade.

Cary effectively ended discussion of the topic of violence. The interviewer's questions may have seemed to question his parents' decisions, or they simply may have been too much for him. Certainly, Cary had gotten his parents' message that some programs are not acceptable, and he articulated an account of media that was consistent with his parents' and older brother's. His assumption that there was a distinct category of forbidden programming demonstrated his creative way of dealing with what his father called an "unspoken rule," which sometimes amounted to a confusing, contradictory set of definitions.

Perhaps as a result of this layering and changing of family policy, Michael and Cary continually renegotiated their interpretation of their parents' interpretations. The complexity and contradiction in the family's media approach prompted the two brothers to construct their own finely tuned scale of R-rated movies, as well as their own explanations of why the family's approach was the way it was. Like the Hartman children, they were media critics in a family environment, constantly considering in some fashion their parents' wishes.

Still, Ryan had a sense that he did not fully control the amount of television watched in his house—a sense that seemed to blur his view of his own role regarding television. "If I had a choice, maybe the TV set would only be on during the weekends, or maybe the TV would only be on once a week. I don't know," he said. This attitude seemed to be connected to his awareness that he seldom watched television because he worked so hard at home and at his job. However, he said he would prefer to watch programs with his sons so that he could understand what they were "exposed to" in media. With this, he expressed an "account of media" that defined television as something to be experienced, perhaps unavoidably.

> The TV's not there to explain things to my children. Maybe the TV's there to expose my children to something. But depending on how I feel at the time, either I do want them exposed to it or not, depending on how comfortable probably I feel about the situation myself and how I'm going to explain it to them after they're exposed to it.

Such exposure was not all bad, as it could also prepare his children for adult life:

> But also at the same time, they need to be exposed to as much as possible so that they can, at the time where it's their turn to go out and make their own way, they have a feeling for, "I want to go do this, or I want to go do that." You know.

He added that he hoped his sons would be adventuresome, that they could "easily move and make a very good living and go see things."

This sense of adventure, of openness to the world, was not necessarily fostered by media, Ryan said, because he did not believe that the media were tools to shape his sons to be this way. Rather, to Ryan the media were forms of entertainment. Indeed, for all Janet's reservations about television and movie content, she also embraced the notion of media as entertainment. They appreciated the wish of Michael, in particular, to be entertained, and at the same time they wished to have some influence over his media choices. Both told the story of the time, a couple of years earlier, when Michael had ordered an R-rated movie from his grandparents' satellite service and assured them that his parents had given him permission. "He was in trouble," Janet said. "Mmmm. Severe," Ryan added.

Then Janet elaborated, in a statement that showed her deep reservations about media, as she noted that the Roelofs had recently subscribed to a satellite broadcast service.

> He [Michael] likes to entertain. Just because I don't like TV, and I grew up in an area where you, you'd only watch a certain amount of it, and I'd rather you read or did outside activities. It's not really fair for me to take away his love of entertainment, because if there weren't people out there who loved entertainment we wouldn't have the actors, we wouldn't have the comedians, you know. There are those people. And just because I don't understand it, doesn't mean it's wrong. As long as it's within reason and he gets his other chores done and is outside occasionally, then at least now he'll be able to select from a little bit bigger variety, a little bit more quality.

This willingness to let the child shape his free time, and Janet's recognition of a difference in orientation between herself and her older son, was not voiced in this way by the Hartmans, although the Hartmans clearly enjoyed certain programs and talked about watching something because it was fun or funny.

The sense of autonomy Janet expressed for Michael was expressed differently in the Hartmans' stories. The Hartman parents, for example, appreciated the fact that Glen liked *Oprah* and *Dharma and Greg* despite Sharon's reservations about the programs' adult topics. But the Hartman parents did not express a worry that their critique of Glen's shows would amount to taking away his love of entertainment. Janet Roelof imagined her son in a social context—his love of entertainment brings about the social good of having actors and comedians. The Hartmans, on the other hand, emphasized the appropriateness of Glen's tastes at his stage of development. This is a very personal orientation, with no mention of any social aspect of those tastes. Thus we see another example of the Hartmans' drawing from a religious framework that emphasizes a personal journey, in contrast to the Roelofs' references to their belief framework in terms of its relationship to the society around them.

CONTRASTING APPROACHES

Is either of these contrasting approaches to media better than the other? Is it better for parental authority to be looming over media use minute by minute, or for parents to stay in the background while the child experiments with parents' more abstract guidelines? These questions are impossible for us to answer. First, what criteria would we use to evaluate the comparative worth of these approaches? If we look at whether either set of children followed their parents' guidelines about media, we would note that in both families the children ended up with accounts of the media that roughly approximated their parents' accounts, although they took widely different paths to do so. It would be fair to say that the children in both families evaluated media somewhat critically in terms their parents had provided.

The children in both families seemed to understand the larger frameworks behind their families' media guidelines, however inconsistently they were applied. In either case, the children struggled to make sense of family approaches to media. In the Hartman family, the children had to figure out what their parents intended to convey when they turned off a television program or video, and the children did so by drawing on fairly consistent meanings from other family interactions and churchgoing. In the Roelof family, the children struggled with less obviously coherent guidelines, and they did so by figuring out ways to interpret their parents' conflicted feelings about movie ratings, violence, and certain shows, for example. Despite the struggle, the Roelof children constructed accounts of the media that were similar to their parents': that media plays a role in daily life, that it affects children, but that it is less important than other things. Likewise, the Hartman children all understood and accepted the family concept of judgment and the notion that parents should have authority over media and should turn off whatever they deemed inappropriate.

Although there was eventual accord within both families concerning media, in the Roelof family there was far less accord on religion than in the Hartman family. We were struck with how often the Roelof parents said they found religion and religious messages in television, while at the same time they said they did not practice any particular religious regime. The Roelof children were far less inclined than their parents to use the term "religion" in connection with media, and indeed Michael was surprised at the idea that there were religious shows on television.

One rather obvious reason for the disconnect between parents and children was that religion was not a daily practice in the Roelof family. The parents chose not to attend a church—where these themes would be part of the language in use—although the parents considered themselves religious, specifically Christian. This is in keeping with what Roof calls the practice of "mainstream believers," a large, culturally mainstream cohort in the United States that infrequently attends church but professes general Christian beliefs.

We would suggest that the interviewer's presence and questions about religion brought about answers that might not have always been at the forefront of the Roelofs' lives—as evidenced by the fact that the Roelof children did not share their parents' religious language or see religious elements in the media they discussed. This is not to say that the Roelof parents had no religious beliefs, but to argue that their beliefs were more often expressed as social ethics; when pressed to explain their beliefs in the context of media, they found their religious belief system alive and well in popular culture. For example, they believed popular television programs such as *Touched by an Angel* were religious—in contrast to the Hartmans—and they cited these programs as possible lessons in religion for their children, although the children did not think of these programs as religious. In this, the Roelofs were "neither very cold nor very hot religiously," in Roof's terms (1999, 195–96). Their beliefs were expressed in ways similar to those held by "mainstream believers." As Roof notes, in this group "[t]olerance and respect for people who are different and treating others as you would like to be treated are more honored than either strict adherence to doctrinal creeds or unrestrained emotions" (1999, 195–96). Had we pressed the Roelofs to articulate their views about their daily lives—their rural environment, their sense of community, and their sense of well-being within their family—we suspect we might have gotten stories from all Roelof family members that were as consistent as the stories the Hartmans told about their religion. Television in particular was not especially important for filtering or clarifying the Roelofs' views about what was really important to them—their life on a ranch—although the parents recalled using television to teach certain principles about the treatment of other living beings. When pressed about religion and media, they responded with some examples of religion in media that seemed, at least in part, aimed at affirming to the interviewer that they were indeed religious.

A question raised by these cases, then, is this: Is religiosity the key way families relate to the media? The answer would be "yes" in the case of the Hartmans, and a qualified "no" in the case of the Roelofs. The Hartmans viewed media through a carefully constructed system of neoevangelical religious beliefs and life practices that we have called "a net of constraints." As a result, the Hartmans regarded television in particular as almost entirely unrelated to their religion, except as an occasional source of mockery about it. This understanding underlay their extensive and enthusiastic engagement with all media and at the same time, somewhat paradoxically, gave them some distance from media. This distancing managed to make media less worrisome for the Hartman parents than for the Roelof parents.

In contrast to the Hartmans, the Roelof parents had far less distance from media. In fact, when our questions prompted them to articulate their approach to media, the Roelof parents found themselves entangled in media, which seemed to them confusing and threatening, yet at the same time they expressed a wish to harness media for good, in the form of ethics lessons for their children. The confusing, threatening elements of media included depictions of violence, about which the Roelof parents complained far more than did the Hartmans. The Roelof parents struggled somewhat unsuccessfully to define and control their children's exposure to media violence. The Roelof children, however, had figured out ways to explain violence in the media they used, a kind of control over media that their parents apparently did not know they exercised.

A key point of this chapter is that these families' accounts of the media were lodged within larger frames of reference, but in these cases the frames of reference were different. For the Hartmans, their framework was their religious beliefs; for the Roelofs, it was more likely their place in a rural environment and community they cherished—and which they couched in religious terms. The Hartman parents approached media practically, regulating it minute by minute, while the Roelof parents, who did not often share their children's media practices, regarded media more abstractly. Their rules, though very different, were part of each family's project of building and maintaining a family identity, in either case one that placed them close to the heart of U.S. culture.

In this fashion, we have presented an answer to a question we raised in the previous chapter: Is it easier for parents to raise children with their desired values regarding media when those values are set within a religious and cultural framework that is distinct from the culture? We have explored this question through the cases of two families whose religious and frameworks are at the heart of U.S. culture, and our answer is complex and incomplete. The Hartman children clearly share their parents' values regarding media, but the Hartmans did not consider themselves distinct from the culture in general, as evangelicals. In certain particulars, however, the Hartmans saw clear distinctions: Their view of sin, for example, was very different from what they saw on television. They maintained their values regarding media and made sure their children shared them by practicing constant vigilance in the way they engaged in media and in their religion. But how important was it to the Hartman parents to raise children with their desired values regarding media? Not so important as their wish to raise them in their evangelical tradition. Television was but one barrier to raising children in the way they wished, and it was a weak, controllable barrier to the Hartmans.

The Roelofs, as mainstream believers, also did not consider themselves distinct from U.S. culture, including much of television culture. The Roelof parents succeeded in raising children who voiced some of their media values in general terms, but the children conformed to those values by a complex process of redefining and applying their parents' sometimes contradictory rules. Often, the children ended up watching shows that their parents would not have chosen. The Roelof parents identified with much on television, and they saw spiritual content in many shows, although they also worried about depictions of violence and sex. On the rare occasions that Roelof parents and children watched together, the parents tried to point out moral lessons and discuss concepts of right and wrong in relation to their social values. But how important was it to the Roelofs to raise children with their desired values regarding media? Not so important as their initial accounts of the media would have suggested. When Janet in particular sought to present a picture of accord on media and religious beliefs, she was presenting some "shoulds": We should be religious and we should connect religion to daily practice. In practice, however, the Roelofs valued other things over media use and religious practice, such as maintaining their ranch and preserving their hard-won niche in a rural environment that they cherished. However, in their accounts of the media, all were intertwined, as indeed they are in U.S. culture.

With this, we focus on another question: Can we clearly separate media use from daily practice and beliefs? The cases of the Roelofs and Hartmans, whose beliefs and practices are intricately intertwined with their media use, suggest that we cannot. How these beliefs and practices are intertwined with media use vary from family to family, as we endeavor to demonstrate with our case-study approach. In the following chapter, we pursue this issue by looking more closely at two families for whom religion seemed far less important than their relationship to the broader culture.

8

Fitting in with the Media: The Price-Benoits and the Franzes

Lee Hood

"Mom says TV makes you stupid," one young television
character says to another.
"No," the other indignantly replies. "TV makes you
normal."

THIS EXCHANGE TOOK PLACE during the premiere episode of the
Fox Television situation comedy *Malcolm in the Middle*.[1] Stevie, whose
mother made the disparaging remark about television, is portrayed as
a bit of a nerd and an outcast, the kind of kid who eats lunch alone.
Malcolm, who tries to set Stevie straight, is a young boy who wants so
desperately to be "normal" that he protests being put into a special class
for gifted children. The conversation succinctly illustrates the tensions
between the negative accounts of the media, which have become such a
common public script, and the feeling that one must somehow engage
with media products to be able to participate in social situations.

How does a family position itself in relation to media and the broader
culture? It is a question we believe all families have to answer for themselves in one way or another. In this chapter we meet two families who
tried *not* to be different from other families in their positioning and
practices related to media—who tried, as young Malcolm might say, to
be "normal." Yet they conveyed tensions between their negative feelings
about some media products and the desire to enjoy media and to fit in
with others by displaying their own media savvy.

Both were white, middle-class, dual-parent households with preadolescent children. Both families reported watching less TV than some of the other families in our study, although both households enjoyed the weekend ritual of renting movie videos and watching them together. Both families, in one way or another, had addressed the question of positioning themselves in relation to media—both for the family as a whole, and for the ways in which the parents wanted their children to be positioned in relation to media.

THE FRANZES

The Franz family consisted of four members.[2] They lived in the medium-sized city where Mark, 36, was a faculty member at a university. Mark's wife, Kirsten, 38, was an elementary-school teacher. Their daughter, Bridget, 11, had just completed fifth grade at the time of the interviews. Paul, the Franzes' son, was 9 and had just completed second grade. The children were involved in what could be described as very normal activities for their ages: music lessons, soccer, and 4-H club.

The Franzes' physical surroundings also did not set them apart from many other middle-class households. They lived in a three-bedroom two-story home in an aging suburban neighborhood. Parked in the driveway were two sport utility vehicles and a small car that was in the midst of some mechanical repairs. When the interviewer arrived, Mark was in the backyard, mowing the lawn. Inside the home, the living room included a large piano, but the only media device was a radio with speakers.

One focal point of the Franzes' media use was the many magazines to which they subscribed, magazines that also reflected conventional tastes: *National Geographic, Reader's Digest,* and *Good Housekeeping,* along with a number of specialty magazines on gardening and woodworking. The Franz children subscribed to *Ranger Rick* and *American Girl.* The family also received the nondenominational Christian magazine *Guideposts,* which Mark Franz described as "pretty subtle," like his family's attitude about religion. Mark and his wife, Kirsten, had grown up in a mainstream Protestant denomination, but the family was "between churches" at the time of the interviews.

The Franzes reported they did not watch much television. They owned only one TV set, which was in the family room on the lower level of their home. They limited their viewing further by not subscribing to cable TV. The show they enjoyed most was the situation comedy *Home Improvement,* which they watched as syndicated reruns an estimated once or twice a week.

One of Mark and Kirsten's main complaints about television was that it is a time waster. Although they did not specify a time limit for their children's viewing, Mark was confident that his children "just know that a lot of TV . . . we don't approve of that." He and his wife said they would ask the children to turn the TV off at the end of a program if it "seems" like they have been watching a lot. He remembered watching much more television when he was young than his own children do—an estimated two hours a day—and said if his children watched as much as he did, he would think, "What a waste of time!"

Like Mark, Kirsten worried about the effects on her children of watching too much television at one time:

> If we let them watch more than a couple of hours, you see it in their attitude afterwards. . . . "Maybe I'm aware that when I watch TV for awhile then it's hard for me to get interested in something else. It's like, once I start, I'm a total 'veg'" and it's hard to get out of the . . . sitting and being entertained mode.

"Vegging" was a common term the Franz family used for some media activities, whether it was watching television or playing computer or video games. Both parents and their son, Paul, all used the term independently of each other, in their individual interviews. They used it to describe a state where, as Paul explained, "your brain stops working."

The Franzes, then, were making a statement about their family identity: *We are not a family that likes to "veg" in front of the television.* Mark compared himself and his family to one of his university colleagues, who, Mark said, "watches *a ton* of TV." At the same time he seemed to be trying not to be judgmental about other people's media habits, it was clear that the level of media engagement was one way by which Mark Franz thought of his family's self-image: "[If] people want to watch television, that's fine, because they can choose to spend their time however they like. You know, we don't live our media lives to try to impress anyone or make a statement or anything. It's simply, we don't see the benefit in spending the time doing that."

He said it was fine for his co-worker's family to watch a lot of TV and to allow their children to see R-rated movies, but "that's just not the way we are." He was defining his family's identity, in part, by its relationship to media use and practices. In effect, he was saying: We are not a family that allows our children to practice the media habits we think other families allow their children to practice.

As with a number of other families we interviewed, the Franzes exhibited some conflicted feelings between wanting to simply enjoy media and feeling uncomfortable with the content. On the one hand, there were times when Mark just wanted to sit and be entertained. "Once the kids have gone to bed, and it's quiet and you're beat, what better than to *zone* in front of the television for those hours," he said. He disliked programs that are "preachy," and he was annoyed by a criticism of the Jim Carrey movie *The Truman Show*.

> The reviewer just ripped it to shreds because he basically said that, "Well, it pretends to have a message but it really doesn't have a message," and I think, "Can't you just watch a movie for fun? Why does everything have to have some really deep meaning to it?" And I guess I view the sitcoms and movies and, you know, prime-time TV as—outside of documentary or news-type programs—as being what I'd call 95 to 99–9/10 percent entertainment value as all I'm looking for.

Yet, Mark did not necessarily want the same things out of media for his children as he did for himself. Both he and Kirsten worried about the content of media messages, especially where their children were concerned. Evidence of the parents' concern over content was in their movie-rental practice. "The kids *never* select a movie on their own," said Kirsten. Instead, the parents closely supervised any selections. They rented some videos that they felt were appropriate for the whole family, and also some that Mark and Kirsten watched by themselves after their children went to bed.

"Anything Goes"

Alhough Mark recalled spending too much time watching TV as a child, he believed that at least the content of shows was better then. "Unlike the '60s, you can't just turn the TV on and let it baby-sit the kid, because you have to worry too much about the bad message," he said. Even watching programs with his children did not always mitigate the effect, in Mark's view. He worried the media delivered a message that "anything goes," and that his children would register that message if he did not contradict it.

> Keep your mouth shut and tacitly you're saying, "Oh yeah, it's okay." So a kid sits there and watches this and no one's saying, "You know, that's really bad." And I guess that's one of the problems is, when you have all these messages out there, if as a parent you're not there to be able to watch right along with them, everything they watch and say, "What do you think about that? Is that really right or not?"

The programs the Franz parents were willing to let the children watch did say something about their broader values as a family. Mark thought Ellen DeGeneres coming out as a lesbian on her situation comedy was "inappropriate." He liked *Seventh Heaven* because it was "real family oriented." He also saw *Home Improvement* as safe, family-oriented content, yet he and his wife were uncomfortable when dating issues came up for the teenage characters. The level of the parents' discomfort was evident in an exchange during the family interview as Paul and his parents described the show.

Paul:	It's fun.
Kirsten:	They like it because we allow them to watch it. It's what they get to watch, I think, to a certain extent. . . .
Mark:	Well, and it's a fun show.
Kirsten:	But it's also a good show, uh, the humor. Family situations.
Mark:	It's mostly family situations. . . .
Paul:	Yeah. Probably less than ten percent of the episodes do they have subject matter that—
Kirsten [jumping in]:	Makes us uncomfortable.
Mark:	—makes us uncomfortable for the kids at this point.

Note that Paul, the 9-year-old, is the one who introduced the discussion of content that he clearly understood to bother his parents. Even though he was cut off in mid-sentence, he knew enough about his parents' objections to enumerate for the interviewer what percentage of the show contained the type of subject matter that was unacceptable in his family.

At the same time, there was not always unanimity in the Franz family about what was acceptable or unacceptable media fare.

The Simpsons

The Fox Television animated cartoon *The Simpsons* was one of the most controversial among the families we interviewed. Some families loved the program, touting its humor and incisive social commentary. Others believed the characters were crude and rude and forbade their children to watch it, fearing they would somehow become like Bart. The Franzes represented what might be called a split decision on *The Simpsons*. Mark liked the program and did not mind having his children watch it. Kirsten, on the other hand, did not want them exposed to it: "I don't like the disrespect that I see on the show. I feel they're, you know, disrespectful towards each other and to teachers or other adults or other children in their community. They just don't need to see that."

Mark understood that his wife worried about the show promoting misbehavior, but he did not believe it was any more "contaminating" than watching *Bugs Bunny.* "I've always thought it was kind of cute," he said. He did not think his children watched it enough for it to be a problem, saying he had not seen an entire episode in the past three years. He did not worry about sexual innuendo in the show because he did not believe his children would understand that, anyway.

He also thought that, instead of glorifying misbehavior, sometimes the show actually carried a "decent moral" message. In one episode Mark watched with his children, Bart got a fake ID, took the family car with some of his friends, and headed to the World's Fair in Knoxville after they found a brochure for it in the car's glove compartment. The problem was, the fair had taken place almost 20 years before. Something happened to the car, and they were stranded hundreds of miles away from home. The moral was what can happen when you lie. Mark added: "Not every episode has a nice little message to it like that. . . . I probably wouldn't feel real comfortable letting the kids just watch it, you know, every episode that was on, all the time. . . . Once in a while I don't think it hurts, if they want to watch it."

The Franz children understood that their parents had different feelings about *The Simpsons.* And while they could echo their parents' words, they had a harder time articulating their specific conflicts over the show. The word "appropriate," for example, was one that children used in a number of our interviews when describing television fare.

Bridget Franz said she would like to watch *The Simpsons* more, and she tried to explain why her mother did not like the show:

Bridget: My dad would let me watch them but my mom wouldn't, because it's not appropriate. Some shows are inappropriate because, you know . . . this one show, for punishment, Bart had to drink beer or something. He's like . . . he's too young to drink beer, you know.

Interviewer: I'm just wondering what you mean by "inappropriate" for TV?

Bridget: I don't know. Well, something *bad.*

Bridget's brother, Paul, also knew there was something his parents did not like about *The Simpsons,* but he had a difficult time articulating what it was.

Paul: They just . . . because Bart and his sister, they just go around and do bad stuff.

Interviewer: Like, what do they do?

Paul: Well, Bart just like makes . . . well . . . I don't know what's bad, but . . .

Interviewer: You don't really know what's bad about it, but they just told you that it's bad?
Paul: Yeah.

Later, he imagined what one of his parents might say if he asked to watch *The Simpsons*: "It's bad for you and you might get habits of doing what they're doing and stuff like that." Still, Paul said he *really* liked *The Simpsons,* and that most everybody in his class watched the show.

While some media content was off limits in the Franz home, the children were not always shielded from content that Mark and Kirsten found uncomfortable. Paul, for instance, reported being a viewer of *Buffy the Vampire Slayer,* a show that begins with a disclaimer about the content.

Kirsten said she or her husband would occasionally change the channel if they did not like the content of a program the children were watching or "hope they're not paying too much attention." Her husband believed part of the issue was not being able to shelter the children from the real world:

> When something that we really wish wasn't there *is* there, we don't cover the kids' eyes and ears or shoo them out of the room or anything. We let it run and say, "Well, that's reality." And they're going to be exposed to that at school and just in society. You see that kind of stuff. But . . . if we can avoid overloading with that, we try to.

This statement reflected Mark's belief in moderation. It was evident in everything from his views on government policies in his professional field to his religious practice, as he found religious right and extremely liberal views "equally distasteful." Even his diet was moderate, as he said French fries were okay in reasonable quantities. As it related to media, this belief was manifest in a set of practices that allowed some flexibility in the family's viewing choices rather than a lot of rigid rules. Yet the family's values, and the ways in which media messages might challenge those values, represented sometimes-conflicting forces that required Mark and Kirsten to make difficult decisions.

The Titanic *Phenomenon*

One incident that illustrated the Franz family's struggles over media beliefs and practices was in deciding to let Bridget see the movie *Titanic.* Even though Mark and Kirsten had some questions about the movie's content and its PG-13 rating, they felt they had to let Bridget see it because of the tremendous social pressure to do so. Kirsten, in her roles as both mother and teacher, could not help but notice the interest in the movie: "The rage about the *Titanic* this year has been a big deal with Bridget.

Fourth through sixth grade girls, or what I'm exposed to, have just gone bonkers over *Titanic,* which is a phenomenon I have not witnessed before as a schoolteacher."

Kirsten said *Titanic* was "probably pushing it" for what they wanted their 11-year-old daughter to see, and Mark said allowing Bridget see it was "a trade-off." But Kirsten said that, because it was so popular, she bowed to the peer pressure and agreed to let Bridget go to the movie, feeling that "to be one of the crowd, she had to have some degree of awareness." To not let Bridget see the movie would have put her at a social disadvantage, and she had to be equipped to be able to participate with her friends and classmates in discussions about the movie—to have what her mother described as a "feeling of normalcy."

> We did give her the opportunity to see the show, which to some degree, I thought was fairly important, because it was such a social issue. I think a lot of times our kids are . . . our children are somewhat socially deprived because they don't, you know, there's a lot of the conversation that goes on at school, I would guess, about TV shows. "What did you watch?" And they can't take part in that very often because they don't watch it. And there was a lot of discussion at school, I'm assuming, about the *Titanic.* So I think it was relatively socially important for Bridget to see it and be aware of it.

Yet Kirsten was not willing to let Bridget see the movie alone. Kirsten went along when she found out the mother of Bridget's friend intended to drop the girls off at the movie theater and was not going to stay with them. By being there, Kirsten was able to judge the movie for herself and to gauge Bridget's reactions. Kirsten concluded that there were "more innuendoes than I really would have wanted her to see," and that a couple of scenes "weren't quite appropriate, but the giggles got us through it." And, in the end, Kirsten decided it was "quite fine" that Bridget saw *Titanic,* after all.

For her part, Bridget reported that "some parts were gross." But she said that before she saw the movie, she felt left out when her friends at school would talk about it. She felt better when she could join the conversation. She also felt better after her parents allowed her brother to buy her the *Titanic* CD. She said she got it "because everyone else had it."

In this instance, therefore, her parents' qualms about the content of *Titanic* were overwhelmed by their desire to let Bridget feel a part of the crowd. They believed the choice they made about the media, in this instance, made the difference for their daughter being able to "fit in" with her peers.

Mark Franz understood how media products could become social currency. He had seen it at work in his own academic department. Many of his colleagues watched *Seinfeld,* a show he did not enjoy. He felt excluded from conversations when that program was the topic. "You talk about feeling like you're on the outside," he recounted later. He would roll his eyes and say, "Well, okay, when you guys are done talking about this, you let me back in." He also first heard about *Home Improvement* from people who talked about it at work. At first he was skeptical, but it eventually became the family's favorite program.

In summary, Mark and Kirsten Franz saw their family as one that had somewhat more restrictive media policies than other families, but they felt it was important that their children be able to participate with their friends and classmates with a "feeling of normalcy," as Kirsten termed it. That "normalcy" included watching certain movies, such as *Titanic,* that the parents might otherwise have not allowed. They were acutely aware of the social currency of media products and judged them in part on that basis.

THE PRICE-BENOITS

The Price-Benoits were also a two-parent family.[3] They had one daughter, 11-year-old Lisette, and their household also included one cat and one dog. They lived in a diverse, older neighborhood of a large city, in a brick ranch-style home with large front and back yards and beautiful flowers blooming. Inside the home, pictures of Lisette were prominently displayed, along with her own artwork that had been tastefully framed.

Like the Franzes, the Price-Benoits said they did not watch much television. They, too, said a large amount of TV viewing was not worthy of their time. And, like the Franzes, they did not have specific rules on the amount of time Lisette could watch television, just a feel for when it was too much. On the night before their family interview, Lisette had asked to be excused to watch television after dinner. She was told, "No," that she had been watching a lot of television lately, so instead the family played cards together on their back patio. During the school year, her parents reported, Lisette's TV-watching time was not an issue because most of her spare time was taken up by homework and school activities. Like the Franzes, the Price-Benoits liked to rent movie videos to watch together on weekends. They said they watched movie videos as a family much more often than they watched TV shows together.

The Price-Benoits voiced objections to their child seeing explicit sexual or violent content, just as the Franzes did. But they were open to Lisette seeing a wider range of content than some other families with 11-year-olds that we interviewed. Mark Price compared himself and his media use to that of his conservative, evangelical Christian sister. "I definitely am much more willing to expose my child and myself to broader things than . . . my sister is," he said. For the Price-Benoits, time, not content, was the deciding factor by which they differentiated themselves. As Mark said:

> I'm just as guilty of wanting to shut my family and myself off from media, but for a different reason from my sister. She's trying to not expose them to all that is tawdry in the world. She's protecting her children from that. And what I say more often is, "This is ridiculous. This is not worthy of our time."

"Daddy" and "Papa"

While the Price-Benoits were similar to the Franzes in some of their media habits and attitudes, they were also different. Mark Price, 42, and Gabriel Benoit, 45, were gay and had adopted Lisette as an infant. Lisette referred to Mark as "Daddy," to Gabriel as "Papa," and to them collectively as "my parents." Gabriel worked as a hairdresser; Mark had left the real estate business and considered himself a "house husband" while he wrote a novel. Both were actively involved in the private school where Lisette was going to be a sixth grader. Their household income, more than $70,000 a year, put them in a higher income range than many of the families we interviewed, and they were getting ready to leave on a month-long trip to Europe at the time of the initial family interview. As we will discuss, however, they saw themselves as very much like any other family, and their media choices and attitudes were as "mainstream" as those of many heterosexual families we interviewed. They saw themselves as fitting into mainstream culture as much as any other family.

Family Focused

The Price-Benoits' media choices largely did not reflect gay themes. Gabriel enjoyed watching TV news magazines and late-night local TV newscasts, but not regular entertainment programming. He read *Time, Newsweek,* and *The New Yorker,* as well as the city's daily newspaper. The night before his individual interview, flipping through the TV channels he happened to come across a gay-oriented news program, *The Lambda Report,* but he was far from a regular viewer. "I've probably watched it two or three times, and I think they said last night it was their 480th show," he said.

Mark noted that he regularly picked up a local gay news magazine— "to see what's going on in that community." But the TV programs he watched were not the overtly gay-themed programs of the time, such as *Ellen* or *Will and Grace.* Instead, Mark's favorite TV programs included *Seinfeld,* which he watched in syndicated reruns while he fixed dinner, and *Ally McBeal,* which he discussed with female friends who identified with the show. He also enjoyed *The Simpsons,* and what he liked about the program was its reflection of family life. "I think *The Simpsons* is insightful," he said. "It makes statements on how American families work. I mean, it's silly, but it really talks about how we work and how we are."

It is clear from Mark's un-self-conscious use of *we* that he considered his family in the same terms as the two-parent, vaguely middle-class family suggested on *The Simpsons,* which has become a kind of public script in U.S. society. When asked if his particular family situation influenced his media choices, Mark gave the same answer many other parents did: "I definitely make selections when we go to the video store based on what I think Lisette would like to watch, or what's appropriate for her. There are things I know in advance clearly would not be appropriate for her. X-rated movies. That influences my choices."

Mark was interested in news because he wanted to understand "how my family and I are going to be impacted," and his examples mostly reflected the same concerns many other parents have, such as property-tax increases and education debates, rather than issues involving the gay community specifically. He expressed how upset he was over the shootings at Columbine High School in 1999 because he empathized with the parents. "You're watching children getting off the bus to go home and parents grabbing them and taking them . . . and then there are a group of parents that, they're probably not going to have their kids," he said. Both Mark and Gabriel said family was the most important thing in their lives.

When Lisette was asked about how she saw her family fitting into the broader culture, she answered, "I guess we've kind of got the normal things, you know, with the pets and . . . we're together, we spend a lot of time together." The difference she saw between her household and others was that she believed other families had more family meetings than hers did. She did not believe her particular family situation influenced her media practices. "I have friends [from] all kinds of different families, and most of us have the same kinds of rules, so I don't think that really has much to do with it," she said. Having gay parents, she said, sometimes affected the discussions she had with her parents around media choices, such as the rock music station she liked to listen to that sometimes made fun of gays. "That gets my Dad mad," she said. "And most parents don't like that, but it doesn't get them as mad, because it doesn't really affect them or their immediate family in that way." For her part, Lisette said she usually changed the station if she heard too much talking, because she would rather listen to music.

It was perhaps because the Price-Benoits thought of themselves as a regular family unit that Gabriel Benoit, in particular, was sensitive to any attempts that would suggest otherwise. He nixed a request from *Time* magazine to do an article on his family:

> I don't want that out there in front of the whole world, for them to feel like they've got a right to make a judgment, because I know what we've done has been fantastic. I mean, I see one of the strongest, free-thinking little girls that you could meet. That didn't happen just on its own. That happened because we put a lot of time and energy into the whole thing. And I don't want somebody reading an article like that and deciding just because we're a male couple it was totally wrong. I don't want to give them that right.

Open Discussions

But while they were not always open with the outside world about their family make-up, Mark and Gabriel believed being gay parents had made them more open with Lisette. This philosophy of openness with Lisette was part of how Mark and Gabriel approached parenthood from the very beginning, believing that being able to talk with her parents was the way Lisette could handle having a family unlike the "norm." Mark noted that they intended from the beginning to help Lisette have the strength to deal with people who did not approve of her parents being gay:

> One of the pacts we made was, if we're going to do this, then we have to make sure that she is very strong. We have to make sure that she is able to handle it, that she can go out into the world and say, "Okay, this is who my family is and it's okay, and if you don't like it then suck eggs."

That openness has extended to their media use, as well. Mark elaborated:

> I think probably if I were not gay, I would not spend so much time asking Lisette—and myself—to think about what that person is saying on the news or what the newspaper article says, and consider whether it's the truth or whether it's an opinion that may have a valid opposite.

For all types of media, her parents felt it was important to discuss issues frankly and openly with Lisette. "I'd rather her watch anything with us than [with] somebody else," Gabriel said. They frequently discussed programs or movies, as well as news, which Lisette often watched with both parents. Lisette said she felt comfortable watching any media content with her parents because they talked about it. "I like to talk to my parents . . . because I can get information from them," she said.

There were also more subtle, yet obvious ways, in which Lisette's parents reflected their own media attitudes to her. Mark, for instance, believed some of the network primetime news magazines—he named ABC's *20/20* and NBC's *Dateline NBC*—were sensational. Although he did not restrict Lisette from watching them, he said, "I make a point to laugh at it in front of Lisette so that she knows that it's not something to be taken seriously."

Lisette and her parents described her as "self-policing" when it came to deciding what to watch and what not to watch. Sometimes they fast-forwarded through scenes they found objectionable in movies they otherwise thought were worthwhile, and R-rated movies were not off limits. Often, family members agreed, it was Lisette who decided to fast-forward or to stop watching. "We have very few rules," Mark explained. "Lisette has more rules for herself than we have for her." Lisette elaborated:

> In the movies that are bloody or news shows that are bloody and gory, I *can* watch it, but if it's getting too bad then I'll just stop myself. My parents don't really care what I watch as long as I'm willing to talk to them about it if I have questions. And I can get up and leave. I don't feel like I have to stay there. I kind of have the discipline, so they trust me with it.

An example shortly before the family interview was the Academy Award–nominated movie *Elizabeth*. They all thought Lisette would enjoy it because of her interest in history. "And I knew it would be scary, because that was hard times," she said. "But I didn't realize it would be like that. It was really graphic." She said the movie made her cry, and about halfway through she "just couldn't take it anymore."

Besides Lisette's own self-discipline concerning media fare, the family's openness to discuss issues was another reason her parents did not worry about setting rules for restricting particular program choices. Programs such as *The Simpsons* and *Beavis and Butthead* were not off limits, as they had been in a number of other households we visited. Lisette said she could watch these programs if she chose to, but she thought they were "stupid," to which Gabriel added "rude." Still, he and Mark believed that talking about the programs mitigated any potential negative impact that watching might inspire. As Gabriel said:

> Most everything we've watched, we've had an understanding [that] "other people might do something. We don't." And that's what we've talked about with Lisette. I mean, you know, with any movie, any sitcom, any anything . . . it might be appropriate behavior for one family or for one person, doesn't mean it is for us. And a program like *The Simpsons*, they're belching, they're whatever . . . it's just like foul language in programs. Lisette's heard it all, and she knows that's not how we talk and she doesn't talk that way. You just talk about it with your kids.

Gabriel believed the media had prompted the family to talk about a lot of different issues, such as the time he was watching a program in which someone had committed suicide, prompting Lisette to ask,

"What's suicide?" She was about four years old at the time. In relating this story, Gabriel noted that children cannot be sheltered from everything, the same sentiment the Franz parents voiced in allowing their daughter to see *Titanic*.

Also like Mark Franz, Gabriel Benoit looked at much of media with an eye toward being entertained, and he did not view media as particularly threatening to his family. He said:

> Basically media has been family entertainment, something to inform you, something that, if anything, has helped open Lisette's mind up to things, has caused family discussions. So as far as I'm concerned, media is a good thing. It's not something we've tried to protect, keep her away from the whole thing. I think it's a tool, it's an education thing. It shows what's going on all over the world. Like I say, it's given us some good conversations.

BEING "NORMAL"

Like the TV character Malcolm, the families here wanted to be considered "normal" when it came to media. For the Franzes, that meant allowing their daughter to see a movie they might otherwise forbid so that she could keep up with her friends. For the Price-Benoits, "normal" also had a social context: they thought of their family as part of the mainstream of U.S. society. In some ways, both sets of parents sought to distinguish their families from others: for the Franzes, they believed they did not allow as much television watching as other families with whom they compared themselves; the Price-Benoits also distinguished themselves by the limited time they felt they spent with media, but they also believed they more openly discussed media issues with their daughter. Still, both of these families positioned themselves as families that were not outside of the mainstream in their views and practices related to media.

The next chapter will introduce two families, the Carsons and the Vogels, who *were* more engaged in media than many of the families we interviewed.

9

"Couch Potatodom" Reconsidered: The Vogels and the Carsons

Joseph G. Champ

Perhaps no better term reflects Americans' ambivalent attitude toward media—especially the burgeoning electronic varieties—than "couch potato." A computer search for the phrase in only a few months' coverage of major newspapers, magazines, and broadcasting companies revealed it in hundreds of stories. In many cases "couch potato" communicated a certain harmless, resigned comfort, evoking the image of settling into a soft chair to enjoy an evening's programming. But in others, "couch potato" had sinister connotations, suggesting the notion of valuable time lost, precious attention distracted, and imagination stymied.

If one subscribes to the public script that "couch potato" refers to those who watch a lot of television, it would not be a stretch of the imagination to hang the moniker on the Vogels and the Carsons, the families discussed in this chapter. Indeed, the term could also be applied to their use of other media—movies, the Internet, computer games, and books also figured prominently in their lives. They were surrounded and saturated by media and proud of, if not a little defensive about, their media-heavy way of life. The Vogels and the Carsons, as we shall see, wrestled in some fashion with both senses of the term "couch potato." But before we explore the accounts of these two families, we must further examine the concept of "couch potato." Doing so reveals problematic assumptions.

Working Mother magazine (Bowen 2000) updated the term "couch potato," expanding its scope, with the more inclusive "tech potato"—the child who suffers from excessive exposure to TV, computers, and video games. We are warned that children are now "absorbing more sophisticated information earlier and faster than we [adults] ever did," thus creating "a brood of precocious media masters," a "new—and often unhealthy—breed of child." The author focused on a warning by the American Academy of Pediatrics (AAP) of the potentially harmful effects of media technology on children's health. The AAP found that because watching television, playing computer games, and surfing the Internet is taking increasingly more time out of children's days, their fitness levels are dropping precipitously, putting them at risk of minor eye and back fatigue, as well as more serious repetitive stress injuries. The AAP advised parents to encourage a "healthy approach to technology," including limiting the time their children spend in front of a screen (Bowen 2000, 74).

This is only one of many responses children's advocates have made in the face of an increasingly ubiquitous electronic media. The American Psychological Association has repeatedly warned of the dangers of television, citing numerous studies that found violent content had negative effects, including causing children to become desensitized to the pain and suffering of other people, to have an increased fear of the world around them, and to show increased aggression in daily life. But concern over media effects, especially electronic media, has taken on even more nuanced forms. Proponents of a philosophy known as "media literacy" worry that children will grow up blindly believing what they experience via media because they do not possess the ability to question, evaluate, and analyze TV shows, computer games, and Web sites; without skills of critical interpretation, they are destined to grow up at the mercy of attractive, persuasive messages. Still others, anxious about what might be called "*religious* media literacy," wonder whether a lifetime of exposure to less-than-desirable values portrayed in media might harm the spiritual potential of children. Meanwhile, feminist theorists worry about the effects of the objectification of women, and scholars who study changing *environmental* meanings are troubled by representations of "exoticized" nature that do not account for human impacts on local environments (Davis 1997, Papson 1992, Price 1999).

As we have argued at other points in this book, these fears are based on a fundamental assumption about what we, as humans, are, and the role media may play in our lives. From Ferdinand Tönnies (1887), to Walter Lippman (1922) and John Dewey (1927), to the more recent Surgeon General (1972) studies of media violence and children, it has been commonly assumed that the mass human, isolated from potential supportive social relations, and bombarded by mass communication, is seemingly at the mercy of those who communicate, as this early-twentieth-century passage by James Bryce makes clear:

> In examining the process by which opinion is formed, we cannot fail to note how small a part of the view which the average man entertains when he goes to vote is really of his own making. His original impression was faint and perhaps shapeless: its present definiteness and strength are mainly due to what he has heard and read. He has been told what to think, and why to think it. Arguments have been supplied to him from without, and controversy has imbedded them in his mind. Although he supposes his view to be his own, he holds it rather because his acquaintances, his newspapers, his party leaders hold it. His acquaintances do the like. Each man believes and repeats certain phrases, because he thinks that everybody else on his own side believes them, and of what each believes only a small part is his own original impression, the far larger part being the result of commingling and mutual action and reaction of the impressions of a multitude of individuals, in which the element of pure personal conviction, based on individual thinking, is but small (quoted in Janowitz and Hirsch 1981, 5).

The idea seems to have not diminished over time. As each medium, from books, to newspapers, radio, television, and then computers and the Internet, has been introduced and developed, tension has mounted over its "impact" on society. "Each new mode or medium . . . stimulated research," George Gerbner and Wilbur Schramm wrote, "as well as controversy about the consequences for children, the 'lower classes' and culture in general" (Gerbner and Schramm 1989, 16). The concern made sense to those who viewed modern society as a mass of atomized individuals, in a Lockean sense, *telementing* with one another (Taylor 1992). If one bought this notion of communication, then one believed the receiver of a message could reach an understanding about the general meaning of the message—but it was a one-sided affair. Critical theorist John B. Thompson wrote of the process he called "mediazation":

> . . . while mass communication involves the exchange of symbolic forms, the kinds of communication established thereby are quite different from those involved in ordinary, day-to-day conversation. . . . Unlike a dialogical situation of a conversation, in which a listener is also a potential respondent, *mass communication institutes a fundamental break between the producer and receiver,* in such a way that recipients have relatively little capacity to intervene in the communicative process and contribute to its course and content. (Thompson 1990, 15; emphasis in original)

But if one also believed that, according to the Enlightenment view, a large number of receivers (i.e., "children, the 'lower classes', and culture in general") are not even capable of rationally intervening, then one might conclude that the receivers may blindly take the meanings as their own. On top of that, growing, ever more pervasive media are commonly believed to have racheted up the danger level. It is no longer a one-to-one, or one-to-thousands, transfer of meaning. If, as the assumption goes, a single institution could be in touch with literally millions of people at the same time, then there is *a lot* of meaning transfer going on, a *one-to-millions* transfer of meaning. To many communication theorists and their followers, the thought of a nation of "tech potatoes," suffused within a stream of mediated discourse and mindlessly absorbing the meanings of dominant culture, seemed dangerous.

In light of this brief media history, the story of Isabel Vogel, a mother who had relatively few rules about her 12-year-old daughter's media use, even taking her to the theater to see R-rated movies, and encouraging her to watch films and TV programs with evil and violent themes, might give many of the media critics just described cause to shudder. The same is true of the Carsons, a family whose children admitted to having regularly watched more than 18 hours of television a day and participated in 36-hour video-game marathons. And yet, by tracking and analyzing the reflexivity and the "accounts of the media" of these unrelated families, we will provide evidence supporting the argument that even these families, seemingly highly suffused within the discourses of the media (absorbed even), can express a nuanced, complex, reflexive positionality vis-à-vis media. While their differences may be striking, what is most important are similar ways in which they provide evidence for our argument that media-saturated families maintain well-crafted, self-conscious relationships to mass communication. We turn now to the story of the Vogels.

THE VOGELS

Isabel Vogel, 43, and her husband Elton, 44, grew up in Southern California.[1] They met, had a relationship, and then a daughter. But marriage was not right for them and they went their separate ways, Isabel enrolling in a graduate program and Elton pursuing his home-remodeling career. Years later, after Isabel took a job as a university professor in the western United States, she and Elton decided to permanently reunite. The Vogels were married and, with their 12-year-old daughter, Renee, considered themselves a "traditional" family.

For some, their self-description may seem way off the mark because the Vogels also repeatedly told our interviewer that Renee had literally no prohibitions about what she could see or hear via media. Her freedom was supposedly unlimited. The 12-year-old watched R-rated movies with her parents, and she spent large periods of time alone in her room sampling programming off the satellite. She was encouraged to view whatever she wanted. "We tape her feature films that are R-rated that are more complex in their nature . . . and she enjoys them," Elton said. Renee was also urged to join her mother while Isabel watched rather dark films and television shows that focused on stories about evil. Violence is often a core element of these shows; all the better, according to Isabel. This superficial, rather sensational description of the Vogels' relationship to media underscores how easily we can reach quick (and perhaps negative) judgments about practices like these. As we hope to make clear in the following discussion, such judgments are often based on suppositions we all carry around about the proper role of media in the lives of families, especially children. As we tell the story of the Vogels, one begins to understand how our seemingly unquestionable assumptions often turn out to be misguided and wrong.

We begin with the Vogels' foundational beliefs. Although his mother was Lutheran, the Darwinist philosophies of Elton's father stuck with him. Elton was inclined to believe that he and the rest of humanity were more the product of fortunate twists of evolution than the plan of an omniscient God. Similarly, Isabel said she connected earlier in life with one parent's beliefs, her father's Southern Baptist faith, but later, after her parents' separation, she increasingly identified with her mother's belief system—the Native American Peyote church.[2] Sitting in a living room adorned with a diversity of aboriginal artifacts, it was obvious that Native Americanism was an important thread in Isabel's life and, by association, the identity of the rest of her family. Isabel described herself as "mixed blood," three-quarters Native American and one-quarter Hispanic. Elton labeled himself a "mutt," a mixture of European ancestry, while Renee largely identified with her American Indian heritage. Though Elton said his beliefs coincided well with most of Isabel's, he good-naturedly reminded Renee that she was half European: "I always like to throw that in in this family because I sometimes get overrun with the Native American." While exhibiting skepticism about large aspects of modern life, Renee showed great reverence for Native American traditions, especially Pow-wows in which she danced and wore a ceremonial dress handed down through the family from her grandmother. The white, ornamented dress hung in the hall just around the corner from the living room.

The Vogels' rustic home sat in a picturesque canyon in the Rocky Mountains. Inside, the living room was nestlike, with large leather couches and chairs covered with pillows. A rather large TV, aimed at the couch, sat on a stand on one side of the room. An adjoining office had two computers, Isabel's and Elton's. Another computer and television was in Renee's bedroom down the hall. The parents' bedroom had its own TV. The computers were linked in a home network (Internet, email access), and the televisions were all connected to subscription satellite dishes. Renee had her own, so parents and child were free to watch what they wanted.

Because the Vogel parents had time-consuming, deadline-oriented, demanding jobs, they said they were very careful about planning their schedule: when to work; when to relax and how; when and how to engage in explicit "family time." They agreed that their most significant activities together took place outdoors; skiing and rafting were their major sports. Elton explained: "That's probably been a very fundamental thing in the way that our family . . . cohesion . . . in our family because we have to work together in order to have a fun day." Isabel and Elton also relaxed in the hot tub together at the end of many days, especially in the winter when they were busiest. Renee was not allowed to bother them, so they were free to relax with a beer and "Talk about whatever's bothering us, or whatever we did that we did well, or bad," Elton said. "That's our counseling session every evening, and when we get out of the hot tub, we don't talk about the day anymore, that's it."

What is especially significant for our research was the important position of media in the Vogels' lives. Immediately striking about this family was the *comfort* with which they related their relationship with media. For instance, one often hears estimates of the amount of television the average family watches per week, but it was a bit jarring to have a respondent casually and with no visible signs of regret report watching 30 hours a week, as Elton did during the family interview. The Vogels matter-of-factly—almost proudly—reported having several media "rituals" in which the whole family regularly participated together, such as gathering to watch the sitcom *Dharma and Greg* on Thursday nights, or the dark drama *Millennium* on Friday evenings. They did not have a dining table and often set up TV trays in the living room, eating their dinner while watching these shows and others. Another family media ritual, something Isabel jokingly referred to as their "civil religion," involved Sunday afternoon trips to town to catch movies at the "big screen" theater. Renee accompanied her parents and sometimes watched another movie showing in the theater at the same time, sometimes alone or with a friend. On a less scheduled basis, the Vogels enjoyed movies together on one of the satellite independent film channels, a favorite of the parents. But more often, just Isabel and Elton watched together, or separately, with Renee retreating to her own room, sometimes watching the same film. Meanwhile, Isabel said she and Renee liked to pair up to watch "girl flicks" and "love stories" that Elton did not care for.

Individually, Elton reported using media less than Isabel and Renee. Besides enjoying the independent film channel, Elton caught CNN every morning and scanned the local paper before driving Renee into town for school. In the car, they listened to what Elton described as a "pretty straight little talk show" that seemed appropriate for Renee, with "stupid little jokes," but as soon as she was out of the car he switched over to a talk show with more adult humor, such as mature themes and sexual innuendo. Throughout the day, driving from one job site to another, he would switch back and forth between talk and music-oriented radio stations.

Because Isabel taught about and researched Native American topics, she made use of media presentations by and about Indians, such as films, documentaries, and several academic journals. Because she taught and needed to "know what's happening on a daily basis," Isabel drew her news from a variety of sources. She often worked at home and said she liked to have CNN on for hours in the background, "Something's interesting, I'll get up and go watch it." She said she would also watch *Larry King Live* and *Face the Nation,* and she would read the local paper every day, despite criticizing it for its lack of coverage of Native American issues. A "guilty pleasure" was occasionally watching the soap opera *All My Children,* something she had been doing since she was nine years old. *All My Children* was always a favorite of her mother's.

Renee's individual use was, in some ways, predictable for her age. She said she was drawn to action movies. When asked to come up with an example, she noted *Mercury Rising,* which was rated R. Isabel defended her daughter's experiences with R-rated movies by explaining that, as long as she maintained A's in school, completed her homework, and finished her chores, she could watch whatever she wanted. In an interesting reversal to what we heard in almost all of our family interviews, Elton actually made it clear that Renee was allowed to watch other movies besides those with an R-rating. "We're not like as soon as it says 'R-rated,' or 'PG-13' that that's the only thing that she's allowed to see." An unusual aspect of Renee's media use, especially for her age, was an interest in stories and information about oppression. Renee and her parents explained that books such as *Exodus* and *The Diary of Anne Frank,* and Art Spiegelman's *Maus* series, as well as the movie *Schindler's List,* educated Renee about the Nazi Holocaust. *The Navajo Long Walk* and *Medicine River,* as well as movies like *Smoke Signals,* helped her reach a greater understanding of Native culture. Renee also used the computer games *Myst* and *Riven* (she usually played *Riven* with a friend who owned it) and watched the soap opera *All My Children* when she got the chance and would tell her mother what happened on the episode.

The Vogels' "Accounts of the Media"

In an interview with another family participating in the study, the mother pointed out how most of her son's friends, themselves from families with "good educations" with "very high values," were allowed to see violent and sexually explicit films.[3] This fact mystified her. So far, our stories about the Vogels's highly suffused relationship to media have been mostly that—stories. A deeper investigation of their liberal approach to media might tell us how so-called respectable families could act this way. As we will demonstrate, what at first might seem like rather unrestrained experiences with media (especially relative to the sensibilities of the mother who was just quoted) were actually based upon a well-formulated, highly constructive positionality vis-à-vis media that in the end reveals important similarities to families who essentially walled themselves off from media.

Early in our study, we often associated "accounts of the media" with a listing of what our respondents told us media "should" and "should not" do for them. As we have said, we conceptualized "accounts of the media" to include the common "public scripts" about the dangers and proper uses of media from which people draw to present themselves to the stranger-interviewer. It was assumed that, whether people actually followed these scripts or not in their daily life with media, they were important identification markers that positioned them in relation to the rest of society. But we quickly realized that the Vogels presented something different. They believed, for instance, that media should provide pleasure and an oasis in their rewarding, but hectic, lives. While this might, on its face, seem to provide damning evidence of the couch potato existence discussed earlier, closer inspection revealed a great deal of thought at the base of this "account of the media" as well as a recognition of a less rational, but important, functionality. For Elton, a medium such as television simply did not hamper his lifestyle and in fact served as a tool "enhancing" his "relaxation" when he needed it. Isabel expanded on Elton's assessment, listing all the ways a media presentation such as the soap opera *All My Children* functioned for her. Describing herself as regularly "hyper," grinding through her daily schedule to fulfill her numerous responsibilities, Isabel said she needed something like an occasional "mindless" soap opera for a little decompression. This was possible both within the specific practice of paying attention to a soap opera, as well as practices related to *not* paying attention to the program. The show allowed Isabel to physically get away from her desk, to free her mind for a short time from more challenging reading, research, and writing. Less directly, it might prompt her to think of her mother (who also liked the show), eat lunch (something she might not otherwise take the time to do), or do laundry during the commercials. "It is a time," she explained, laughing, "when a lot of things are going on. Not necessarily the soap opera. But it gives—that's a whole little routine that I have *with* it. Not just staring and listening to it." Isabel concluded that the practice of experiencing her soap opera "attaches to other things."

Indeed, an observation of the Vogels participating in their weekly ritual of watching *Dharma and Greg,* their favorite sitcom, revealed them "attaching" the practice to "other things." The show seemed to function as a great escape for the family, especially Isabel, who laughed uproariously at the succession of funny situations. The commercials also served a purpose. At 12, Renee was probably interested in learning more about mainstream culture through the advertisements. She paid close attention. For Isabel and Elton, however, the commercials were a chance to leap up, let the dogs in from outside, pour a beer, and catch up on each other's day. But Isabel made it clear that her media enjoyment was more than rationally functional. In a similar way to her appreciation of family kayaking and skiing trips, Isabel *just liked* to use media, especially watching TV and movies with other members of her family. "I think for a family, we watch a lot of TV," she said. "We go to a lot of movies compared to friends I know. I think that we spend a tremendous [amount of] time engaged in media, but, I actually personally really *like* it." Isabel was clear that media use should not dominate one's life. For her, and her family, it was a luxury they deserved to enjoy:

> I mean we do other things. We do, in conjunction with watching mindless TV sometimes, as some people would view it, I think we produce a tremendous amount, it takes a tremendous amount of work to upkeep our own property outside of our own lives and work, what we do. To be an "A" student, or, to write three books at one time, to build a house, you know, or to work on our own property, is that, you know? I don't think that, you know, the TV is affecting my productivity by any stretch of the imagination.

The Vogels also believed media should inform. Elton said it was important as a functioning member of society to use media to keep abreast of important issues for communication with others. Isabel said, as a university professor, it was her duty to keep up with current events as an aid to teaching. Furthermore, though being realistic about the ideological and institutional limits imposed upon media, Isabel extolled their potential as a "powerful tool" for change, allowing "voices to be heard and stories to be told," perhaps enabling "a much better environment, and society, if we could work with our media to sort of send better messages."

Renee agreed, saying shows critical of social injustice of any kind should be informing people about oppression. The Vogels also felt strongly that media should not *mis*inform. Elton criticized the media "manipulation" of corporations, such as oil companies that called themselves environmental stewards while engaging in practices that harmed the ecosystem. Isabel and Renee both shared a disdain for inaccurate media portrayals of Native Americans. Most of the time, the representations were rather humorous, such as the time the supposed "Cheyenne" Indians in the adventure show *Walker, Texas Ranger* were dressed as Apache and Lakota Sioux. Other times, they were deeply disturbing, such as a Christian children's cable show that equated Indians with the "depths of sin" for their non-Christian religious beliefs.

Though the Vogels believed that, by now, Renee should have the foundations of her value system in place (further discussion follows), there was a time when they thought it was important to expose her to positive images and life lessons available in media. For instance, Isabel used to watch the feel-good drama *Touched by an Angel* "for" Renee. Isabel also pointed to the "good lessons" available on the program *Early Edition.* Elton added that afternoon PBS nature shows such as *Kratt's Creatures* were positive as well, teaching children about the natural world. When Renee informed her parents during the interview that she did not regularly use mediated environmental discourse such as *The Discovery Channel* or *National Geographic* televised specials and magazines, both Elton and Isabel admonished her, saying they wished she would.

Being informed about basic facts and values was not the full extent of what the Vogels hoped media would provide for them. Elton, and especially Isabel, desired something more from media, something more abstract. It was evident in their growing appreciation of the independent film channels available on their satellite service, and it was underscored by Elton's criticism of a TV program like MTV's *Beavis and Butthead:* "If Renee or anybody wants to watch them, it's fine by me. But to me it's more, it's on such a basic level of entertainment. I like to have a little more complexities in film and media than [he sees] in some things. Like sitcoms—I don't like sitcoms at all. Um, I *hate* those."

What Elton liked were "reality films," current social commentaries on "what's happening." He liked a movie that "gets you in that mode of thinking." It did not have to be movies about oppression (a favorite genre of Renee's). The existential science fiction movie *Contact,* for instance, made Elton think deeply about ontological issues; he remembered that it "moved me spiritually," made him consider the "beyond" the "whole picture of things," carrying him outside the limited view that "we are the only human beings governed by one God and the only God on this planet."

Even complex storylines and characters were not enough for Isabel. She wanted complex storylines and characters *that are evil.* What's more, she wanted Renee to experience these presentations as well. The topic was introduced in the family's discussion about their ritualistic viewing of the Friday night TV show *Millennium.* Despite the fact that Renee said she did not care for the show and Elton expressed only mild interest, Isabel required that, if they were home when it was on, she be allowed to sit down with her dinner and watch it. Because they were a close-knit family and regularly used media together, the other two usually joined her, though sometimes with reluctance:

Isabel: Renee will say, "God, I can't believe we're watching this gore and guts while we eat, Mom!" Like that. *[Elton laughs.]*
Interviewer: Okay. What is the attraction of *Millennium?*
Isabel: Oh, I just like those kind of movies. I love them.
Renee: She has a sick sense of—
Isabel: *Millennium, Reservoir Dogs,* and Fox, you know, sort of, *X-Files,* and a dark, deep, and a—
Renee: Gooey.
Isabel: "Gooey?!" Nah, I don't think they're bloody per se, I just think they're, they're things that make me ponder the "depthness" of evil in our society.
Renee: She likes to ponder that.
Isabel: I like those evil moments of my life.

To Renee's challenge that shows such as *Millennium* and *X-Files* are no more complex than a program like *Touched by an Angel* (which Isabel criticized for its simplicity), Isabel suggested that Renee had not had the life experience to grasp her interpretation. Throughout the interviews and observation, Isabel repeatedly returned to the theme and justified her attraction to a certain kind of mediated presentation of wickedness:

> *Millennium* and *X-Files* are that kind of evil. I'm *very* drawn to that. I'm not really drawn to violence per se like *Scream* or *Halloween* shows, those are absolutely ridiculous. I mean those are almost like too much, based on I'm sure some very true stories in the world today, but, you know, that's just too much, I like that, sort of *hidden* under the tables, *complex* kind of evil. Kind of a more calculated, stemming, trying to figure out where it's stemming from, where is it going, and how is it going to be dealt with. I just love those kind of shows.

It might seem that Isabel was arguing the antithesis of her "account of the media" that media should expose young children to "*positive* images and life lessons," but she was making the point that once a child reaches a certain age, it was time she learned something about the dark underside of human existence. Further, malevolence does not always broadcast its existence with a Freddy Krueger mask. Sometimes, Isabel warned, the vilest being is the seemingly nice person living next door. In fact, what is presented on TV and in the movies is "mellow," Isabel said, "compared to what's really out there." Renee, she explained, was not being raised in the impoverished conditions with the potential for violence that Isabel was. For instance, one of Isabel's four brothers was violently murdered. It had a deep impact on her life, and she believed mediated presentations of evil might serve Renee as a protective reminder.

But for Isabel it went even further than personal safety. It was connected to the Native American spirituality she drew from her mother. For instance, death is feared in modern society, yet it is a part of life. We should not be taught to dread it and run away, but to embrace death for a holistic and balanced existence. Isabel explained:

> The general theme that you would find in Native spirituality is a sense that evil is always, and has been, and will always continue to be part of that natural cycle of life. For me it is not a bad thing, it just is here. You have to have both evil and good, to have a balance.

It was true, the stories were often predictable enough that Isabel could accurately foretell what would happen from one scene to the next. Despite that, the experience provided her with the opportunity to constantly question the motives of the evil character as she asked:

> [W]hy would somebody *be* so deviant? Why would someone *do* something like that? You know, and trying to see how the movie's going to present, you know, what has led someone to do this. What does it *all* mean, what is the *meaning* of it all? The violence.

And if she could reach a deeper understanding of that, Isabel felt she would better understand her existence.

It may seem especially jarring to some sensibilities when one reads this passage from an interview with Renee (her mother was sitting nearby and joined in), in which daughter playfully chided mother for openly laughing during some particularly heinous moments on the screen:

Renee:	But I don't think you need to *laugh* about it like you do! *[Isabel laughs hard, and the interviewer laughs.]*
Isabel [Almost yelling]:	I DON'T *LAUGH* ABOUT IT!
Renee:	YOU THINK THOSE SHOWS ARE *COMEDIES!*
Isabel [laughing]:	That's true, some of them they are. Well because they're *silly!*

Interviewer:	Well which, well wait, which shows?
Isabel:	Well, some . . . some . . .
Renee:	*Millennium* she watches—
Isabel:	No!
Renee [Interrupting—mimics Isabel]:	"OH THE GUY'S GONNA COME OUT AND STAB HER! *[Wicked laugh, almost a cackle]* Ha, ha, ha!!"

Now that we understand something about its context, the interaction takes on a much different meaning. While other families may express "accounts of the media" in relation to conservative religious worldviews, or more liberal notions of the so-called politically correct modern family, the Vogels, especially Isabel, were conscious of nonmodern sensibilities, such as Native American spiritualism, and constructed their value systems and subsequent approaches to media accordingly. Evil, according to Isabel's American Indian beliefs, is part of life. Like anything else, it can be feared, but it can be laughed at. Taken this way, the Vogels seem much less exotic than they at first appeared.

And what of their seemingly open-ended policy about Renee's watching R-rated movies? Again, the Vogels were quite reflexive in their discussions of what children should be allowed to watch, and their reflexivity speaks a discourse of subtle limits. The Vogels agreed with the common theory that children, like Renee, develop their critical abilities over time, and they need to be guided in their use of media. For instance, Isabel pointed out how Renee "does live a gendered life. You know, in reality, is that she—through commercials for lipstick, through billboards, you know, through *Seventeen* magazine—there's all of this sexual innuendo, you know, little girls looking like adult women kind of thing."[4]

Though Renee disagreed at times during the interviews, the Vogels said she used to believe everything she saw on television. Elton said it served as a wake-up call: "Without parent supervision, that sort of thing becomes dangerous because then they don't have any input as to what is reality." The Vogels responded by editorializing to Renee. For example, in response to their daughter's naïve belief in some advertising claim, Isabel said she would exclaim, "Quit being so lame! Can't you see they're fooling you?" According to Elton, Renee also asked a lot of questions while they watched TV and movies together. "It's almost like a little conversation at the time we're watching the movie." Isabel said she was not comfortable with demeaning sexual portrayals of women, especially because Renee was a young teen coming into her own sexuality. She countered this by talking about sex in an informational way, and she once had Renee watch 40 videos about AIDS she used in teaching. After that, Isabel said, Renee could be critical of depictions of women "flaunting their breasts" in the media. And finally, the Vogels said they taught by example. They modeled. Instead of choosing *Baywatch Babes*—the Vogels' term for *Baywatch*—off the satellite, Isabel might select something that she and Elton considered to have some redeeming social value—even complex, evil violence—but not mindless sex.

But where the Vogels may part ways with most media literacy guidelines was in their opinion of the point at which a child like Renee should be encouraged, and, indeed, required to make her own decisions about media. While Renee's apparent freedom and the absence of media rules may be construed as a *lack* of interaction, it was in fact an overarching theme in relations with one another and their entire approach to media in the household. The Vogels pointed to outside criticism about their lifestyle. For instance, Elton recounted a time when someone in line outside a movie loudly commented that an R-rated film they were about to see was inappropriate for Renee. Other criticism came from one of Elton's sisters, who was very restrictive about her children's media use and would view all movies, start to finish, before allowing her children to see them.

Elton: But I think those sorts of rules are detrimental to a child's growth.
Isabel: They don't allow the child to make decisions.
Elton: I think that—
Isabel: You have to learn to make decisions.
Elton: —a kid raised like that is going to have problems making his own decisions.

Elton went on, explaining that media use is an "interactive" process that must be learned. If it is not, it is possible that one will not restrict oneself from media, but instead will leave the television on all day "so they're just, they're jelly." Because the Vogels believed Renee was smart enough, and emotionally balanced enough, and had the self-discipline to avoid mindless sex and violence, not to mention getting her homework and chores done, they could give her the independence to make her own decisions about media. And when she needed help, she had historically turned to them first. "I think we're pretty much the leading value maker in Renee's life without any competition at all," Elton said. Isabel concluded:

> I'm always astounded when people say, "You know the influence that the TV has on my children is much more than I do." I think, "Gees, then you're not parenting right." There's something going on with parenting if you have to really compete with the media. I think I'm teaching her to analyze it, and then that way you can't be as influenced by it. If you look at it and read it carefully.

We end our analysis of the Vogels where we began. What at first seemed to be the example of laissez-faire parenting is in fact based on a well-considered public script any media-literacy advocate could feel proud of. Renee Vogel may be sitting on a couch and watching a lot of television (indeed, much of it unsettling for most sensibilities), but in their stories of her media use her parents insisted that she developed the ability to critically engage with what she saw and heard. Renee was not at the mercy of attractive, persuasive messages; the potato metaphor is inappropriate.

THE CARSONS

A mere seventy-five miles separated the Vogels from the Carsons, but the context of their lives seems worlds apart.[5] Whereas the Vogels enjoyed the pristine serenity of a mountain lodge, our interviewer characterized as "ominous" the scene that greeted him as he entered the main living space of the Carson family, the rented unfurnished basement of a central-city bungalow. Walking down the stairs into a windowless, dark space, he saw two figures lying on a mattress next to massive furnace and utility conduits. The flicker of a television, nestled somewhere among the pipes, out of sight, illuminated the young men. This was the room of 18-year-old Mark Carson and his 20-year-old cousin, Jacob. Just as the interviewer admitted to being a bit unsettled at first by the sight, the facts of the Carson family's life—especially their media use—might lead many people to the same reaction. The Carsons could readily tell stories of watching television every waking hour, day after day. They reported playing video games for days on end without sleep. One boy used to regularly repeat the mantra, "TV is my friend," and he hoped for a life "that's more like an adventure story."

The Carsons treated us to perhaps one of the more surreal exchanges of the project. Here, Mark described how he dealt with the isolation of living with his manic depressive mother:

Mark:	I just watched television constantly and *[he pauses]*.
Interviewer:	Did you—?
Mark:	I did have a little fort in the woods, but—*[he and brother Raoul laugh]*.
Interviewer:	Uh-huh.
Mark:	I didn't go there much because there was no television *[laughter]*. My mom wouldn't let me string a cord. I even asked her *[more laughter]*.
Interviewer:	So, were there any particular shows or was there any particular music that you—

Mark:	Television!
Interviewer:	—that you wanted to—
Mark:	Radio!
Interviewer:	Just anything?
Mark:	Yeah.
Interviewer:	Had to be on pretty much the whole time?
Mark:	Unless I was asleep, and even then, if I were asleep. Even now I can recognize the sound of a television, no sound on it, just the electron gun in the back *[laughter]*.
Raoul [his cousin]:	I can hear that too.
Mark:	It's a skill that you get—
Interviewer:	That is a skill.
Lester [a cousin]:	Yeah, for a while I could find out how many were on in the block.
Interviewer:	Yeah?
Jacob [a cousin]:	It's deafening in a library. You're like *[he contorts his face; Raoul laughs]*. Yeah, electron gun.

What sort of family has conversations like this? Would it be appropriate to describe the Carsons as the quintessential "postmodern" family, living in Jean Baudrillard's hyperreal world of disconnection and simulacra (Baudrillard1987)? Perhaps it has become the comfortable, even expected, route in the assessment of cases like these. However, an investigation and analysis of their lives, especially their lives with media, reveals a self-conscious approach to media that is different in its specifics—much less reflexive, perhaps—from what we saw with the Vogels, yet similar in purpose. This somewhat uneven, and yet in places quite sophisticated, collection of "accounts of the media" helped the Carsons relate to one another while defending themselves (often unsuccessfully) against a greater culture they often found enigmatic.

Middle-aged Rob, a 47-year-old dry waller and graduate student in mathematics, was the patriarch, sharing his home, at times, with two sons, Mark and Trent, 15.[6] At the time of the interviews, three nephews were also living in the Carson home—Jacob, 15-year-old Lester, and 12-year-old Raoul.[7] While Rob had custody of each of his nephews at some point, all of the children had physically resided somewhere else within the three years prior to the interviews (usually with various parents). The constant ebb and flow was an association of relatives, with Rob the resident elder. They truly seemed to enjoy and appreciate one another, most of the time; a sense of camaraderie and good-natured teasing leavened their interactions. Their family and individual stories of home life pointed to long years of knowing and caring for one other. Rob spoke of the responsibility and great challenge and fun of raising this motley crew as a single parent, praising their intelligence, mentioning their triumphs, and voicing concerns about their education, friendships, and motivation. It was hardest for him when one was separated from the group: "The experiences that they were suffering in, the dangers that they were in, were *[pause]* they were more important than my job, more important than my education, more important than my church. *[pause]* I can't think of anything else. Well, more important than my nonexistent love life *[he laughs]*."

In describing the challenges of blended families, Mark only half jokingly mentioned "abusive parental others." Rob quickly followed up by saying: "I guess I'd like to explain a little bit what Mark was talking about, which is that maybe I shouldn't be the one to say this, but I'm a little bit more sane and easier to get along with than some of the other parents involved *[he laughs]*."

For Raoul, it was the opposite problem:

Raoul: I never really knew my dad—
Interviewer: Mm-hmm.
Raoul: —in fact I still don't know his name, but—
Interviewer: You still don't know his name?
Raoul: Yeah. I knew it once, but I forgot. Well, he lives somewhere in [the city] and I think I met him once.

It was a "hard childhood," Mark concluded, that meant "learning to adapt to strong emotions." He further stated, "We're all pretty emotionally strong, 'cause we've lived through hell, I guess."

The Carsons rented the basement space for $50 a month, which helped ease their financial situation. At the time of the interviews they reported annual earnings of $15,000. Their income was a little difficult to define because of the fluid nature of their employment. Some family members reported working for several months at a job, then leaving in order to start new work, to return to school, or just to take a break. Activities and purchases had to be adjusted to fit the flow of dollars into the house at any moment. Their income was also dependent on who was living in the home at any one time, which could be quite variable. Jacob said the lower income experience had left him feeling marginal in relation to greater society. He felt the need to be careful about where he went and with whom he associated. For instance, he had learned to steer clear of the very rich and the very poor. "I've viewed kids getting arrested for just walking in a rich neighborhood, you know, being poor, and I've seen poor people killing each other and stuff, so both of those I try to avoid."

Lester said his upbringing used to make him feel the same way around the middle class:

Lester:	[When I was] younger, I was really uncomfortable, especially around, like, middle class, you know, but then my TV education helped me, 'cause I'd watched enough sit-coms about middle-class individuals to be able to, one, mimic their habits and—
Interviewer [in surprise and interest]:	Hmm.
Lester:	—sort of control them in a way to make it so that they would, well, cloak myself so that I seemed just like one of them. You know, like, complain about heady, pathetic things or that sort of thing and I was pretty successful. You know, I had parents offering to adopt me, saying to their kid that they should be more like me.

In addition to enduring poverty together and facing the challenges of being a dynamic, blended family, the Carsons shared a system of values. Rob's longtime interest in Eastern worldviews, such as Bushido, Ninjitsu, and Zen Buddhism—what Jacob called, "Three sides of the same philosophy"—had been a catalyst for the boys.[8] They learned from Rob and his collection of readings, and they gathered their own knowledge from various forms of martial arts training, which they practiced for years. Mark also combined Zen teachings with the cosmology of a role-playing game called *Mage: The Ascension*. Even though they did not always invoke Buddhism, conversation with the Carsons often returned to what seemed to be a Zen-influenced search for "enlightenment" and "true consciousness." Mark explained: "Well, I believe there's more to this reality than you can see, just like I believe that in television. I believe that as soon as you see things for what they really are, then reality just becomes infinite and immensely powerful, whereas now it is contained and restrained."

Mark summarized that the religion they shared, the poverty, and the disruptive families were but a few of the commonalities binding them. The fact that "we can identify in each other," Mark said, was the greatest support. They also shared a long history of seemingly pathological

exposure to media. While many of our study families might fondly remember important historical moments in their lives, such as vacations,
birthdays, and graduations, the Carsons exhibited the same nostalgia
for early media. For example, Rob told of buying Mark his first computer at the age of three and a half. "It was a primitive, cheap Timex,
one-hundred-dollar one," he recalled. "One kilobyte of RAM. The programming language was Basic." Rob explained that he used the computer
to make flash cards for Mark, so his son could learn his numbers and
the alphabet, to which Mark exclaimed, "So you're saying I was raised
by a computer?" Over time the sophistication of the Carsons' computers
increased until they had a windfall—a close relationship with Dan, their
landlord. Dan lived in the upstairs portion of the home, was very close to
Rob and the boys, and allowed them to use his media equipment when
he was at work or not using them. "Dan's game and computer tradition
is very important to all these kids," Rob explained. "He's worked with
them very closely in many different situations."

Even though the Internet was still a fairly new phenomenon for most
people at the time of the interviews in 1996, some of the Carsons exhibited
a great familiarity with it, using it for general Web site surfing, research,
chat room participation, and game playing. Their Internet/email use took
place mostly at school or the library, but they also had some experience at
home. For instance, Raoul got into some trouble with his brother Jacob
when he ran up a rather large America Online bill playing the game
Never Winter Nights. Mark and Raoul both reported enjoying "strategic
war game" software such as *Fantasy General* and *Warcraft*. The boys also
enjoyed playing *Masters of Magic, Magic Carpet*, a flight simulator game,
as well as games on their Super Nintendo. The Carsons had access in
their home to four computers (one state of the art at the time of the
interview, and the rest older models), a great deal of software ("Dan has
always had a huge amount of software," Rob explained), and a Super
Nintendo Entertainment System. In this exchange they might have been
putting on the interviewer a bit, but it is probably not a stretch to say
their level of media use was much higher than other study families.

Jacob:	Yeah, Raoul's been pulling the 36-hour gaming sprees. *[Mark laughs.]* You know, consecutively: sleep for 12 hours, play for 36.
Interviewer:	My Lord. *[Rob laughs.]*
Jacob:	And it's been driving me nuts, too, 'cause it's like, "Roll Raoul over and do something," and he's just in the way when he's like that.
Raoul:	Like what?

Mark:	36-hour gaming *blaah*—
Raoul:	Oh, yeah. *[He laughs.]*
Interviewer:	Actually, 36 hours, man, I can't even *[laughter]*, I can't even imagine that.
Mark:	Oh, it's not that bad *[laughter]*. Three days in a row and video games start taking over your life, but 36 hours isn't that bad.
Jacob:	Yeah, I only do that for a really good game *[more laughter]*.
Mark:	And plus it helps you keep awake.
Jacob:	Yeah, you can't stay up for three days without video games.
Mark:	If you need to, for some unreal reason.

Whatever amount of time they spent, the Carsons' media use was hardly limited to computers. Despite their relatively limited income, the family had a radio, a telephone,[9] a "digitalized" answering machine, newspapers, books, and comic books. However, the media that competed with, and often surpassed, their computer use were a pair of televisions,[10] a VCR, and video tapes (both purchased and rented). The "flicker" that illuminated Mark and Jacob during our interviewer's first visit was a show called *Ned and Stacey.* The boys did not particularly care for the sitcom, but it did not seem to matter. They watched TV simply for the sake of it. "Yeah, we watch TV all the time," Jacob un-self-consciously reported. They watched what they like every night, such as reruns of *The Simpsons, Seinfeld,* and *Friends.* But they also watched programs they really did not care for, such as *Baywatch, Rugrats,* soap operas, and talk shows. Like their computer gaming, television viewing could become an ultra-marathon:

Mark:	[I] spent a summer, sleeping two hours a night and watching TV the rest, and I think that was the peak, but I can't remember when that was.
Interviewer:	Say again? Two hours of sleep and then the rest television?
Mark:	Yeah.

Lester remembered a time when he was watching television every waking moment and then some: "When I was younger I watched way more television, for a while even *[chuckling while talking]* eighteen hours a day—or more and often slept in front of the TV."

Despite suffering from a limited movie budget during the time of the interviews, the Carsons could praise and critique a number of titles they had seen in the theaters and at home on video. A particular video favorite—one for which the entire family repeatedly expressed great appreciation and that we will consider further later on—was a series of Japanese animated cartoons called *Ranma ¹/₂.* Characterized by Jacob as "a Japanese animation version of Shakespeare," family members carefully detailed *Ranma*'s plot line and its artistic and, for some of them, spiritual values. "It's just very intensely worked fine art, from beginning to end," Rob explained. "Even though it's very frivolous and fun—it's just a goofy Saturday morning cartoon—it's also very fine art, as far as I'm concerned." Jacob was more earnest in his endorsement: "It's a good combination of philosophy and art and humor and, basically, all the things that I feel are important—and martial arts, even though the martial arts is basically silly, it's still, if I could live a perfect life, it would be as a character in that show and, I just love that show so much."

But their media experiences were about more than just consuming television shows, videos, or computer games. These practices presented the opportunity to participate in a common activity. That was something the Carsons appreciated. They described "group stuff": gathering together to watch *The Simpsons, Seinfeld, Friends,* or *Ranma* ½ tapes. They preferred, all the boys said, to use media together so they could share their humor, or excitement, or criticism, depending on what they were watching. Indeed, a couple of times during the interview, mentioning *The Simpsons* prompted the boys to launch into commonly known dialogue from the show, which brought laughter all around. But the Carsons also told stories of heated interactions: discussions, arguments, and battles over media. Jacob accused others of spreading his comic books "randomly across the house—you jerks!" Rob did not agree with their "multitasking," for example, using the computer while watching TV and listening to music. "I'll say *[taking on a mocked-crazed voice]*, 'This is driving me crazeee!'" Media, for the Carsons, were something they could enjoy together or disagree about, but it all happened within the safety of their family. Media provided the community and the difference they needed to thrive together.

But a significant change was detected in their stories of interactions *outside* the immediate family. It was there that the Carsons seemed more sensitive—most vulnerable. It is the place that we can begin to understand how what might be interpreted at first as a seemingly simple, barely considered, suffused relationship to media is in fact just the opposite—a highly complex and intentional one. Jacob hinted at this when he told the story of relationships that have soured. "The only time that movies are a problem is when girls are involved," he said. He imitated a past date: "'[This] makes me feel bad. I hate the movies you take me to.'" Jacob also said that acting like characters from the *Ranma* video "just got me into trouble," so he stopped doing it. Jacob said he liked to watch *Ranma* with friends and would get a sore neck turning around to see if they laughed at what he thought was funny. He said he was "mortally injured" if the friend did not like what he did. Mark and Lester said they also wanted to make sure that their media interpretations were appreciated by their friends and acquaintances.

The Carsons' "Accounts of the Media"

As one reads through the interview transcripts, a specific idea of "use" continues to emerge. Media provided the Carsons with something they needed and could *use*. But it is not enough to declare that people simply *use* media and then leave it at that. We must determine what their expressions of use tell us about their worlds, about the ever-pervasive media they are aware of, and ultimately, about them. We pay attention to the different ways people use media to satisfy emotional needs, such as pleasure, excitement, or solace. We also track their claimed uses of media for what they consider rather straightforward information, such as news of the world, weather, fashion, and gossip about celebrities. The Carsons exhibited all of those uses, as rather elegantly stated by Jacob when he said, "Video games are to forget, music is to soothe, and TV is to encourage and excite." But a use that the Carsons allowed us to explore in a way no other case family in our study could relates to what we call "grounding" in the world. For the reasons stated earlier, because the Carsons largely viewed themselves as having an identity *outside* what they considered the cultural norm, they felt it was important to know as much as they could about the greater world and how they fit into it. The media provided the constant stream of information they needed to better understand who they were.

To apply this interpretation to the entire family is a bit misleading. For instance, 12-year-old Raoul was not mature or experienced enough yet to present a coherent "account of the media"—he could not yet finesse a story of his identity using the symbols and meanings of mediated presentations. On the other hand, Rob had reached a point in his life in which the inventory of symbols and meanings could no longer augment his tales of living. At this stage, media merely provided entertainment or factual information. Rob reported that what he experienced via media might have occasionally accented his creative urges,[11] but the motivation was largely his own. Little credit could be given to the media producers.

The three middle Carsons who participated in the interview were less firmly established in their worldviews, however, and in different ways they mined the media for meanings. Several clues have already been hinted at. For instance, as we've already quoted, Lester said that when he was younger he "was really uncomfortable, especially around, like, middle class, you know, but then my TV education helped me." Lester explained that his greatest challenge in life was interacting with other people. He struggled with that handicap by closely analyzing television shows to try to better understand people. He assumed that because the producers create the product for the audience, "you can get a certain amount of perspective into the general populace. And since most shows are made to be enjoyed by the general populace, then you get an understanding of what they think is entertaining."

By watching TV, Lester gained another view of the elusive world. Mark hinted at a similar idea in the quote, "I believe there's more to this reality than you see," followed by "just like I believe that in television." The admittedly confusing final sentence fragment relates to Mark's apparent personal project of self-enlightenment. Like Lester, Mark took television to be "just another teacher" or "resource with which I can explain things," revealing social patterns. He watched any kind of television, often for long periods of time, for the social patterns he saw behind the more immediate characters and story lines. "I don't discriminate based on plots, because I read for what's deeper in there," he said. "So any television show really does what I need." Unlike Lester, however, Mark was more confident in his approach. The knowledge he gained added to his "perspective"—his "open-minded pool of resources." Some day, he expected to be complete (perhaps like Rob) and might no longer need to watch television to learn about the world and his place in it. But for the time being, television was still a resource.

The final discussion in this section has been saved for Jacob and his rather strong connection to the *Ranma* $^1/_2$ video series, summed up in the earlier quote, "If I could live a perfect life, it would be as a character in that show." Indeed, for a period of time, Jacob *did* try to live the perfect life:

> I find myself thinking to myself, you know, "How would Ranma react to this?" and I identify with how Rioga [a male character] feels a lot of the time and I say, you know, "Man, I wish that I could've done things so they could have been closer to this ideal." And basically everything about the show makes me happier. For a while I was trying to base my life on being a character in that show or something like that. The style of humor in my life changed because of the show and actually, for me, I learned a lot about human relationships and females in particular through the show, because I haven't had too much exposure with them.

But his complete identification eventually wore thin:

Jacob: I still identify with him [Rioga], but I'm not going to mimic his lifestyle. I'm going to learn from his mistakes, and avoid the ones that I already know about.

Interviewer: Mm-hmm.

Jacob: So—and besides, they are pretty much, they're sort of caricatures and they're sort of regular people, so I don't know—

You just have to be careful how you, how you actually view it, because if you, if you base your life—I had a horrible relationship with a certain girl, because I started acting a lot more like Ranma and she was acting like Akane [a female character], only she didn't actually like me very much, so we were just fighting anyway. And it was fairly destructive for both of us, so I decided that if I was one of those people, one of those characters, then I could act that way, but since I'm not, then I have to act like me.

Jacob admitted that he was so enamored with *Ranma ¹/₂* that he lost himself for a time in its story and characters. Indeed, he incorporated meanings from the program into his life, such as the mantras: "You can't take yourself too seriously," and "Relationships are very confused." In the end, however, he realized its limitations. His account of media presentation made it clear that his absorption in the show was probably always a means to an end that, ultimately, helped him work through where he stood in relation to a world he often found enigmatic and confusing.

"COUCH POTATO" RECONSIDERED

At the end of her individual interview, Isabel Vogel told the tragic story of a brother who was murdered. It was experiences like that and others, she explained, that set the pattern for her media use and the stories she would tell about it. As we tried to make clear at the beginning of this chapter, Isabel expressed an attraction to evil, violent media presentations because they told her something she needed to know about the way her world is:

Isabel: The way people read media is sort of like the way people read literature, is you read it through your experiences, through your religion through, you know, through your age and that's how I read media. That's what sort of like what will speak to me before *Leave it to Beaver* does, my mother didn't vacuum the house with pearls on and high heels. I'm *sorry! [She and the interviewer laugh.]* But—my brother got stabbed to death. So, you know, which one will I be more at home with watching on TV?

Interviewer: Yeah. It helps you work out the issues that you faced.

Isabel: And not even necessarily "work them out," it's just understanding them. It's just being able to watch something or read a book that you can really sort of understand where it's coming from.

The significant differences between the Vogels and the Carsons were in their orienting frameworks. For example, as we have seen, the Vogels were heavily influenced by a premodern Native Americanism, while the Carsons followed a Zen-like, interconnectedness-of-all-life philosophy in their struggle with the challenges of poverty and complex family situations. There also was a developmental issue. The Vogels seemed to have more of a cohesive family project—one that solidified into a plan for raising their daughter, Renee. In the Carson family, it appeared to be a plan in development, especially in the stories of Jacob, Mark, and Lester. But in both cases—the Vogels and the Carsons—these families that we could so easily marginalize for behavior that seems absorbed or suffused within media, are, in fact, interacting with media from a well-defined or developing framework—an intentional and sophisticated relationship. Their "accounts of the media" reveal a pair of families for whom media encompass a tremendous portion of their identity. But it would be a critical error to conclude that media *is* their identity. Media, even after supposed thirty-six-hour computer gaming sessions, are always integrated (or not) in relation to fundamental beliefs. Again, media may significantly *inform* those beliefs, but, as we saw with the two most highly involved families of our study, the Vogels and the Carsons, we cannot yet say that the media *determine* what they believe. After carefully considering both cases, it is hard to imagine that there are families that operate outside of a relationship with some assemblage of cultural values. No family is suffused. Everyone has at least some form of a self-conscious relationship to media. As Isabel put it, "people read media" in relation to their constructed frameworks, such as one's experiences, and religion, and age. The stories they tell are their expressed identities. It is only when we have carefully listened to their talk, including their "accounts of the media," that we can imagine the fullest possibilities of what that identity might look like. Today, media play a significant role in who we are. But it is never the only role.

CONCLUSION: The "Intentional and Sophisticated" Relationship

Diane F. Alters
Lynn Schofield Clark

At the end of every interview we conducted, the interviewer asked family members some version of the same question: Do you think that the interviews we've done with your family have accurately reflected your experiences with the media in your home and in your family life? Mark Price, whose story was highlighted in Chapter Seven, illustrates the kind of self-conscious response we sometimes received in answer to that final question:

Mark: I really had to think about whether it was really true, that we did what we said, or that kind of stuff.

Interviewer: It's interesting to us not only what people say they do, but what they want to think of themselves as doing. So that's part of it as well, how you want to think about your family.

Mark: Exactly. When we were telling you we really don't watch much television, you know, and then I think, "Do we really not watch much television?" And then I'm sitting there watching *Martha Stewart* this morning when you pulled up, and I said, "Lisette, we should turn off the television. The media lady's here!" *[He laughs heartily.]*

Interviewer: And we don't try to catch people in contradictions—

Mark: And you're not here to make any kind of—
Interviewer: No, no, certainly no judgments about it. But we do find it interesting that what people tell us they do says something about how they want to think about themselves and their relationship to media.
Mark: Right.
Interviewer: Whether or not that's what they actually do is really another question. . . .
Mark: But that's also really important, how you perceive—how you want to be perceived. That's very important, 'cause it's like a goal. It's how you want to be.

Indeed, as we have argued throughout this book, it is impossible to separate statements of media practices within families from the fact that parents are aware that such statements say something about them *as* parents: Such statements are always related, as Mark observes, to "how you want to be" and "how you want to be perceived" as a parent. When Mark was asked to make claims about his family's media practices, he found himself caught in a contradiction, much like the father in the introduction to this volume who claimed that he fast-forwarded through violent and sex-filled videotapes. Mark wanted to present himself to the interviewer as someone who carefully controlled the television-viewing habits of himself and his daughter, yet laughed as he admitted that they'd quickly turned off *Martha Stewart* just before the interviewer arrived.

Of course, having a good sense of humor helps as parents negotiate the challenges of consistent and effective parenting. Yet as Mark recognized, the contradiction between statements and practices about media use become especially interesting and important in the sense that they inadvertently give expression to a parent's goals about and self-perceptions regarding parenting. These expressions occur in a context shaped by larger, cultural expectations of parental responsibilities that highlight a balance between the need to protect children from dangers and the need to nurture in children the ability to navigate their own course with discernment.

Almost all of the parents we interviewed believed that the media had effects on their family life, and on their young children especially. We have argued that when families talked about such effects, they tended to borrow from what we have termed the "public scripts" about media effects, or what Seiter has called the "lay theories of media effects" (Seiter 1999, 58). The public scripts we heard most often were that media, particularly television, affect children and are often too violent and sex-filled for children's consumption. Most important, moreover, was a subtle script that every family wrestled with in some way: How we deal with media defines how we are as parents and family (or, others judge us and we judge them by how we deal with media). This last public script came across in several different tones: It was said with worry and anxiety in some families, in celebration in at least one family, and in all with a fair degree of thoughtful contemplation. All families, moreover, were concerned to explain how they negotiated these public scripts: They hastened to put them in the context of their own histories and experiences, both as individuals and families, and in some framework or philosophy of life that they fashioned as a family. This negotiating of public scripts and families' own experiences produced the accounts of the media on which we focused in this study.

Parents deemed it important to act on these "public scripts," usually by regulating or explaining media use to their children in some way, or by choosing to experience media with them. Thus, most of the parents with whom we spoke thought that they had been quite intentional in their approach to media policies in their home, in at least one case going so far as to post guidelines on the family refrigerator door, as we found in the Ahmed home. Indeed, in that home and in the Payton household, discussed in Chapter Six, the parents seemed to formulate their media beliefs and practices in relation to what we termed an alternative culture. In this way, these families were able to sidestep the problem of having to constantly sort "good" and "bad" media by maintaining a fairly constant set of guidelines by which all media were to be judged. Thus, it was not that the rules were necessarily consistent, but that there was a presumed consistency behind the worldviews that informed judgments about the media.

Family rules were also "intentional" in that they indicated parental intentions, if not always their actions. While such rules reflected both parents' worries about the values they saw in media products and their hopes that carefully policing media use would somehow better their children's lives, their media rules often also reflected wishful thinking on the parents' part, as family media practices were not so easily shaped by formal rules. Even the strictest of parents were well aware that they were not always consistent in which shows they allowed their children to watch, and why—and they discussed this situation thoughtfully, as the Hartman parents did in Chapter Seven. The most lenient of parents also had a kind of "intentional and sophisticated" relationship with the media, as argued in the previous chapter. This holds for all the families that participated in this study, not just the families of media enthusiasts discussed in Chapter Nine.

It is worth noting that none of the parents or children we interviewed seemed surprised that our questions assumed that there was a link between parenting responsibilities and media use in the home. On the contrary, most parents had thought about the relationship between these with a great deal of intentionality and sophistication. Yet what we gained from our interviews with parents was not an abstract hierarchy of preferred media behaviors but stories about media use that parents—and in some cases, their children—constructed in a way that was consistent with what they envisioned about their family's collective life and practices.

Many complex stories from our interviews were at the heart of our project of studying family meaning making in modernity, as we focused on what families tried to present about their media use and its relation to their identity as a family. A father said he fast-forwarded through sex scenes on videos—and his family laughed at his story because they could not imagine him actually doing so. A child said she wanted a happy, prosperous family like she saw on television—and her family mocked the idea with good-natured humor. A mother said her family saw religion in television—a suggestion that surprised and confused her preadolescent son. The stories had much value, because they offered us a chance to explore and analyze media use as an important, historically and socially situated process, among others, in which families negotiate their own meanings and identities. In this book we have argued that identity, most commonly viewed as an individual project, can helpfully be seen as it is formed and negotiated collectively in the context of family life. As we have observed, individuals interact with one another to figure out who they are as a family; often everyday struggles, such as those involving media practices, become the stage on which such family identity construction is set.

Such careful, attentive, and collective approaches to media by audience members are often ignored in media studies. Indeed, at first we did not fully appreciate how thoroughly the people we talked with contemplated media—even television, perhaps held in the lowest regard of all media considered in this book. As we began to understand the importance of these multilayered accounts of the media, we realized that the stories people told us said a great deal about U.S. society as well as about these particular families. Such reflections on media and life gave expression to many tensions in contemporary U.S. society.

Given the variety and texture of each family's discussions about family media use, we felt that an in-depth case study approach could best address the context and nuance in family accounts. By positioning two different families in some detail in each chapter, we could learn much by comparing and distinguishing between them. In sorting out what we wished to emphasize, we were reminded of David Morley's defense of the study of "the complex and contradictory" in cultural studies:

> The point, however, is in my view an *empirical* one: The question is one of understanding (and here I believe that Bourdieu [1984] has much to offer in this respect) just *how* "complex" or "contradictory" it is, for *which* type of consumers, in *which* social positions, in relation to *which* types of texts or objects. The "distinctions" are all, in this respect . . . they are what we need to look for. (Morley 1996, 323; emphasis in original)

Thus we tried to understand and articulate the distinctions family members made as we described the complexity of their practices and their statements about their practices. We thus interpreted their stories through the lens of social theory rather than viewing our task as simply one of providing stories of media use and presumed related behaviors.

We believe that the notion of accounts of the media introduced in this book deserves further development in audience research, as we believe it is an important way of understanding and analyzing how families deal with the embeddedness of the media in contemporary American life. We look at media engagement as part of a process of reflexivity in dealing with modern life, as media brings us the world in some ways or, more precisely, a particular set of statements about the world that invite some kind of negotiation. We have argued that the talk about the media in this study served as an important, concrete expression of the more general project of self-aware parenting in a world defined by risk and change.

This world includes significant post–World War II changes in family structure and in definitions of the family over the lifetimes of parents in this study. Furthermore, such changes coincide with the lifespan of television itself, as television sets first entered families' living rooms in great numbers in the late 1940s and early 1950s and today represent a complex array of programs, delivery methods, and watching styles. Many parents we talked with brought up and contemplated what most considered simpler television programming of their childhoods, programs that demanded less negotiation and worry from parents. In fashioning this memory of simpler times, we argued, parents recognized the complexity of contemporary social life and the tensions contained in public scripts surrounding all media today. Such complexity and tension seemed to demand from parents a greater effort than they believed their own parents had made to contemplate and engage in the media as part of the process of parenting. The parents we interviewed felt pressured to be "responsible" by limiting media use in a number of ways.

In particular we were interested in parents' negotiations about media and their children's involvement with all kinds of media. These parents engaged in what we came to call "reflexive parenting," a way of living in modernity that involves calling on immediate and distant surroundings, including media, memory, and experience. Parents' sense of accountability as parents was particularly pronounced. Parents thought and worried about the media and took various overlapping paths to control it—some by imposing time limits or trading off book reading for television watching or video gaming, for example, and others by insisting on (or thinking of insisting on) discussing with their children the media they used. In these ways, parents tried to disembed media, particularly television, from their lives in order to examine and try to control them. At the same time, they listened to, engaged in, and reflected upon the public scripts of the media that they in effect helped fashion.

We often think about media as a children's issue. For example, a child-based subtext of many accounts of the media reads something like this: How children deal with the media will affect their character, now and in the future. Yet here we see media engagement as a whole family project, sometimes in the name of children but nevertheless always involving the family as a group. Children often worked very hard to figure out parental intentions behind conflicting rules, as the Roelof children did. We found that children tried to negotiate the slippery slope of media use, taking pleasure in some television programs or movies their parents disdained but also working out why their parents felt the way they did. In turn, parents told us about their anxieties as parents over the media. In all these discussions, we found that what people said to us about media use had relevance beyond that immediate subject, as the stories we heard also suggested and even described outright family members' dreams and hopes for their family, for society, and even for media themselves.

In this study, we drew upon the work of distinct but related areas of media studies: British cultural studies, European reception analysis, and U.S. audience research. We were particularly interested in the work that attempted to examine both society and individuals (or individual families) in relation to society, as in the traditions of pragmatism and symbolic interactionism in the United States and in critical cultural studies particularly in Britain. We have focused on family struggles to negotiate a place in society, a process that includes media engagement and involvement in the home, and we have drawn on a variety of audience research in the cultural studies traditions on both sides of the Atlantic.

We have also argued in this book that our somewhat unusual method of long-term collaboration and intensive discussion contributed much to the study. This method helped us define our own terms for the study, in a journey from postpositivism to constructivism, from assuming we would find quantifiable information to a focus on a more complex, qualitative case-study approach that allowed us to consider each family in context. Our weekly meetings were a collaborative effort to develop the theory that underlies this work. We developed these ideas over time, relating them always to the differing theories each member of the research team brought to the project as well as to other experiences within our specific historical context.

Our method also helped each of us grasp the significance of various facets of each family's stories and to fashion a way for us as a group of scholars to try to understand and interpret the stories and the families in relation to media. Through our extensive discussion and collaboration, we realized that each of us had been impressed by family members' contemplation of the media and how they saw themselves in relation to the taken-for-granted notions about the media that constitute public scripts. From this we began to develop our concept of the importance of family accounts of the media. We saw that meanings were made in the larger context of public scripts and accounts of the media, and we acknowledged their contingency on other cultural narratives. From this collaboration our book emerged, along with a number of single-author works and individual scholarly interests as each of us, inevitably, has gone our separate ways.

Because of the nature of U.S. scholarship, most of us are unlikely to have such a collaborative experience in these particular ways again. Still, the directions each of us chose indicate ways we think these concepts and methods can be explored. As this project concluded, Stewart Hoover and Lynn Schofield Clark began supervising another set of researchers in another collaborative study, the Symbolism, Meaning, and New Media @ Home project and the Teens and the New Media @ Home project, both funded by the Lilly Endowment, Inc. In the first of these projects, Hoover is working on his notion of "plausible narratives of the self," in which he theorizes that human beings make meaning from an inventory of symbolic resources. Drawing from symbolic interactionism, Hoover argues that people self-consciously produce meaning in such plausible narratives, and that the self is always constructed with some reflexive understanding. The notion of "plausible" means that which makes sense in a given context, and a "plausible narrative of the self" is a person's attempt to make sense of himself or herself vis à vis a particular context and one's internalization of a generalized other. Hoover's theory is based in part on the research team's observations that people often cite media and other cultural commodities as they attempt to form self-narratives.

Clark's work has moved toward a greater examination of social networks that include but also extend beyond the immediate family, an area of influence that is particularly relevant among the teenage population that she studies. Based on research employing similar family- and group-interviewing methodologies, she has come to believe that most Web sites assume a much more rational, individualistic approach to the Web than is most commonly found among teenage Web-related practices. She argues instead that decision making about values and ideas occurs in teen on-line settings less as an experience of an individual seeker searching for information on the Web and more frequently as the result of ongoing conversations with peers in such places as instant messages, private chat rooms, or extended email conversations. This builds upon the notions of the "public" nature of thought and of decision making, as well as the reflexive and uncertain nature of life as experienced by teens and others today, as described in part in this book.

In addition, Clark has published her own analysis of the relationship between popular entertainment media and popular religious beliefs among teens. She argues in *From Angels to Aliens* (Clark 2003) that, contrary to the assumption that there are basically two different ways in which teens encounter religion in media (as true believers or skeptics), there are at five different approaches to how teens incorporate or reject fictional stories of the supernatural in relation to their own claimed religious or spiritual beliefs. She also argues that part of the appeal of the supernatural at this point in history is due to the rise in evangelicalism as well as its historic attention to a supernatural battle between good and evil and the desire among its leaders to claim the cultural authority to continue to define "good" and "evil" in universalizing terms. Clark's work was based on her own extensive research with teens as well as on some of the interviews from the present study.

Diane Alters is interested in the social processes of cultural production, and in particular the roles of class and taste in families' media engagement as expressed in their experiences with a long-lived and contested television show, *The Simpsons*. She examines what she identifies as a conflicted process of legitimation of television, how parents historicize and contextualize television by talking about it in terms of how they experienced television over the course of their children's lives, and how that compared to their own childhood experiences with television. Her dissertation examined class and taste in cultural work, and she continues to contribute to new approaches to audience research, emphasizing her interest in the social relations of audience work by drawing on the work of Pierre Bourdieu and Raymond Williams.

For Joseph Champ, the Symbolism, Media, and the Lifecourse project served to provoke his interest in evolving cultural narratives about the environment. His dissertation investigated the way families use the symbols and meanings of natural history films, television, and magazine, and he has pursued his study of discourses about the environment as they emerged from family talk about the media. His current research includes qualitative investigations of the role of nature—both direct and mediated—in contemporary identity work.

Since this project, Lee Hood's research has focused on local news and sense of place, examining how news (particularly television news) is implicated in locality, place-based identity, and viewers' sense of grounding. Her research in this area so far has been audience focused, using methods and analysis similar to this project. She plans to explore how sense of place and local grounding interface with the potential loss of some local media in the age of increasing corporatization within the media industries. She also hopes to write more about gay and lesbian families as media audiences, stemming from research begun with this project.

Like the families we interviewed, we have tried to disembed the media from their close, intricately intertwined presence in daily life in the United States, in order to examine media and society more precisely. In doing this, we have tried to detail the many ways in which media are integral to family life, and we hope we have done so more thoroughly than has been the norm in past reception research. We have emphasized the social nature of contemporary media use, and—not so paradoxically—its important role in the project of building family identity within each family discussed in this book.

More ethnographic-style work needs to be done to help situate media use in social and cultural contexts. But such studies are not simple or easy. They demand a great deal of time and commitment on the part of all involved. Knowing this more acutely than we did when we began, we are doubly grateful to the family members who gave us so much of their time. They allowed us into their homes and sometimes delayed dinner, canceled meetings, or postponed other daily activities for the dubious privilege of patiently explaining what sometimes seemed so obvious to them.

In the process, the interview families helped us understand some fundamental issues in contemporary life. Often, after a particularly contemplative interview, someone would offer some version of this sentiment: "Well, I never talked about this before, never put it together quite like this." We share this sentiment, as we also discovered new ways to look at our mediated lives within U.S. society. By presenting these accounts, we hope to contribute to an ongoing conversation about media, home, and family in U.S. society, and the "intentional and sophisticated" relationship among them.

NOTES

Chapter 1

1. All names of interviewees are pseudonyms. The Kandinskys were interviewed by Lynn Schofield Clark.
2. Much media research in the United States just before and after World War II was focused on behavior thought to result from watching movies. The most well known of these was a series known collectively as the Payne Fund Studies, which includes Charters (1933). For a history, see Jowett, Jarvie, and Fuller (1996), cited in Butsch (2000). This "direct effects" literature has increasingly been supplanted by work that asks other questions, such as how audience members make meaning, a research strain that includes this project. However, because we did not study behavior, and indeed our method would preclude any attempt to do so, our research neither confirms nor denies that media directly affects behavior.
3. For example, the American Academy of Pediatrics warned of the harmful effects of television on children in American Academy of Pediatrics (August 1999), "Media Education (RE9911)," Policy Statement, vol. 104, No. 2, pp. 341–43. From the Web site *www.aap.org/policy/re9911.html* [last accessed 2 May 2003]. The Center for Media Literacy has also repeatedly admonished parents to help their children watch critically.
4. Generally, parents in our study did not articulate opinions on the kind of authority or responsibility they thought teachers or childcare givers should assume. We did not study schools or day care centers as sites of media engagement and control, in contrast to Seiter (1999). Our focus is on interviewees' perceptions of media and particularly parental and familial responsibilities regarding media.
5. Interviewed by Diane F. Alters.
6. Interviewed by Joseph G. Champ.
7. Interviewed by Diane F. Alters.
8. Interviewed by Diane F. Alters.
9. Interviewed by Lynn Schofield Clark.
10. Interviewed by Joseph G. Champ.
11. We are using the term "accounts" in a somewhat different sense than Garfinkel's notion of tacitly employed mutual knowledge, and our emphasis on media accounts is different than his (Garfinkel 1967).

Chapter 2

1. Interview by Henrik Boes.
2. Examples of this approach are in Jensen and Jankowski (1991, 1–11); Hoijer (1992); Silverstone, Hirsch and Morley (1992); and Moores (1993).
3. The notion of generalizing from people to the culture was developed by Clark (2003).
4. For a full discussion of this idea, see Clark (1998).
5. Reflexivity in this study is based on several considerations, including the parenting experiences of the researchers mentioned earlier. We were also aware that we were limited by the fact that all of us are middle class and white. The diversity of our geographic experiences stretches some limits, too: Lynn grew up in the Northeast, Diane in the West, Joe in the Upper Midwest, and Lee and Stewart in the Rocky Mountain region.

Chapter 3

1. In particular we discussed the European reception theory as represented by Jensen (1987) and Linderman (1997); U.S. qualitative media studies, as represented by Lindlof (1987, 1995) and Lull (1980, 1988, 1990); and British Cultural Studies, including Morley (1986, 1992, 1996), Brunsdon (1983, 1989), and Brunsdon and Morley (1978). Stewart M. Hoover, the principal investigator on our project, was an early practitioner of qualitative audience research. In his study of religion and media, Hoover gathered life stories of evangelicals and focused on how interacting with media intersected with people's religious beliefs and experiences (Hoover 1988, White 1994).
2. These include Ien Ang (1985, 1991, 1996), Elizabeth Bird (1992a and 1992b), Charlotte Brunsdon (1983, 1989; Brunsdon and Morley 1978), John Fiske (1987, 1992), David Gauntlett and Annette Hill (1999), John Hartley (1999), Dorothy Hobson (1982), Klaus Bruhn Jensen (1987, 1991), Alf Linderman (1997), Sonia Livingstone (1998), James Lull (1988, 1990), Knut Lundby (1993), Shaun Moores (1993a, 1993b), David Morley (1986, 1992, 1996), Virginia Nightingale (1996), Ellen Seiter (1989, 1999), Roger Silverstone and Eric Hirsch (1992), Roger Silverstone (1994).
3. Meeting with Elizabeth Bird, International Communication Association meeting in San Francisco, May 1999.
4. Bird argues that we need to understand why people read what is considered perhaps the most "low-class" media—supermarket tabloids—and what they get out of them, rather than simply dismissing such practices altogether. She therefore communicated with readers, much as we have done by talking with people about a practice they might abhor but still participate in: watching television (Bird 1992a).
5. There are noteworthy exceptions, such as Charlotte Brunsdon and David Morley's study of audiences that watched the British news program *Nationwide* (Brunsdon and Morley 1978) and David Gauntlett and Annette Hill's (1999) study of diaries completed by TV audience members over a five-year period which traced how respondents' attitudes to the media they consumed changed as they encountered new experiences in their own lives.
6. As we try to make clear throughout the book, we no longer think of these families as "outliers," nor do we use this term, which is more commonly found in survey research.
7. Also related are works by Blumler and Katz (1974) and Rosengren, Wenner, and Palmgreen (1985).
8. Linderman, a sociologist at University of Uppsala in Sweden, spent a year at the University of Colorado at Boulder, attended early project meetings, and helped discuss transcripts.
9. We made this change as a result of a suggestion by David Morgan, an art historian and leader in the field of visual cultural analysis and Phyllis and Richard Duesenbert, Duesenberg Chair in Christianity and the Arts at Christ College, Valparaiso University.

10. Bourdieu offers a contextualized, case-study approach to interviewing that addresses such issues (Bourdieu et al. 1999).

11. Other symbolic interactionist works that Hoover cited included Cooley (1902), Glaser and Strauss (1967), and Blumer (1969).

12. Mead (1910). Significantly, Stuart Hall (1982, 67) has also speculated as to the potential value of interactionism to cultural studies, although he focuses on inteactionism's approach to symbols. It should be noted that a significant stream of interactionist research has been driven to understand these issues in the context of individual psychological development.

13. Also relevant were Csikszentmihalyi and Rochberg-Halton (1981) and Kubey and Csikszentmihalyi (1990).

14. This is argued in Alters (2003).

15. During this time, we also moved from talking about "discourses of" to our current terminology, "accounts of," because we did not want to be limited to a structuralist mode of considering language as primary, as we thought the term "discourses" would suggest.

16. *Veggie Tales* is a series of animated videos by Big Idea Productions, Inc. The videos were first sold in Christian bookstores, and then in 1998 in national chains. Each of the plots are built around Bible stories, with vegetables as the main characters (Lyman 1998). The *Veggie Tales* characters were also featured in the 2002 animated feature, *Jonah*. We learned about the series from the children in the evangelical Hartman family (interviewed by Alters).

Chapter 4

1. Interviews by Diane Alters.

2. Habermas' distinction between public and private is well known, as is the insightful critique by Nancy Fraser (Fraser 1989; Habermas 1987, 1989).

3. Interviewed by Lee Hood.

4. Interviewed by Diane Alters.

5. Interviewed by Henrik Boes.

6. Many scholars have noted the transformation of family structure throughout the twentieth century. Demographers Frey, Abresch, and Yeasting (2001, 123–24) cite U.S. Census figures to note that "only from 1920s to 1970s did the majority of American children live in nonfarm, two-parent households." And a minority of children during that time lived in "ideal" nuclear families of two parents with a breadwinner father and stay-at-home mother. By 2001, a child was far more likely to have both parents working in the labor force, or only one parent as primary caregiver. Due to rising divorce rates and more children born outside marriage, there are fewer two-parent families and more female-headed families. (Frey et al., 123–24)

7. Interviewed by Lee Hood.

8. Interviewed by Diane Alters.

9. Interviewed by Lynn Schofield Clark.

10. Interviewed by Lee Hood.

11. Interviewed by Lee Hood.

12. Interviewed by Lee Hood.

13. Interviewed by Diane Alters.

14. In fact, *The Andy Griffith Show* draws fans that would agree with Jim Mills. Bible study groups have formed around the show, and Joey Fann, who created "The Mayberry Bible Study" concept, says that "the show is filled with basic morals and Christian principles taught by the Scriptures" (Terwilliger 2001, 2D).

15. Interviewed by Lynn Schofield Clark.
16. The way Paula Pearson-Hall told this story was important to what she said, and therefore we have treated words without a final "g" as words in themselves, as the speaker does, and have not used an apostrophe to denote a missing letter. This in the spirit of making stories "look like they sound," as the folklorist Henry Glassie described his own style of transcription (Glassie 1982, 40).
17. Interviewed by Diane Alters.
18. Interviewed by Lynn Schofield Clark.

Chapter 5

1. For example, Martin Allor (1988) in the uses and gratifications tradition makes these points, as does David Morley (1996) from cultural studies.
2. The term "cultural competence" is also used by Morley (1992), building on an earlier conception of the term from Pierre Bourdieu (1984), who applied it to his description of the capacity to interpret high art. Fiske and Morley apply the term more broadly, and we use this broader application here.
3. Interviewed by Lee Hood.
4. These feminist researchers note that women's pleasure and leisure activities have historically been denigrated by patriarchal society.
5. For example, Nick Stevenson (1995, 89–101) criticizes Fiske's theory of pleasure, arguing that Fiske incorrectly assumes that a nondominant reading of a text is resistance. Stevenson also criticizes Fiske for offering only "one-dimensional" readings of popular texts, and for substituting his own experiences for those of the audience. Similarly, Shaun Moores criticizes Fiske for "an overly optimistic and rather romantic perception of everyday life in the postmodern world" (Moores 1993, 103).
6. Interviewed by Lee Hood.
7. Interviewed by Lee Hood.
8. Interviewed by Joseph G. Champ.
9. Interviewed Joseph G. Champ.
10. Interviewed by Lee Hood.
11. See also Morley (1986); Silverstone, Hirsch, and Morley (1990).
12. Interviewed by Lee Hood.
13. Interviewed by Lee Hood.
14. Interviewed by Lee Hood.

Chapter 6

1. Lynn Schofield Clark interviewed Jemila and the four children together, then interviewed each of them separately on a subsequent visit. Clark and Henrik Boes came to their home to observe their media practices one evening during a school spring break. Boes interviewed Umar Ahmed, who had been unavailable for interviewing earlier. Umar may have been hesitant to participate in a research situation with a female researcher. It is also possible that he viewed the interests of the research project in general as of the domestic, and hence female, realm. Finally, Clark spent additional time with the family about a year after the initial contacts because she recruited Hasan, the oldest son, to lead a discussion group about media use with his friends as part of a more in-depth study of teens.
2. Jemila's birth name is Anglo-Saxon; she legally changed her name with her conversion, although her birth family still calls her by the former name. She had discovered Islam prior to courtship, but she officially converted after marriage. In Islam, while it is

preferred that men and women marry within the faith, it is more acceptable for a man to marry outside it than it is for a woman. This is because it is assumed that children will be raised in the religious tradition of the father. See, for example, Yamai (1998).

3. The interviewer witnessed this during both an afternoon and an evening observation.

4. In fact, Hasan expressed exasperation that his parents did not enforce the rules more strictly.

5. On the other hand, Saleem, 13, asserted that he enjoyed death and shock rock music, rather clearly using music as a form of rebellion against his family's preferences.

6. Interestingly, Saleem also pointed out that Libya was Arab rather than African. (His mother had used the term "Arab-African" to describe their racial/ethnic background.) "African is like Zulu and stuff like that. That's just totally different from Libya," he said.

7. Interviewed by Joseph G. Champ.

8. In a previous paper, Hoover, Clark, and Alters (1998) began to explore this concept in relation to conservative Christianity and institutions such as Focus on the Family, which create cultural resources attempting to facilitate a world view similarly distinct from the perceived mainstream.

Chapter 7

1. Interviewed by Diane F. Alters.

2. The Roelofs said their elder son, Michael, also read a lot. In interviews they made no other references to reading books or to plots of books, in contrast to the Hartmans, so it is difficult to compare the reading habits of the two families.

3. Interviewed by Lee Hood.

4. This is in contrast to what he had said earlier about his mother's reaction to *Jurassic Park* and *Alien.*

Chapter 8

1. January 9, 2000.

2. Interviewed by Joseph G. Champ.

3. Interviewed by Lee Hood.

Chapter 9

1. Interviewed by Joseph G. Champ.

2. While formal definitions and analyses of the Peyote Church highlight its eclecticism (such as the combination of Native American and Christian elements), Isabel's discussion of the belief system foregrounded the balance of spirits, both good and bad, in all nature, including *human* nature.

3. Murphy-Gordons, interviewed by Lee Hood.

4. This seemed to be supported by Renee's behavior during the interviewer's observation of the Vogels watching *Dharma and Greg.* Renee watched the commercials for beauty products and other cultural accoutrements with rapt attention, while her parents did anything but pay attention.

5. Interviewed by Henrik Boes.

6. Trent did not participate in the interviews.

7. Rob and his sons are European American. Jacob, Lester, and Raoul have the same European-American mother. (Jacob and Lester have the same African American father. Raoul has a different father, also an African American).

8. Often compared to the chivalry codes of the European knights, Bushido is the "way of the warrior" life code of the Japanese Samarai. Ninjitsu, another martial arts philosophy with roots in Asia, stresses self defense of the body, mind, and spirit. The more commonly known Zen Buddhism emphasizes the interconnectedness of all life. The philosophies are often combined in martial arts training.

9. Two phone lines came into the house, but their landlord disconnected one when they could not get them both to function properly.

10. The Carsons did not have cable television, but Jacob explained, "Cable is not something that you should pay for yourself. . . . That's what you have friends for."

11. Rob was an amateur poet and songwriter.

REFERENCES

Chapter 1

Aguilar, Louis. 2002. Rich-poor gap grows at slower rate than U.S. *Denver Post,* 24 April, C1.

Ang, Ien. 1985. *Watching* Dallas: *Soap opera and the melodramatic imagination.* London: Routledge.

———. 1991. *Desperately seeking the audience.* London: Routledge.

———. 1995. *Living room wars: Rethinking media audiences for a postmodern world.* London: Routledge.

Bird, S. Elizabeth. 1992a. *For enquiring minds: A cultural study of supermarket tabloids.* Knoxville: University of Tennessee Press.

———. 1992b. Travels in nowhere land: Ethnography and the "Impossible" Audience. *Critical Studies in Mass Communication* 9: 250–260.

Brunsdon, Charlotte. 1983. Crossroads: Notes on a soap Opera. In *Regarding television: Critical approaches—An anthology,* edited by E.A. Kaplan. Frederick MD: University Publications of America.

———. 1989. Text and audience. In *Remote control: Television, audiences and cultural power,* edited by Ellen Seiter, Hans Borchers, Gabriele Kruetzner, and Eva-Marie Warth. London: Routledge, 116–129.

Brunsdon, Charlotte, and David Morley. 1978. *Everyday television: "Nationwide."* London: British Film Institute.

Butsch, Richard. 2000. *The making of American audiences: From stage to television, 1750–1990.* Cambridge, UK: Cambridge University Press.

Carey, James. 1989. *Communication as culture: Essays on media and society.* London: Unwin Hyman.

Charters, Werrett Wallace. 1933. *Motion pictures and youth.* New York: Macmillan.

Denver Post. 2001. Census reflects new mix, 21 March, B10.

Denzin, Norman K. 1992. *Symbolic interactionism and cultural studies.* Malden, MA: Blackwell.

Finke, Roger, and Rodney Stark. 1992. *The Churching of America, 1776–1990: Winners and losers in our religious economy.* New Brunswick, NJ: Rutgers University Press.

Fiske, John. 1992. British cultural studies and television. In *Channels of discourse, reassembled.* 2d ed, edited by Robert Allen. Chapel Hill: University of North Carolina Press.

Florio, Gwen. 2001. Census survey gets personal, results reveal new facts about Colorado housing, pay, education. *Denver Post,* 6 August, A1.

Garfinkel, Harold. 1967. *Studies in ethnomethodology.* Englewood Cliffs, NJ: Prentice-Hall.

Gauntlett, David, and Annette Hill. 1999. *TV living: Television, culture and everyday life.* London: Routledge and British Film Institute.

Giddens, Anthony. 1979. *Central problems in social theory: Action, structure and contradiction in social analysis.* Berkeley: University of California Press.

———. 1991. *Modernity and self-identity: Self and society in the late modern age.* Stanford, CA: Stanford University Press.

Greene, Susan. 1998. Four counties in Colorado lead in growth. *Denver Post,* 18 March, B1.

———. 2001. Colorado's new face: Front Range catapults 90s population explosion. *Denver Post,* 20 March, G1.

Guba, Egon G., and Yvonna Lincoln. 1994. Competing paradigms in qualitative research. In *Handbook of qualitative research,* edited by Norman Denzin and Yvonna Lincoln. Thousand Oaks, CA: Sage.

Hobbs, R. 1998. The seven great debates of the media literacy movement. *Journal of Communication* 4, 1: 16–32.

Hoijer, Birgitta. 1992. Socio-cognitive structures and television reception. *Media, Culture, and Society* 14: 583–603.

Hoover, Stewart M. 1988. *Mass media religion: The social sources of the electronic church.* Newbury Park, CA: Sage.

———. 1996. Working prospectus: Symbolism, media and the lifecourse. University of Colorado at Boulder. Unpublished manuscript.

Hoover, Stewart M., and Shalini Venturelli. 1996. The category of "The Religious": The "Blindspot" of contemporary media theory? *Critical Studies in Mass Communication* 13: 251–265 (September).

Hughes, Jim. 2000. Douglas remains richest, county's median income tops in U.S. *Denver Post,* 22 November, A1.

Jensen, Klaus Bruhn. 1987. Qualitative audience research: Toward an integrative approach to reception. *Critical Studies in Mass Communication* 4.

Jensen, Klaus Bruhn, and Nicholas Jankowski, eds. 1991. *A handbook of qualitative methodologies for mass communication research.* London: Routledge.

Jowett, Garth, Ian Jarvie, and Kathryn Fuller. 1996. *Children and the movies: Media influence and the Payne Fund controversy.* Cambridge, UK: Cambridge University Press.

Kosmin, Barry A., and Seymour P. Lachman. 1993. *One nation under God: Religion in contemporary american society.* New York: Harmony Books.

Lindlof, Thomas R., ed. 1987. *Natural audiences: Qualitative research of media uses and effects.* Norwood, NJ: Ablex.

———. 1995. *Qualitative communication research methods.* Thousand Oaks, CA: Sage.

Linderman, Alf. 1997. Making sense of religion in television. In *Rethinking media, religion, and culture,* edited by Stewart M. Hoover and Knut Lundby. Thousand Oaks, CA: Sage.

Lopez, Christopher. 1995. 55,000 Colorado households live in poverty. *The Denver Post,* 27 December, B3.

Lull, James, ed. 1988. *World families watch television.* Newbury Park, CA: Sage.

———. 1990. *Inside family viewing: Ethnographic research on television's audience.* London: Routledge.

Martín-Barbero, Jesús. 1987. *Communication, culture and hegemony: From the media to mediations.* Translated by Elizabeth Fox and Robert A. White. London: Sage.

Mintz, Steven, and Susan Kellogg. 1988. *Domestic revolutions: A social history of American family life.* New York: The Free Press.

Moores, Shaun. 1993. *Interpreting audiences: The ethnography of media consumption.* London: Sage.

Morley, David. 1986. *Family television: Cultural power and domestic leisure.* London: Comedia.
———. 1992. *Television, audiences and cultural studies.* London: Routledge.
———. 1996. The geography of television: Ethnography, communications, and community. In *The Audience and Its Landscape,* edited by James Hay, Larry Grossberg, and Ellen Wartella. Boulder: Westview Press.

Morley, David, and Charlotte Brunsdon. 1999. *The "Nationwide" television studies.* London: Routledge.

Morley, David, and Roger Silverstone. 1991. Communication and context: Ethnographic perspectives on the media audience. In *A Handbook of Qualitative Methodologies for Mass Communication Research,* edited by Klaus Bruhn Jensen and Nicholas W. Jankowski. London: Routledge.

Nathanson, A.I. 1999. Identifying and explaining the relationship between parental mediation and children's aggression. *Communication Research* 26, 2: 124–143.

Narvaes, Emily. 1997. State a leader in high-tech job concentration. *Denver Post,* 4 February, C1.

Nightingale, Virginia. 1996. *Studying audiences: The shock of the real.* London: Routledge.

Olinger, David. 2001. West's growth still tops, census finds region fastest for fourth straight decade. *Denver Post,* 3 April, A1.
———. 2002. Census reflects a state in flux, population growth a mixed blessing for Colorado cities. *Denver Post,* 5 June, A1.

Robey, Renate. 1996. People continue to flock to Colorado, pace among nation's highest. *Denver Post,* 31 December, B5.

Schneider, Alfred R. with Kaye Pullen. *The gatekeeper: My thirty years as a TV censor.* Syracuse, NY: Syracuse University Press.

Schwab, Robert. 1999. Low-skilled workers struggle to ride wave of state's prosperity. *Denver Post,* 28 February, A28.

Seibert, Trent. 2002. GOP voter edge grows in Colorado, gap widens to 176,000 as population increases; independents also soar. *Denver Post,* 13 August, A1.

Seiter, Ellen. 1999. *Television and new media audiences.* Oxford, UK: Oxford University Press.

Seiter, Ellen, Hans Borchers, Gabriele Kruetzner, and Eva-Marie Warth, eds. 1989. *Remote control: Television, audiences and cultural power.* London: Routledge.

Silverstone, Roger, and Eric Hirsh, eds. 1992. *Consuming technologies: Media and information in domestic spaces.* London/New York: Routledge.

Silverstone, Roger, Eric Hirsch, and David Morley. 1992. Listening to a long conversation: An ethnographic approach to the study of information and communication technologies in the home. *Cultural Studies* 5, 2: 204–27.

Spigel, Lynn. 1992. *Make room for TV: Television and the family ideal in postwar america.* Chicago: University of Chicago Press.

Spock, Benjamin. 1957. *Baby and child care.* Revised ed. NY: Pocket Books.

Stacey, Judith. 1990. *Brave new families: Stories of domestic upheaval in late twentieth century America.* New York: Basic Books.

Wagner, Roy. 1981. *The invention of culture.* Chicago: University of Chicago Press.

Westkott, Jim. 2002. Press release. Colorado Division of Local Government, 20 December.

White, Robert. 1994. Audience "interpretation" of media: Emerging perspectives. *Communication Research Trends* 24, 3: 3–32.

Woodard, E.H., and Natalia Gridina. 2000. *Media in the Home 2000: The Fifth Annual Survey of Parents and Children.* Report of the Annenberg Public Policy Center of the University of Pennsylvania, Survey Series No. 7.

Zaldivar, R.A. 1994. Poverty highest in decade. *Denver Post/* Knight-Ridder News Service, 7 October, A1.

Chapter 2

Ang, Ien. 1996. *Living room wars: Rethinking media audiences for a postmodern world*. London: Routledge.

Babcock, Barbara. 1980. Reflexivity: Definitions and discriminations. *Semiotica* 30, 1/2: 1–14.

Bird, S. Elizabeth. 1992. *For enquiring minds: A cultural study of supermarket tabloids*. Knoxville, TN: University of Tennessee Press.

Bloom, Allan. 1987. *The closing of the American mind*. New York: Simon and Schuster.

Blumler, Jay G. and Elihu Katz [Eds.] 1974. *The Uses of Mass Communication: Current Perspectives on Gratifications Research*. Beverly Hills, CA: Sage.

Blumer, Herbert. 1969. *Symbolic interactionism*, Englewood Cliffs, NJ: Prentice-Hall.

Cirksena, Kathryn, and Lisa Cuklanz. 1992. Male is to female as _____ is to _____: A guided tour of five feminist frameworks for communication studies. In *women making meaning: New feminist directions in communication*, edited by Lana Rakow. New York: Routledge.

Clark, Lynn Schofield. 1998. Identity, discourse, and media audiences: A critical ethnography of the role of media in religious identity-construction among teens. Ph.D. diss., University of Colorado at Boulder.

———. 2003. *From Angels to Aliens: Teenagers, the Media, and the Supernatural*. Oxford, UK and New York: Oxford University Press.

Clifford, James. 1988. *The predicament of culture: Twentieth-century ethnography, literature, and art*. Cambridge, MA: Harvard University Press.

Collins, Douglas. 1980. *Sartre as biographer*. Cambridge, MA: Harvard University Press.

Cooley, Charles. 1902. *Human nature and the social order*. New York: Scribner's.

Denzin, Norman. 1992. *Symbolic interactionism and cultural studies: The politics of interpretation*. Oxford, UK: Blackwell.

Denzin, Norman, and Yvonna Lincoln, eds. 1994. *Handbook of qualitative research*. Thousand Oaks, CA: Sage.

Drew, Robert. 2001. *Karaoke Nights: An Ethnographic Rhapsody*. Walnut Creek, CA: Afta Mira Press (A Divison of Rowman & Littlefield Publishers, Inc.)

Durhom, Meenakshi Gigi. 2003. Adolescent girls and media culture: Unpacking the politics of pleasure. Paper presented at annual meeting of the International Communication Association, San Diego, CA, May.

Garnham, Nicholas. 1995. Political economy and cultural studies: Reconciliation or divorce? *Critical Studies in Mass Communication* 12: 62–71.

Geertz, Clifford. 1973. *The interpretation of cultures*. New York: Basic Books.

———. 1980. Blurred genres: The reconfiguration of social thought. *The American Scholar*, 49(2): 165–79.

Gibson, Timothy A. 2002. Beyond cultural populism: Notes toward the critical ethnography of media audiences, *Journal of Communication Inquiry* 24: 253–273.

Glaser, Barney, and Anselm Strauss. 1959. *The discovery of grounded theory*. New York: Aldine de Gruyter.

Goffman, Erving. 1959. *The presentation of self in everyday life*. Garden City, NY: Penguin.

Grossberg, Lawrence. 1989. The Circulation of Cultural Studies. *Critical Studies in Mass Communication* 6: 413–20.

Guba, Egon G., and Yvonna Lincoln. 1994. Competing paradigms in qualitative research. In *Handbook of qualitative research*, edited by Norman Denzin and Yvonna Lincoln. Thousand Oaks, CA: Sage.

Hammersley, Martyn. 1989. *The dilemma of qualitative method: Herbert Blumer and the Chicago Tradition*. London: Routledge.

Hoijer, Birgitta. 1992. Socio-cognitive structures and television reception. *Media, Culture, and Society* 14: 583–603.

Hoover, Stewart. 1996. Working prospectus: Symbolism, media and the lifecourse, University of Colorado at Boulder.

Jensen, Klaus Bruhn. 1991. Introduction: The qualitative turn. In *A handbook of qualitative methodologies for mass communication research*, edited by Klaus Bruhn Jensen and Nicholas Jankowski. London: Routledge.

Jensen, Klaus Bruhn, and Nicholas Jankowski, eds. 1991. *A handbook of qualitative methodologies for mass communication research*. London: Routledge.

Katz, Elihu and Tamar Liebes. (1984). Once upon a time in Dallas. *Intermedia*. 12(3): 28–32.

Lincoln, Yvonna, and Egon Guba. 1985. *Naturalistic inquiry*. Beverly Hills, CA: Sage.

Lindlof, Thomas. 1995. *Qualitative Communication Research Methods*. Thousand Oaks, CA: Sage.

Lull, James. 1990. *Inside family viewing: Ethnographic research on television's audience*. London: Routledge.

Malinowski, Bronislaw. [1922] 1961. *Argonauts of the western Pacific: An account of native enterprise and adventure in the archipelagoes of Melanesian New Guinea*. New York: Dutton.

McRobbie, Angela, and Jenny Gerber. 1976. Girls and subcultures: An exploration. In *Resistance through rituals: Youth subcultures in post-war Britain*, edited by Stuart Hall and Tony Jefferson. London: Hutchinson.

Mead, George Herbert. 1910. *Mind, self and society*. Chicago: Unwin Press.

Modleski, Tania, 1986. *Studies in Entertainment: Critical Approaches to Mass Culture*. Bloomington: Indiana University Press.

Moores, Shaun. 1993. *Interpreting audiences: The ethnography of media consumption*. London: Sage.

Nagar, Richa. 1997. Exploring methodological borderlands through oral narratives. In *Thresholds in feminist geography: Difference, methodology, representation*, edited by John Paul Jones III, Heidi J. Nast, and Susan M. Roberts. Lanham, MD: Rowman and Littlefield.

Natrajan, Balmurli, and Radhika Parameswaran. 1997. Contesting the politics of ethnography: Towards an alternative knowledge production. *Journal of Communication Inquiry* 21, 1: 27–59.

Nightingale, Virginia. 1996. *Studying Audiences: The Shock of the Real*. New York: Routledge.

Parameswaran, Radhika. 1999. Western romance fiction as English language media in postcolonial India. *Journal of Communication* 49, 2: 84–105.

Press, Andrea. 1991. *Women watching television: Gender, class, and generation in the American television experience*. Philadelphia: University of Pennsylvania Press.

Radway, Janice. 1984. *Reading the romance: Women, patriarchy, and popular literature*. Chapel Hill: University of North Carolina Press.

Rosengren, Karl E, Lawrence A. Wenner, and Phillip Palmgreen, (Eds.). 1985. *Media Gratifications Research*. Beverly Hills, CA: Sage.

Seiter, Ellen. 1999. *Television and new media audiences*. Oxford, UK: Clarendon.

Silverstone, Roger, and Eric Hirsch, eds. 1992. *Consuming technologies: media and information in domestic spaces*. London: Routledge.

Silverstone, Roger, Eric Hirsch, and David Morley. 1992. "Listening to a long conversation: An ethnographic approach to the study of information and communication technologies in the home." *Cultural Studies* 5, 2: 204–27.

Stacey, Judith. 1990. *Brave new families: Stories of domestic upheaval in late twentieth century America*. New York: Basic Books.

Tsing, Anna Lowenhaupt. 1993. *In the realm of the diamond queen: Marginality in an out-of-the-way place*. Princeton, NJ: Princeton University Press.

VanMaanen, John. 1988. *Tales of the field: On writing ethnography*. Chicago: University of Chicago Press.

Van Zoonen, Lizbet. 1994. Feminist Media Studies. London: Sage.

Visweswaran, Kamala. 1994. *Fictions of feminist ethnography.* Minneapolis: University of Minnesota Press.

Chapter 3

Alters, Diane F. 1998. Identity and meaning: The project of self-reflexivity in a family. Paper presented at annual meeting of the Society for the Scientific Study of Religion, Montreal, Quebec, November.

———. 1999a. Conflict and historical memory: A comparison of two families. Paper presented at the Popular Communication Division, International Communication Association, San Francisco, California, May.

———. 1999b. Media, religion, and the dark, dark room: One family's struggle with contemporary culture. Paper presented at the Third International Conference on Media, Religion and Culture, Edinburgh, Scotland, July.

———. 2001. The family audience: Media, nostalgia and change. Paper presented at the annual meeting of the International Communication Association Annual Meeting, Washington, DC, May.

———. 2002a. The family audience: Class, taste, and cultural production in late modernity. Ph.D. diss., University of Colorado at Boulder.

———. 2002b. They hid Jesus in the bulrushes: Children's understandings of religion in popular culture. Paper presented at the annual meeting of the Society for Scientific Study of Religion, Salt Lake City, November.

———. 2003. We hardly watch that rude, crude show: Class and taste in *The Simpsons*. In *Prime time animation: Television animation and American culture*, edited by Carol A. Stabile and Mark Harrison. London: Routledge.

Ang, Ien. 1985. *Watching* Dallas: *Soap opera and the melodramatic imagination*. London: Routledge.

———. 1991. *Desperately seeking the audience*. London: Routledge.

———. 1996. *Living room wars: Rethinking media audiences for a postmodern world*. London: Routledge.

Berger, Peter L., and Thomas Luckmann. 1967. *The social construction of reality: A treatise in the sociology of knowledge*. Garden City, NY: Anchor Books.

Bird, S. Elizabeth. 1992a. *For enquiring minds: A cultural study of supermarket tabloids*. Knoxville: University of Tennessee Press.

———. 1992b. Travels in nowhere land: Ethnography and the "impossible" audience. *Critical Studies in Mass Communication* 9: 250–260.

Blumer, Herbert. 1969. *Symbolic interactionism*. Englewood Cliffs, NJ: Prentice-Hall.

Blumler, Jay G., and Elihu Katz, eds. 1974. *The uses of mass communications: Current perspectives on gratification research*. Beverly Hills, CA: Sage.

Bourdieu, Pierre. 1984. *Distinction: A social critique of the judgement of taste*. Translated by Richard Nice. Cambridge, MA: Harvard University Press.

Bourdieu, Pierre and Alain Accardo, Gabrielle Balazs, Stéphane Beaud, François Bonvin, Emmanuel Bourdieu, Philippe Bourgois, Sylvain Broccolichi, Patrick Champagne, Rosine Christin, Jean-Pierre Faguer, Sandrine Garcia, Remi Lenoir, Françoise Œuvrard, Michel Pialoux, Louis Pinto, Denis Podalyds, Abdelmalek Sayad, Charles Soulié, Loïc J.D. Waguant, 1999. *The weight of the world: Social suffering in contemporary society*. Translated by Priscilla Parkhurst Ferguson, Susan Emanuel, Joe Johnson and Shoggy T. Waryn. Stanford, CA: Stanford University Press.

Brunsdon, Charlotte. 1989. Crossroads: Notes on a soap opera. In *Regarding television: Critical approaches—An anthology*, edited by E. Ann Kaplan. Frederick MD: University Publications of America.

———. 1989. Text and audience. In *Remote control: Television, audiences, and cultural power,* edited by Ellen Seiter, Hans Borchers, Gabriele Kreutzner, and Eva-Maria Warth. London: Routledge.

Brunsdon, Charlotte, and David Morley. 1978. *Everyday television: "Nationwide."* London: British Film Institute.

Carey, James. 1989. *Communication as culture.* Boston: Unwin and Hyman.

Champ, Joseph G. 1999a. Finding transcendence in nature: Thoughts on the intersection of religion, the environment, and media. Paper presented at the Third International Conference on Media, Religion, and Culture, Edinburgh, Scotland, July.

———. 1999b. Media and the meaning making of environmental families: A constructivism-differentiation model. Paper presented at the annual meeting of the International Communication Association, San Francisco, CA, May.

———. 1999c. Seeding the boundary: A family's defense against media and greater culture. Paper presented at annual meeting of the International Communication Association, San Francisco, CA, May.

———. 2001. "Media, identity, and the environment: Popular religiosity and spectacular nature." Ph.D. diss., University of Colorado at Boulder.

Clark, Lynn Schofield. 1996. Media, meaning and religious identity in the postmodern context: The case of adolescents and their families. Paper presented at the annual meeting of the Society for the Scientific Study of Religion, Nashville, TN, November.

———. 1997a. Case study methodology in media research. Paper presented at the Symposium on Methodology in Reception Studies, Uppsala, Sweden, May.

———. 1997b. How audiences talk about *Touched by an Angel:* Religion and spirituality in contemporary public discourse. Paper presented at the annual meeting of the Society for the Scientific Study of Religion, San Diego, CA, November.

———. 1997c. Teens, television, and religious identity. Paper presented at the Symposium on Youth and Religion, San Diego, CA, November.

———. 1998a. Baby boomers and their millennial kids: Constructing religious identity in a mediated environment. Paper presented at the annual meeting of the Society for the Scientific Study of Religion, Montreal, Quebec, November.

———. 1998b. Identity, discourse, and media audiences: A critical ethnography of the role of visual media in religious identity-construction among U.S. adolescents. Ph.D. diss., University of Colorado at Boulder.

———. 1999a. The funky side of the supernatural: Angels, aliens and "legitimate" culture. Paper presented at the meeting of the International Study Commission on Media, Religion, and Culture, Boulder, CO, January.

———. 1999b. Ideology, religion, and class in a mediated environment: A critical reception study of *Touched by an Angel.* Paper presented at the annual meeting of the International Communication Association, San Francisco, CA, May.

———. 1999c. If you stay away from Nintendo, You'll read the Qur'an more: Media, the family, and Muslim identity. Paper presented at the International Conference on Media, Religion and Culture, Edinburgh, Scotland, July.

———. 1999d. Learning from the field: The journey from post-positivist to constructivist methods. Paper presented at the annual meeting of the International Communication Association, San Francisco, CA, May.

———. 1999e. Media, religion, and family identity: The symbolism, media, and the lifecourse project. Paper presented at the annual meeting of the Society for the Scientific Study of Religion, Boston, November.

———. 2000a. "Angels." In *Encyclopedia for contemporary American religion,* edited by Wade Clark Roof. New York: Macmillan.

———. 2000b. Touched by a (vampire named) angel: Teen girls, beliefs in the supernatural, and delegitimated popular culture. Paper presented at the annual meeting of the Society for Scientific Study of Religion, Boston.

————. 2001a. Creating family media policies: A case study comparison of how two families regulate media use for their children, and how their children interpret those policies. Paper presented at the annual meeting of the International Communication Association, Washington, DC, May.

————. 2001b. Fundamentalists and the entertainment media. In *Encyclopedia of fundamentalism,* edited by Brenda Brasher. New York: Routledge.

————. 2001c. The history of media studies in media, religion, and culture scholarship. Paper presented at the pre-conference on Media, Religion, and Culture, American Academy of Religion, Denver, CO, November.

————. 2002a. The "funky" side of religion: Religion, media, and the supernatural in the ethnographic narratives of U.S. adolescents. Paper presented to the annual meeting of the American Academy of Religion, Toronto, Ontario, November.

————. 2002b. Overview: The "Protestantization" of research into media, religion, and culture. In *Practicing religion in the age of the media: Explorations in media, religion and culture,* edited by Stewart M. Hoover and Lynn Schofield Clark. New York: Columbia University Press.

————. 2002c. U.S. adolescent religious identity, the media, and the "funky" side of religion. *Journal of Communication* 52, 4: 794–811.

————. 2003a. Baby boomers and their millennial kids: "Folk" definitions of religion and their relationship to culture. In *Defining religion: critical approaches to drawing boundaries between sacred and secular,* edited by Arthur L. Greil. New York: JAI Press.

————. 2003b. *From angels to aliens: Teens, the media, and beliefs in the supernatural.* Oxford, UK: Oxford University Press.

————. 2003c. "Touched by an angel." In *Encyclopedia of television,* 2nd ed, edited by Horace Newcomb. New York: Routledge.

————. 2003d. U.S. teens, the media, and the "funky" side of religion. In *Readings in media, religion, and culture,* edited by Jolyon Mitchell and Sophia Marriage. London: Continuum.

————. 2003e. "The WB Network." In *Encyclopedia of television,* 2nd ed, edited by Horace Newcomb. New York: Routledge.

Cooley, Charles H. 1902. *Human nature and the social order.* New York: Scribner's.

Csikszentmihalyi, Mihalyi. 1990. *Flow: The Psychology of Optimal Experience.* New York: Harper and Row.

————. 1997. *Finding Flow: The Psychology of Engagement with Everyday Life.* New York: Basic Books.

Csikszentmihalyi, Mihalyi, and Eugene Rochberg-Halton. 1981. *The meaning of things: Domestic symbols and the self.* Cambridge, UK: Cambridge University Press.

Denzin, Norman K. 1992. *Symbolic interactionism and cultural studies: The politics of interpretation.* Oxford, UK: Blackwell.

Fish, Stanley. 1980. *Is there a text in this class? The authority of interpretative communities.* Cambridge, MA: Harvard University Press.

Fiske, John. 1987. *Television culture.* London: Routledge.

————. 1992. British cultural studies and television. In *Channels of discourse, reassembled,* 2nd ed., edited by Robert Allen. Chapel Hill: University of North Carolina Press.

Fiske, John, and John Hartley. 1978. *Reading television.* London: Methuen.

Gauntlett, David, and Annette Hill. 1999. *TV living: Television, culture and everyday life.* London: Routledge and British Film Institute.

Geertz, Clifford. 1983. *Local knowledge.* New York: Basic Books.

Giddens, Anthony. 1991. *Modernity and self-identity: Self and society in the late modern age.* Stanford, CA: Stanford University Press.

Glaser, Barney G., and Anselm Strauss. 1967. *The discovery of grounded theory.* New York: Aldine de Gruyter.

Goffman, Erving. 1959. *The presentation of self in everyday life.* Garden City, NY: Doubleday.

Hall, Stuart. 1979. Culture, the media and the "ideological effect." In *Mass communication and society,* edited by James Curran, Michael Gurevitch, Janet Woollacott, John Marriott, and Carrie Roberts. London: Sage.

———. 1981. Notes on deconstructing "the popular." In *People's history and socialist theory,* edited by Raphael Samuel. London: Routledge.

———. 1982. The rediscovery of "Ideology": Return of the repressed in media studies. In *Culture, society and the media,* edited by Michael Gurevitch, Tony Bennett, James Curran, and Janet Woollacott. London: Methuen.

———. 1986. On postmodernism and articulation. *Journal of Communication Inquiry* 10, 2: 45–60.

Hartley, John. 1999. *Uses of television.* London and New York: Routledge.

Hay, James, Larry Grossberg, and Ellen Wartella, eds. 1996. *The audience and its landscape.* Boulder, CO: Westview.

Hobson, Dorothy. 1982. Crossroads: *The drama of a soap opera.* London: Methuen.

Hood, Lee. 1999a. From *Unsolved Mysteries* to *Walker, Texas Ranger:* Children talk about God in the media. Paper presented at the conference of the International Study Commission on Media and Religion, Boulder, CO, January.

———. 1999b. Ghosts, spirits and Schwarzenegger: Children's connections to God in mediated culture. Paper presented at the Third International Conference on Media, Religion and Culture, Edinburgh, Scotland, July.

———. 1999c. Mixed messages: Children negotiating meaning in media violence. Paper presented at the annual meeting of the International Communication Association, San Francisco, CA, May.

———. 2000. From angels to outlaws: How children find God in visual media. Paper presented at the Religious Communications Congress, Chicago, IL, March.

———. 2001. The local news audience and sense of place: A home in the global village. Ph.D. diss., University of Colorado at Boulder.

Hoover, Stewart M. 1988. *Mass media religion: The social sources of the electronic church.* Newbury Park, CA: Sage.

———. 1998a. Media scholarship and the question of religion: Evolving theory and method. Paper presented at the 48th Annual Conference of the International Communication Association, Jerusalem, July.

———. 1998b. *Religion in the news: Faith and journalism in American public discourse.* London: Sage.

———. 1998c. Toward a nominative theory of symbolism. Paper presented at the Roundtable on Meaning, jointly sponsored by the Network for Qualitative Audience Research and the Working Group on Media, Religion, and Culture, International Association for Mass Communication Research, Glasgow, July.

———. 2000a. Media and the visual imagination of religion. Paper presented at the invitational conference "The Visual Culture of American Religions," Valparaiso University, Indiana, August.

———. 2000b. Media, meaning and visual religion. Paper presented at the Association for the History of Religions, Durban, South Africa, August.

———. 2000c. Recovering religion in media ritual. Paper presented at the annual meeting of the International Communication Association, Acapulco, June.

———. 2001. Religious meaning-making in media households: Fieldwork on social-scientific study of religion and the media. Paper presented at the annual meeting of the Society for Scientific Study of Religion, Columbus, OH, October.

———. Forthcoming. *Religion in the Media Age.* London: Routledge.

Hoover, Stewart M., and Lynn Schofield Clark. 1998. Children, families and the media in the context of postmodern religion: A report on research in progress. Paper presented at the annual meeting of the International Communication Association, Jerusalem, July.

Hoover, Stewart M., Lynn Schofield Clark, and Diane F. Alters. 1999. Children, families and the media in conflict: A culturalist field research perspective. Unpublished paper, available online at www.mediareligion.org.

Hoover, Stewart M., and Knut Lundby, eds. 1997. *Rethinking media, religion, and culture.* Thousand Oaks, CA: Sage.

Jensen, Klaus Bruhn. 1987. Qualitative audience research: Toward an integrative approach to reception. *Critical Studies in Mass Communication* 4, 1: 21–36.

———. 1991. Introduction: The qualitative turn. In *A handbook of qualitative methodologies for mass communication research,* edited by Klaus Bruhn Jensen and Nicholas Jankowski. London: Routledge.

———. 1994. News of the world: Preliminary findings and theoretical implications. Paper presented at the 19th conference of the international association for mass communication research, Seoul, Korea.

Kubey, Ronald, and Mihalyi Csikszentmihalyi. 1990. *Television and the quality of life: How viewing shapes everyday experience.* Hillsdale, NJ: Erlbaum.

Liebes, Tamar, and Elihu Katz. 1990. *The export of meaning: Cross-cultural readings of Dallas.* New York: Oxford University Press.

Linderman, Alf. 1996. The reception of religious television: Social semeiology applied to an empirical case study. In *Acta Universitatis Upsaliensis, Psychologia et Sociologia Religionum* 12, Stockholm: Almquist and Wiksell International.

———. 1997. Making sense of religion in television. In *Rethinking media, religion, and culture,* edited by Stewart M. Hoover and Knut Lundby. Thousand Oaks, CA: Sage.

Lindlof, Thomas R. 1987. *Natural audiences: Qualitative research of media uses and effects.* Norwood, NJ: Ablex.

———. 1995. *Qualitative communication research methods.* Thousand Oaks, CA: Sage.

Livingstone, Sonia. 1998. *Making sense of television: The psychology of audience interpretation,* second ed. London: Routledge.

Lull, James. 1980. The social uses of television. *Human Communication Research* 6, 3: 198–209.

———, ed. 1988. *World families watch television.* Newbury Park, CA: Sage.

———. 1990. *Inside family viewing: Ethnographic research on television's audience.* London: Routledge.

Lundby, Knut. 1993. *Mediekultur.* Oslo: Universitetsforlaget.

Lyman, David. 1998. Vegetables star in surprise kiddie video. *Denver Post,* 18 May, 2E.

Mead, George Herbert. 1900. What social objects must psychology presuppose? *Journal of Philosophy, Psychology, and Scientific Methods,* 7: 174–80.

———. 1910. *Mind, Self and Society.* Chicago: Unwin Press.

Moores, Shaun. 1993a. *Interpreting audiences: The ethnography of media consumption.* London: Sage.

———. 1993b. Satellite television as cultural sign: Consumption, embedding and articulation. *Media, Culture and Society* 15, 4: 621–39.

Morgan, David. 1998. *Visual piety: A history and theory of popular religious images.* Berkeley: University of California Press.

Morley, David. 1986. *Family television: Cultural power and domestic leisure.* London: Routledge.

———. 1992. *Television, audiences and cultural studies.* London: Routledge.

———. 1996. The geography of television: Ethnography, communications, and community. In *The audience and its landscape,* edited by James Hay, Larry Grossberg, and Ellen Wartella. Boulder, CO: Westview Press.

Morley, David, and Charlotte Brunsdon. 1999. *The "Nationwide" television studies*. London: Routledge.

Newcomb, Horace, and Paul M. Hirsch. 1983. Television as a cultural forum. *Quarterly review of film studies,* Summer 1983.

Nightingale, Virginia. 1996. *Studying audiences: The shock of the real*. London: Routledge.

Rosengren, Karl Erik. 1994. *Media effects and beyond: Culture, socialization, and lifestyles*. London: Routledge.

Rosengren, Karl Erik, Lawrence A. Wenner, and Philip Palmgreen, eds. 1985. *Media gratifications research: Current perspectives*. Beverly Hills, CA: Sage.

Seiter, Ellen. 1995. *Sold separately: Parents and children in consumer culture*. New Brunswick, NJ: Rutgers University Press.

————. 1999. *Television and new media audiences*. Oxford, UK: Oxford University Press.

Seiter, Ellen, Hans Borchers, Gabriele Kruetzner, and Eva-Marie Warth, eds. 1989. *Remote control: Television, audiences and cultural power*. London: Routledge.

Silverstone, Roger. 1981. *The message of television*. London: Heinemann.

————. 1988. Television, myth and culture. In *Media, myths and narratives*, edited by James Carey. London: Sage.

————. 1989. Television: Text or discourse? *Science as Culture* 6: 104–123.

————. 1994. *Television and everyday life*. London: Routledge.

Silverstone, Roger, and Eric Hirsch, eds. 1992. *Consuming technologies: Media and information in domestic spaces*. London: Routledge.

Silverstone, Roger, Eric Hirsch, and David Morley. 1990. Information and communication technologies and the moral economy of the household. Discussion paper for Centre for Research in Innovation, Culture and Technology, Brunel University. Reprinted in Roger Silverstone and Eric Hirsch, eds. 1992 *Consuming technologies*. London, Routledge.

White, Robert. 1994. Audience "interpretation" of media: Emerging perspectives. *Communication Research Trends* 24, 3: 3–32.

Chapter 4

Bourdieu, Pierre. 1996. On the family as a realized category. *Theory, Culture and Society* 13, 3: 19–26.

Coontz, Stephanie. 1992. *The way we never were: American families and the nostalgia trap*. New York: Basic Books.

————. 1997. *The way we really are: Coming to terms with America's changing families*. New York: Basic Books.

Coontz, Stephanie, with Maya Parson and Gabrielle Raley, eds. 1999. *American families: A multicultural reader*. New York: Basic Books.

Fraser, Nancy. 1989. *Unruly practices: Power, discourse and gender in contemporary social theory*. Minneapolis: University of Minnesota Press.

Frey, William H., Bill Abresch, and Jonathan Yeasting. 2001. *America by the numbers: A field guide to the U.S. population*. New York: New Press.

Gerstel, Naomi R. 1994. Family. In *The Blackwell dictionary of twentieth-century social thought*, edited by William Outhwaite and Tom Bottomore. Oxford, UK: Blackwell.

Glassie, Henry. 1982. *Passing the time in Ballymenone: Culture and history of an Ulster community*. Philadelphia: University of Pennsylvania Press.

Habermas, Jürgen. 1987. *The theory of communicative action, vol. 2: Lifeworld and system: A critique of functionalist reason*. Translated by Thomas McCarthy. Boston: Beacon Press.

————. 1989. *The structural transformation of the public sphere: An inquiry into a category of bourgeois society*. Translated by Thomas Burger. Cambridge, MA: MIT Press.

Lipsitz, George. 1988. "This ain't no sideshow": Historians and media studies. *Critical Studies in Mass Communication* 5: 147–161.

———. 1990. *Time passages: Collective memory and American popular culture.* Minneapolis: University of Minnesota Press.

Mintz, Steven, and Susan Kellogg. 1988. *Domestic revolutions: A social history of American family life.* New York: The Free Press.

Moores, Shaun. 1993. *Interpreting audiences: The ethnography of media consumption.* London: Sage.

Morley, David. 1986. *Family television: Cultural power and domestic leisure.* London: Routledge.

———. 1992. *Television, audiences and cultural studies.* London: Routledge.

Murdock, George. 1949. *Social structure.* New York: Macmillan.

Roschelle, Anne R. 1997. *No more kin: Exploring race, class, and gender in family networks.* Thousand Oaks, CA: Sage.

Spigel, Lynn. 1992. *Make room for TV: Television and the family ideal in postwar America.* Chicago: University of Chicago Press.

Stacey, Judith. 1996. *In the name of the family: Rethinking family values in the postmodern age.* Boston: Beacon Press.

Taylor, Ella. 1989. *Prime-time families: Television culture in postwar America.* Los Angeles: University of California Press.

Terwilliger, Cate. 2001. *Mayberry* a religious experience to some. *Denver Post,* 25 March, 2D.

Tichi, Cecilia. 1991. *Electronic hearth: Creating an American television culture.* New York: Oxford University Press.

Chapter 5

Allor, Martin. 1988. Relocating the site of the audience, *Critical Studies in Mass Communication* 5, 3: 217–33.

Ang, Ien. 1985. *Watching* Dallas: *Soap opera and the melodramatic imagination.* London: Methuen.

Bourdieu, Pierre. 1984. *Distinction: A social critique of the judgement of taste.* Translated by Richard Nice. Cambridge, MA: Harvard University Press.

Fiske, John. 1987. *Television culture.* London: Routledge.

Hall, Stuart. 1993. Encoding, decoding. In *The cultural studies reader,* edited by Simon During. London: Routledge.

Hobson, Dorothy. 1982. Crossroads: *The drama of a soap opera.* London: Methuen.

Katz, Elihu, and Tamar Liebes. 1985. Mutual aid in the decoding of *Dallas:* Preliminary notes from a cross-cultural study. In *Television in transition: Papers from the first international television studies conference,* edited by Phillip Drummond and Richard Paterson. London: British Film Institute.

Lull, James. 1980. The social uses of television. *Human Communication Research* 6, 3: 198–209.

———. 1991. *Inside family viewing.* London: Routledge.

Moores, Shaun. 1993. *Interpreting audiences: The ethnography of media consumption.* London: Sage.

Morley, David. 1986. *Family television: Cultural power and domestic leisure.* London: Comedia.

———. 1992. *Television, audiences and cultural studies.* London: Routledge.

———. 1996. The geography of television: Ethnography, communications, and community. In *The audience and its landscape,* edited by James Hay, Larry Grossberg, and Ellen Wartella. Boulder, CO: Westview Press.

Radway, Janice A. 1984. *Reading the romance: Women, patriarchy, and popular literature.* Chapel Hill: University of North Carolina Press.

Silverstone, Roger, Eric Hirsch, and David Morley. 1990. Information and communication technologies and the moral economy of the household. Discussion paper for

Centre for Research in Innovation, Culture and Technology, Brunel University. Reprinted in Roger Silverstone and Eric Hirsch, eds. 1992. *Consuming Technologies.* London: Routledge.

Stevenson, Nick. 1995. *Understanding media cultures: Social theory and mass communication.* Thousand Oaks, CA: Sage.

Chapter 6

Awass, Omer. 1996. The representation of Islam in the American media. *Hamdard Islamicus* 19, 3: 86–102.

Denny, Frederick. 1994. *An introduction to Islam, second ed.* New York: Macmillan.

Djait, Hichem. 1985. *Europe and Islam.* Berkeley: University of California Press.

Gallup, George H., and Michael Lindsay. 2000. *Surveying the religious landscape: Trends in U.S. beliefs.* Harrisburg, PA: Morehouse Publishing.

George H. Gallup Institute. 1999. *The spiritual life of young Americans: Approaching the year 2000.* Princeton, NJ: George H. Gallup International Institute.

Gourevitch, Philip. 1999. A husband for Dil: Can tradition make a young woman happy? *The New Yorker.* Feb. 22 and March 1.

Hood, Lee. 1999. Mixed messages: Children negotiating meaning in media violence. Paper presented at the annual meeting of the International Communication Association, San Francisco. May.

Hoover, Stewart M., Lynn Schofield Clark, and Diane F. Alters 1999. Children, families and the media in conflict: A culturalist field research perspective. Unpublished paper. Available online at www.mediareligion.org.

McIrvin Abu-Laban, Sharon. 1991. Family and religion among Muslim immigrants and their descendants. In *Muslim families in North America,* edited by Earle H. Waugh, Sharon McIrvin Abu-Laban, and Regula Burckhardt Qureshi. Edmonton: University of Alberta Press.

Mir-Hosseini, Ziba. 1988. "Rethinking gender: Discussions with Ulama in Iran." *Critique,* Fall: 45–59.

———. 1996. Women and politics in Post-Khoumeini Iran: Divorce, veiling and emerging feminist voices. In *Women and politics in the Third World,* edited by Haleh Afshar. London: Routledge.

Nash, David. 2002. Religious sensibilities in the age of the internet: Freethought culture and the historical context of communication media. In Stewart M. Hoover and Lynn Schofield Clark (Eds.), *Practicing religion in the age of the media: Explorations in media, religion, and culture.* New York: Columbia University Press.

Ramazani, Nesta. 1993. Women in Iran: The revolutionary ebb and flow. *Middle East Journal* 47, 3: 409–28.

Ross-Sheriff, Fariyal, and Azim Nanji. 1991. Islamic identity, family and community: The case of Mizari Ismaili Muslims. In *Muslim families in North America,* edited by Earle H. Waugh, Sharon McIrvin Abu-Laban, and Regula Burckhardt Qureshi. Edmonton: University of Alberta Press.

Said, Edward. 1978. *Orientalism.* New York: Pantheon.

———. 1981. *Covering Islam.* New York: Pantheon.

Spivak, Gayatri Chakravorti. 1988. Can the subaltern speak? In *Marxism and the interpretation of culture,* edited by Cary Nelson and Lawrence Grossberg. Basingstoke, UK: Macmillan Education.

Tucker, Judith E. 1985. *Women in nineteenth century Egypt.* Cambridge, UK: Cambridge University Press.

Waugh, Earle H., Sharon McIrvin Abu-Laban, and Regula Burckhardt Qureshi, eds. 1991. *Muslim families in North America.* Edmonton: University of Alberta Press.

Yamai, Mai. 1998. Cross-cultural marriage within Islam: Ideals and reality. In *Cross-cultural marriage: Identity and choice*, edited by Rosemary Breger and Rosanna Hill. New York: Oxford.

Chapter 7

Alters, Diane F. 1999a. Conflict and historical memory: A comparison of two families. Paper presented at the annual meeting of the International Communication Association, San Francisco, CA, May.

———. 1999b. Media, religion, and the dark, dark room: One family's struggle with contemporary culture. Paper presented at the Third International Conference on Religion, Media and Culture, Edinburgh, Scotland. July.

Hoover, Stewart M., Lynn Schofield Clark, and Diane F. Alters. Under review. Children, families, and the media in conflict: A culturalist field research perspective.

Hulsether, Mark. 1996. It's the end of the world as we know it. *American Quarterly*, 48, 2: 375–384.

Roof, Wade Clark. 1999. *Spiritual marketplace: Baby boomers and the remaking of American religion*. Princeton, NJ: Princeton University Press.

Chapter 9

Baudrillard, Jean. 1987. The ecstacy of communication. In *Continental philosophy: An anthology*, edited by William McNeill and Karen S. Feldman. Malden, MA: Blackwell Publishers.

Bowen, Jon. 2000. Media alert: Excessive TV, computer, and videogame consumption may be turning your kids into tech potatoes. *Working Mother* 23, 2: 74–79.

Davis, Susan. 1997. *Spectacular nature: Corporate culture and the Sea World experience*. Berkeley: University of California Press.

Dewey, John. 1927. *The public and its problems*. New York: Henry Holt.

Gerbner, George, and Wilbur Schramm. 1989. Study of communication. In *International encyclopedia of communication*, edited by Erik Barnouw. New York: Oxford University Press.

Graves, W. Brooke, ed. 1928. *Readings in public opinion*. New York: D. Appleton and Company.

Janowitz, Morris, and Paul M. Hirsch. 1981. *Reader in public opinion and mass communication*. New York: Free Press.

Lippmann, Walter. 1922. *Public opinion*. London: Allen & Unwin.

Papson, Stephen. 1992. "Cross the fin line of terror": Shark week on the Discovery Channel. *Journal of American Culture* 15: 67–81.

Price, Jennifer. 1999. *Flight maps: Adventures with nature in modern America*. New York: Basic Books.

Rivers, William L., and Wilbur Schramm. 1969. *Responsibility in mass communication, revised edition*. New York: Harper and Row.

Surgeon General's Scientific Advisory Committee (1972). *Television and growing up: The Impact of Televised Violence*. Washington, DC: Government Printing Office.

Taylor, Talbot J. 1992. *Mutual misunderstanding: Scepticism and the theorizing of language and interpretation*. Durham, NC: Duke University Press.

Thompson, John B. 1990. *Ideology and modern culture: Critical social theory in the era of mass communication*. Stanford: Stanford University Press.

Tönnies, Ferdinand. 1957. *Community and society*. (Trans. by Charles P. Loomis. Originally published in German as *Gemeinschaft and Gesellschaft*, 1887.) East Lansing: The Michigan State University Press.

Chapter 10

Bourdieu, Pierre. 1984. *Distinction: A social critique of the judgement of taste.* Translated by Richard Nice. Cambridge, MA: Harvard University Press.

Clark, Lynn Schofield. 2003. *From angels to aliens: Teens, the media, and beliefs in the supernatural.* Oxford, UK: Oxford University Press.

Morley, David. 1996. The geography of television: Ethnography, communications, and community. In *The audience and its landscape,* edited by James Hay, Larry Grossberg, and Ellen Wartella. Boulder: Westview Press.

ABOUT THE AUTHORS

Stewart M. Hoover, Ph.D. is a professor at the School of Journalism and Mass Communication at the University of Colorado at Boulder and a Professor Adjoint of Religious Studies and American Studies. He is co-chair of the Religion, Culture, and and Communication Consultation in the American Academy of Religion; a member of the International Study Commission on Media, Religion and Culture; and a member of the Steering Committee of the Uppsala Group. He directed the first international public conference on Media, Religion and Culture, held at Boulder in 1996. He earned his Ph.D. in mass communication at the University of Pennsylvania and also holds an M.A. in ethics. He is the author of *The Electronic Giant* (Brethren Press, 1979), *Mass Media Religion: The Social Sources of the Electronic Church* (Sage, 1988), and *Religion in the News: Faith and Journalism in American Public Discourse* (Sage, 1998); he is coeditor of *Religious Television: Controversies and Conclusions* (Ablex, 1990; with Robert Ableman), *Rethinking Media, Religion, and Culture* (Sage, 1997; with Knut Lundby), and *Practicing Religion in the Age of the Media* (Columbia University Press, 2002; with Lynn Schofield Clark). He is married and lives in Boulder.

Lynn Schofield Clark, Ph.D. is Assistant Research Professor at the School of Journalism and Mass Communication at the University of Colorado at Boulder. A former television producer and marketing professional, Clark is author of *From Angels to Aliens: Teenagers, the Media, and Beliefs in the Supernatural* (Oxford University Press, 2003) and coeditor of *Practicing Religion in the Age of the Media* (Columbia University Press, 2002; with Stewart Hoover). A member of the Academic Advisory

Board for the Pew Internet & American Life Project and a member of the International Study Commission on Media, Religion, and Culture, Clark was a 1997–98 Louisville Institute Dissertation Fellow and a 1998 nominee to the Harvard Society of Fellows. She has a Ph.D. from the University of Colorado and an M.A. from United Theological Seminary. She is currently serving as the secretary to the Popular Communication Division of the International Communication Association, and she serves on the editorial board of the journal *Popular Communication* and on the Latino curriculum advisory board for the Denver-based documentary film company Little Voice. She is married and has two children.

Diane F. Alters, Ph.D. is a postdoctoral fellow at the Resource Center for Media, Religion, and Culture at the University of Colorado at Boulder. She has a Ph.D. from the University of Colorado at Boulder and an M.A. in Public Administration from the Kennedy School of Government at Harvard University. She has taught at the Graduate School of Public Affairs at the University of Colorado. She was a reporter or editor at several daily newspapers, including *The Boston Globe* and *The Sacramento Bee*. She is married and has a son.

Joseph G. Champ, Ph.D. is assistant professor in new media at the Journalism and Technical Communication Department at Colorado State University in Fort Collins, Colorado, and president of Champ Communication Research. After working as a television journalist for ten years, he earned an M.A. from the University of Wisconsin-Madison and a Ph.D. in Communication from the University of Colorado at Boulder. He has taught in the Department of Natural Resource Recreation and Tourism at Colorado State University. He is married and has three children.

Lee Hood, Ph.D. is an assistant professor in the broadcasting faculty at the School of Journalism and Mass Communication at the University of Colorado at Boulder, where she received her doctorate and master's degree. She was a television news producer in Denver and also has experience in radio and newspapers. She is married and has three children.

INDEX